Praise For *Wome*

"Friedl distills her years of researc
tives that, taken together, gradually
in the way that village women brin~~g~~
their carpet looms."
  —*The Philadelphia Inquirer*

"Fascinating . . . The twelve stories are interconnected, revealing a pungent, incisive view of women's society as a whole, and multi-faceted portraits of some memorable individuals."
  —*Publishers Weekly*

"This book is extremely well-written. It is especially valuable to hear the voices of women in an alien place—to hear, in their own words about their everyday lives as they live them in a place narrowed by tradition and war."
  —*The Daily Reflector*

"Friedl's rich descriptions evoke rarely glimpsed scenes with numerous and varied characters. Common life themes—rape, marriage, birth, death—are imbued with the unique perspectives of the people from this little-known region."
  —*Belles Lettres*

"Survival skills in an Iranian village . . . Vivid narratives of women making the best of circumstances narrowed by both tradition and revolution . . . I can smell the dust of the courtyards."
  —Mary Catherine Bateson, author of *Composing a Life*

"The real inside story of Iran, of its people—is told in this book. It is through the eyes of the women who live in a small village that Erika Friedl captures the pain, the growth, the humanity that is Iran. That beautifully written account is far more useful than a foreign policy text in understanding how this ancient nation copes with its turbulent place in history."
  —Judy Woodruff, correspondent, "MacNeil/Lehrer NewsHour"

PENGUIN BOOKS

WOMEN OF DEH KOH

Erika Friedl is a professor of anthropology at Western Michigan University. She received her Ph.D. from the University of Mainz, West Germany, and is currently working on a book about the children of Deh Koh.

ERIKA FRIEDL

LIVES IN AN IRANIAN VILLAGE

WOMEN OF DEH KOH

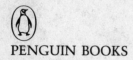

PENGUIN BOOKS

PENGUIN BOOKS
Published by the Penguin Group
Viking Penguin, a division of Penguin Books USA Inc.,
375 Hudson Street, New York, New York 10014, U.S.A.
Penguin Books Ltd, 27 Wrights Lane,
London W8 5TZ, England
Penguin Books Australia Ltd, Ringwood,
Victoria, Australia
Penguin Books Canada Ltd, 10 Alcorn Avenue, Suite 300,
Toronto, Ontario, Canada M4V 3B2
Penguin Books (N.Z.) Ltd, 182–190 Wairau Road,
Auckland 10, New Zealand

Penguin Books Ltd, Registered Offices:
Harmondsworth, Middlesex, England

First published in the United States of America by
Smithsonian Institution Press 1989
Published in Penguin Books 1991

10 9 8 7 6 5 4 3 2

THE LIBRARY OF CONGRESS HAS CATALOGUED THE HARDCOVER AS FOLLOWS:
Friedl, Erika
The women of Deh Koh: stories from Iran / Erika Friedl.
p. cm.
ISBN 0–87474–400–8 (hc.)
ISBN 0 14 01.4993 7 (pbk.)
1. Rural women—Iran—Biography. 2. Rural women—Iran—Social
conditions. 3. Iran—Social life and customs. I. Title.
HQ1735.2.F75 1988
305.4'2'0955—dc19 88–15613

Printed in the United States of America

For Kati and Agnes to remember it by

Contents

Acknowledgments

The many seasons I have spent in Deh Koh over the past two decades were dedicated to scholarly research of the kind one finds documented in scientific journals and were supported by the National Endowment of the Humanities, the Social Science Research Council, the Wenner Gren Foundation for Anthropological Research, and Western Michigan University. All these institutions deserve credit here, because the insights and knowledge on which this book is based I have gained over many years, and incidental to the main research these foundations have sponsored respectively. My profound thanks go to their trust and generosity.

My friends Eleanor Dominek, Mary Hegland, Robert Hinkel, Michael Jayne, and Jan Sloan, and my husband Reinhold Loeffler provided much-appreciated encouragement and critical advice; Royann Anspach lent her admirable typing skills for most of the manuscript; and Judy Sacks improved the book greatly through her sensitive and competent editing. I am deeply in their debt.

No amount of gratitude, however, can balance the generosity the villagers have extended to me and my family, time and again, and the hospitality, loyalty, and openness with which the women have accepted me, an impolitely inquisitive stranger. The original stories are theirs; the reflections in the book, with all the distortions that remembering and writing entail, are mine. I hope that once again, as they have done so often before when I bumbled, the women will smile and say, "It does not matter."

Prologue

Deh Koh means *mountain village*. It is a fictional name for a real village, one of some twenty-six thousand in Iran. Most are oases of huddled houses surrounded by fields and, as the people say, lonely, barren wilderness beyond. Deh Koh is one such village: mud, dust, walls of adobe bricks, walls of stones, hedges of brambles, donkeys, sheep, goats, cows, motorbikes, a few cars, sunburnt people in the shade, and lots of children. Poplar-lined water channels run like lifelines along roads, across alleys, through gardens and fields.

Deh Koh is lucky in many ways. To the north, towering Snow Mountain shelters the oasis of green fields and gardens sloping downwards from its rocky flanks into a gently curved plain. A mile or so up from the village several springs come rushing out from under rocks, and on the east and west ends of Deh Koh's plain two swift, gray-green rivers carry waters from the high peaks all year long—sweet, snow-cold water, seepage from ice that melts away on Snow Mountain only in the dazzling heat of midsummer. Below the Deh Koh plain the two rivers unite in a willow-lined gorge that tosses a deafening echo of crashing wild water through the trees and bushes.

Far above the village the streams channel into ditches and aqueducts along cliffs and through tunnels that were dug out of the rock some time in the distant past, beyond the memory of great-grandfathers.

For the mountains and the water, Deh Koh is a good place—despite its rocky fields; its cold, snow-laden winters; the endless up-down climbs; its seeming solitude. The air is cleaner, people say; the winds are cooler, the views over tree-dotted hills are more pleasing, the apples are sweeter, the sheep are fatter, and the children are healthier than in the stifling heat of the lowlands. Even the flies, it seems, are less of a nuisance here, and the women's wide skirts and long tuniclike shirts, heritage of a tribal past, are much more graceful and colorful than anywhere else. By and large, most of the people of Deh Koh like to be where they are.

To the south, west, and east there are five other villages and hamlets within a two-hour walking distance. More are strung along the river down in the valley, and more still lie in the vast expanse of hills and plains and woods stretching to the lowlands. The closest town formerly was a day's travel away until the Shah built a new road that shortened the distance to two hours by minibus. To get to the next big city (Shiraz), one should plan on a long day's journey in crowded buses. A car, provided no tire blows and the engine doesn't overheat, can make it in six hours. Sometimes a car or a bus goes over a cliff in a hairpin curve because the brakes gave out or the driver was from the city and didn't take the mountains seriously enough. As grisly monuments to mortality and fate, the wrecks slowly rust away in the gorges and on the slopes along the road. "May God have mercy," the travelers cry when they see them. Although the days of caravans are almost over (salt still is transported over Snow Mountain passes by camels), travel to and from Deh Koh is an adventure of sorts. But then, most villages in Iran look, from the outside, isolated and forgotten.

No matter how pervasive, this impression is wrong; it reflects a romantic urban perspective in which villagers on the cities' horizons disappear behind their walls and gates like dwarfs behind mole hills. Despite poverty and illiteracy, there is hardly a village in Iran that does not participate in the wider affairs of the nation and the region. Villages no longer (if they ever did) exist parenthetically, sheltered from another, more real, world, even if they are not hot-beds of political action and social change.

Deh Koh has over two thousand inhabitants and a growth rate of nearly 4 percent—among the highest in the world. The arable land, defined sharply by the availability of irrigation and rainfall and the steepness of the slopes, has not supported the exploding population for several generations. Over the years men have had to find work elsewhere. Some leave for good, some for only a few years; many stay away for the agricultural off-season. More and more young men are learning a trade or going to school. The village has produced many teachers, two doctors, and a handful of university students. Outsiders come and go: the personnel at the government clinic, administrators, high school teachers, even some traders who are turning Deh Koh into a market center for the many villages scattered in the area. Radios have been in use for twenty years, and television since the village got electricity a few years ago. Farsi, the national language, which is quite different from the local dialect, is taught in schools, and all but the most recalcitrant old people can understand it. Young men leave Deh Koh for army service, work, or school and come back changed, and in turn they are changing a village ready for new ways.

Gone are the tribal chiefs, the landlords, the omnipresent gendarmes, the Shah's soldiers. Gone are the days of poppy growing, of dire poverty under the exploitation of landlords who tyrannized villages like Deh Koh with their armed retinue. Gone also are the gazelles, the wild goats, the glorious days of hunting. By now the early days of modest prosperity—when the first schools were opened, water was piped to the village directly from the spring, the first teachers brought the first salaries to their families, the road was built, and the first doctor made his rounds—are barely within recall. Even the first demonstrations and slogans against the Shah, the first revolutionary guard, the first dead soldier, the first of a long series of mullahs, are now history. With the advent of revolutionary functionaries, singing, dancing at weddings, and music have become memories the young ones no longer share.

Life goes on, of course, no matter how dampened it may seem to some. Old people die and are buried with new-order pomp; young people get married, but quietly, almost as if it were a secret; babies

3

are born, but unlike in earlier times most survive. Compromises are forged between old routines and new demands; hopes are scaled down. Fewer families can afford to build new houses of stone and cement in a garden, city-fashion, but new houses are being built. Fewer girls go to school, few young people find the jobs or training they hoped for. Probably for the first time in the village's entire history many people are idle. Young men are waiting for jobs. Women find their traditional chores of milking, butter making, spinning, and weaving petering out as the men decide to sell their animals and to seek income elsewhere.

For village women, the outside world has been shrinking steadily over the past decade. It has become painfully clear that education for women, unlike for their brothers, does not easily lead to a job and a comfortable middle-class life. The new social order of the past decade not only has not offered women many new doors to the world, it also has shut some of the old ones. Empty barns have put a halt to spending summers in high-pasture camps; indoor plumbing makes trips to the communal water wells superfluous; new houses, isolated behind their own walls, make it harder for women to spend casual moments in the company of others; the women's elaborate round-dances at weddings are forbidden; the village is full of strangers and it is not good to be seen among them. Women stay home more as public space has become male space, even in the village.

Less visible than ever before, women in Iran seem to be mere shadows behind their dark veils. Of course they are still there, a silent majority even, but what do they look like? What do they think? Who speaks for them?

These questions are critical. They are the questions of representation, interpretation, and authority. Most of what we hear about women in Iran now comes either from Iranian men who use villagers to reflect their own revolutionary-apologetic or exile-critical political stance, or from middle-class, educated, Westernized Iranian women. Like urban people elsewhere, those women tend to look at their village sisters with a mixture of contempt and pity, applying stereotypes that are as old as the villages themselves: according to most of them, women in villages (by far the majority of Iranian women) are dirty, dumb, downtrodden, filled with superstitions, and in dire need of enlightenment.

Village women like those of Deh Koh know and care about what

4

others think and say about them, but they have no means of redress. A few social scientists have taken them and their affairs seriously; a traveler may have been touched by their hospitality; occasionally a writer has been inspired by their allegedly "beautiful," dignified," or "hard and bleak" lives into recreating them poetically. The second-handedness of the interpretive empathy in these testimonies is what spurred me to listen carefully to what the women of Deh Koh themselves have to say about their own lives and to try to chronicle their stories. I feel that these village women can tell us something about what life is like for them which no scientific account of village life and no poetic interpretation of it can express with equally direct authority. In this sense the stories are stories *of* village women, not *about* them.

Translating and editing always involve choices and therefore interpretation. My own approach to the study of Middle Eastern women grew out of a dissatisfaction with the fragmented nature of the insights into women's lives conveyed in the literature, a fragmentation which neither I as an observer nor the women themselves feel is representative of life on the ground. This is not to say that the various social-scientific analyses of women in the Middle East are "wrong," but rather that analytical approaches do not lend themselves easily to conveying the sense of interconnectedness the people themselves feel as members of their culture. By sketching the cognitive and action-choice boundaries within which life proceeds for women in a small Shiite community in Iran, perhaps we can reach that level of reality in which people are dealing with the quintessential challenges of life—those in which survival and meaning are made real on both practical and philosophical levels. Such an existentialist approach, although hardly novel itself, has not been used much to probe the qualitative dimensions of life for women in Iran. Thus, together with the narrative format which I found to be the most congenial vehicle for exposition, this volume amounts to an experiment in social science reporting.

The "stories" in the book—life histories, sketches of crisis situations, musings, commentaries—are selections from many more I have collected in Iran over the past two decades during a longitudinal study of women in rural Iran. I chose these particular twelve stories (the number has no significance here) because, without much overlap or repetition, they touch on a maximum number of familiar situations in which many women find themselves, wish to find themselves, or hope never to find themselves at one stage or another in their lives. The twelve stories further satisfy an important indigenous criterion for "good" stories in contrast to boring ones, which are called "nothing": they are dramatic. Answering her husband's critical comments on the indelicacy and absurdity of one of her heroes, Mamalus the Master Storyteller once said that nobody could make an interesting story, one worth listening to, of a man or a woman leading a humdrum life. Besides, she said, no one lives peacefully ever after on earth anyway—stories of piety and bliss therefore are bigger lies than her tales are. Things happen all the time. Drama is part of life, no matter the deplorable conditions it may create. Yet despite their dramatic content, none of the events in the stories are extraordinary in the sense of strange or abnormal; they all involve true challenges, albeit ones intensified to a critical, boundary-testing extreme, where choices for action and meaning are narrowed down and focused sharply and the logic of consequences is felt acutely.

Since the stories may strike readers as sad or downbeat, I probably need to explain that I did not select for melancholy and against *joie de vivre*. Much soul searching went into this matter. Life in rural places in Iran demonstrably is hard for most people by all standards, and suggesting anything else would amount to romanticization. My goal is not to decry, as one more voice in a chorus of feminist, critical, or simply ethnocentric noise, the peasant women's poverty or domination or oppression by an ideology that keeps them firmly cemented in dependent positions; all of this is asserted, disputed, affirmed, modified elsewhere in the literature. Rather, I want to fill a gap in our understanding of what women themselves make of their position and of how they use their culture, their relationships, and their philosophy to construct their lives and the lives of those near them. In other words, the stories are meant to testify to the women's emotional and practical resourcefulness, understanding of their world, and gutsiness in gambling their few assets against many odds.

If men seem curiously absent, remote, or even neglected in the stories, it is not due to a feminist-chauvinist denial of their importance on my part, but rather it reflects the local gender segregation. Although they interact, men and women do not congregate. Men create frames of hierarchy and economic interdependence and exert domestic, legislative, and executive authority within which women find ample room to maneuver. The stories follow these maneuvers: Where they take women to the edge of the frame of authority, of men's flexibility or tolerance, men appear as confiners. In daily routine interaction, however, it is more likely to be women who set boundaries for one another's actions and thoughts. Therefore, in Deh Koh, women are more important than men in establishing the thousand pleasant and unpleasant details of everyday existence which add up to a good or middling life for each of them. The emerging picture of life in the village is not gender balanced; it would be arrogant of me to pretend to "know" about the men's universe as I know about the women's. Yet by feeling our way through the women's domain, by listening to the women's discourses with themselves, each other, and men, we can reach a measure of appreciation for village life as a whole.

For almost five of the past twenty years I have lived in Deh Koh as a stranger learning to listen. I have not become a Deh Koh woman—an attempt that would be preposterous in Deh Koh's eyes as well as my own, and one doomed to fail—but at least I have ceased to be conspicuous there. I am odd, but in a familiar way; able to understand yet beyond the power fields of interests, arguments, alliances, and intrigues that make the tight web of kinship ties so secure yet often so unpleasant for the villagers. I feel like I have been on a stage for a minor but legitimate reason while the show is going on, and on a multi-scene stage at that. Against the backdrop of the Shah's pomp, the arrogant displays of an oil-drenched *nouveau riche*, the black-clad frenzy of a revolution and its bloody twin, the endless war, I have observed the goings-on of life in Deh Koh from the close but safe distance of familiar strangeness.

The stories are records of some of these scenes. I call them ethnographic stories not so much because they really happened (which they did) but because the actions and their underlying sentiments are embedded in a particular cultural background, with me functioning as chronicler and translator of what happened and what people say about it. For example, in describing Deh Koh's winters as snow laden, I use a Deh Koh concept ("heavy with snow"); the account of Haji Reza's arrest reflects his neighbors' sense of humor, not necessarily mine; contempt for Aftab is Deh Koh's contempt;

age is rarely given in years because it is not so much a matter of chronology as of how old one feels and acts; complaints about dust and dirt are the villagers' complaints; the terms *love* and *hate* are not used because they don't exist in the local dialect. Some stories (for example, Mamalus's tale in Chapter 8) end with a note of moodiness that was felt by me and others at the time, and this was expressed. The rather extensive use of the auxiliary verb and the overuse of basic verbs like *want, go,* and *say* at the expense of more lively expressions reflect the no-nonsense, matter-of-fact character of local narrative style. Although I do not attempt to simulate the Deh Koh language, the use of a more literary prose style would have infused the stories with coloring, movement, and variety alien to the village. Likewise, again probably to the detriment of color and depth, I have refrained from infusing the accounts with more emotions than were actually expressed at the time and from setting dramatic accents solely on my own judgment, no matter how suggestive they might seem. In any case, the terseness of narration and expression of feelings creates its own style of emotional density. This again does not so much bear the stamp of my interpretation qua my language or bias, but must be seen as a function of the generally low-keyed "view of the world from ground level" (Sarah the Weaver's expression). For example, apropos a discussion among a few women of the scarcity of milk at a certain time in winter, a young woman offered this tale by way of illustration to the rather jolly group of spinners and rice cleaners gathered on the sunny verandah:

> Once there was a girl. Her father's wife had a goat. She milked it and put the pot in front of the girl. She said, "You watch the milk while I go about my chores." When she returned, the foam on the milk had settled, and the pot seemed less full. She said, "What did you do with the milk?" The girl said she had done nothing wrong, the foam had settled. But her father's wife made her a lot of trouble and threw her out. The girl decided to kill herself to get away from this woman. She did so and turned into a bird. Her father came back to his house and asked the woman where his daughter had gone. She said, "She ran away with a man." The bird came, sat down on its father's house, and said, "The goat's milk was bitter, was foamy, was rotten. My father's wife troubled me. I wanted to kill myself, I hanged myself." Her father divorced the woman and threw her out.

It is hard to imagine that more expansive storytelling could have produced a better taste of poverty, injustice, and suffering within a core social group than this minimalist, unsentimental narrative.

I personally witnessed many of the happenings. For example, I was present when Shala was born (Chapter 1), mercifully relegated to an ignorable position in the background; and again when Turan's rape (Chapter 6) was discussed (melting into the shade and uttering no more than grunts of understanding and sympathy). In the story of Mamalus's tale, in which I figure as a prompter for explanations and asides, I use the perspective of the other women to describe myself in third-person narrative so as not to break the pattern in which the stories are told. Other events were told to me personally or were freely discussed in the village. For example, I have met only one of Setara's four husbands (Chapter 10), and I had never exchanged more than greetings with Butterfly before her mother took her back home (Chapter 11), but Setara talks freely about her past to me and to others, and many villagers voice their opinions about Butterfly's problems.

Some of the stories have no satisfactory end by standards of good literature: problems remain unsolved, characters are unchanged, a happy end is tentative, a peace is temporary. I cannot help this. Life itself offers only temporary truce and temporary arrangements, but more important, this perception conforms to local sensibilities. Life's events are seen in Deh Koh as intertwined, one leading into another, going on no matter what, according to a grand scheme designed and set in motion by God through the forces of nature, destiny, chance, human and superhuman powers, and evil. Illiterate Mamalus, not only a teller of tales but also a born philosopher, once said that washing clothes at a water channel often makes her think of life: water is forever coming and going, never the same for the individual drops that indeed might be dirtied by her wash, swallowed by a thirsty goat, dried on somebody's field—like people who may fall sick, be taken out by death, or get caught in one spot.

For essentially pragmatic-realistic people who for generations had to sustain themselves in an environment of scarcity, danger, and oppression, the notion of God as distant mover deals with fundamental existential questions in an emotionally unsatisfactory way. In the eyes of many women God behaves like a powerful, remote shah, essentially good and wise but inattentive to the details of life that matter most to them. Unless one successfully can appeal to His mercy and justice through extraordinary efforts (by invoking saints, for example), one merely is swept along in the stream of life for better or worse. Thus, for a great many women only death means a true end to hardship (or joy, as the case might be); in this sense death is seen not as a hopeful release from earthly shackles into the pleasures of heaven but as release into nonexistence, back-to-dust finality. The ultimate motivation for the many suicide attempts of women in Deh Koh is quoted as a wish "to be at rest, quiet, out of it forever." This view of death does not carry a consolation for the tough conditions of this life, but the hope for dry-bone rest seems realistic to people like the villagers of Deh Koh, who model their observations on the workings of nature. The Islamic notion of judgment and afterlife in heaven or hell does coexist, however, with the notion of death as great silence and can be evoked in the same breath. In Chapter 6, for example, Banu, a devout and knowledgeable believer who agrees to the merits of observing prayers, fasting, and giving aims (locally the three most important of the five pillars of Islam), advocates suicide as the most reasonable way out of Turan's dilemma yet proclaims it a grave sin at the same time. "Only a dead woman is a free woman," another woman once declared in a different context, meeting no protest from her audience. Yet even death, of course, does not end life; it only changes social parameters for the survivors and triggers new situations. It too is a force of nature, a mover of people and events.

For the sake of providing anonymity I have taken liberties with names and with details of events. Each of the many names, however, is used only for one person in the stories, and the pseudonyms all are popular in the village and reflect changing fashions. A few incidents that happened to other people or at different times are collapsed and telescoped for the sake of brevity and camouflage. The stories nevertheless are crowded with actors—I deliberately have not shrunk the large kinship networks to the point of losing the sense of complexity of relationships the villagers actually are living with.

These adjustments, I feel, do not impinge on the verity and reality of events described in the stories. In an undertaking like this, no absolute "truth" is to be had anyway. Nobody ever will find out what really happened to Gouhar's jewelry (and I seriously doubt she herself knows), or when Butterfly "actually" started to be different, or who neglects whom in Sarah's marriage, or whether or not there really was a rape. But what women say about themselves and others, what they think has happened, and what kind of truth they base their preferences, aversions, and actions on amounts to precisely the level of reality on which individuals formulate their existential problems and manipulate their culture in distinct ways. It is on this level that the drama of life is observed in these stories.

1

About Having a Late Child and How Perijan Dealt with This Embarrassment

After her sixth child (the fourth boy) was weaned and no longer tolerated or demanded being carried and cuddled, Perijan started to dress and feel like an old woman. Over her two floor-length, workaday skirts of red-print cotton (some fourteen yards of fabric each) she pulled a dark green skirt when she went out, and her long tunic-like shirt was a dark color, too. She discarded the white, gauzy headscarf for a dark red one, which made her small face even smaller, her nose bigger, the wrinkles around her eyes and across her tired cheeks deeper. Married before the onset of puberty, as was the custom then, she had had four miscarriages before her first child was born. He died soon afterward. Desperate for children under the critical and expectant eye of her husband's mother, she had amulets written for herself, made pilgrimages, promised the saints sacrifices, and had Ahmad, her husband, give alms.

Her next six children stayed alive. They filled the two small rooms of their house and emptied the storage bins in the thick mud walls faster than Ahmad could fill them with wheat. With only a few tiny plots of land and a few skinny animals they all barely survived, with nothing to spare for comfort. Altogether, she felt, she had been through a lot of life, more hardships than ease. She had done her duty without complaints, as well as she had known how to. When her mother's sister died—old, and not missed much—Perijan got herself for propriety's sake a length of dark blue, shiny synthetic material with blotchy purple blossoms for a shirt, as suitable for mourning as for her new image of a matron stepping back to let the young ones carry the burden of work and children. She was out of it all. She had shown who she was—what kind of a wife, mother, daughter, sister, mother-in-law. As the saying went, she could sit down now.

But despite projecting the image of a woman who is through with her purpose in life, she got pregnant again when her youngest was five. First annoyed, then confused and mortally embarrassed, Perijan sat through months of back pain, exhaustion, food cravings and crying spells, hardly leaving her house for fear of the gossip, the inevitable comments, the raw jokes. "Never again," she said, "no way."

Her daughters—both married, and the older one pregnant herself—consoled her. "What happened, happened," they said. "God wants to give you another child, so what. Be thankful, there is nothing to be ashamed of."

So they all said, her sisters, her husband's brother's wife, her sister-in-law, her brothers. Her old and decrepit mother even said, "Good, good, the more the better." The old women! Her husband Ahmad said nothing, he never did, but he looked pleased.

The baby, a girl, bigger and stronger than any of her other children had been, was born one stormy winter evening in the good room of their house, with the midwife and five other women in attendance. A lot of coming and going brought cold drafts and a little snow inside. The kerosene pressure lamp was snuffed out by a sudden cold blast, throwing them all into pitch-dark confusion until a storm lantern appeared from the kitchen room. Squatting on a rug next to the glowing woodstove, gurgling and burbling her waterpipe in a wispy cloud of smoke, Perijan's elder sister Maryam, the widow, gave directions and commands no one paid much attention to. The younger daughter made tea. A dispute about firewood was carried on with one of Perijan's sons through the open door. Perijan was asked the whereabouts of the sugar scissors used to cut

13

the hard cone of sugar into little pieces, the good tea glasses, more matches, the funnel for the kerosene, the box of cookies (for the midwife). "No," she said, in between her moaning and groaning, "not this tray, the red one, and the swaddling clothes are in the topmost suitcase behind the curtain, the other curtain. The big water kettle, well, I don't know, maybe your father has it in the other room—be careful, don't wake him." The midwife was drinking tea and lecturing on the blessings of the pill, saying that having more children than one could well care for was backwards. "Even the Shah has only four," she said. "Here in the village we are like cows, every year another calf, always in milk."

The women nodded. "Right, right," Perijan's sister said. "Now, when my youngest was born last year, I remember . . . "

Perijan was walking up and down the few steps the small, crowded room permitted. She sat down on the shabby old rug she had carefully arranged as her childbed so as not to soil a good one, only to get up again, clutching her sides and gnashing her teeth. "Lie down, Aunt Perijan," said the midwife, without a trace of hope for compliance.

"Oh, Fatima," Perijan cried, "Oh, holy Mary, Oh, holy Sarah." She knew when to push. She knew when the baby's head would appear. When it was time, she squatted on the rubber mat the midwife had spread on top of the flimsy rug. "Now," she gasped, and the baby was born. Thanks be the Lord, praise to God. The umbilical cord was cut; the baby was wiped down with a rag, swaddled, bedded on a pillow with a piece of an old veil over her; the afterbirth was inspected and carried out; more tea was poured; the soiled clothes disappeared outside; more snow came in.

The midwife gave Perijan an injection—"for strength," she said—and measured her blood pressure, then threw her paraphernalia into a big bag. She was tired. Three births in two days, on a salary half that of a teacher, who never had to get up in the night. And then having to put up with these stubborn women like Aunt Perijan who wouldn't lie down as the doctor had said they should, walking around instead like a caged beast, squatting as in the days of the old midwives—the superstitious illiterates like her own grandmother, with their stupid customs of feeding a newborn a mixture of butter, sugar candy, and herbs against evil powers and what not. They even used to bleed babies to let out the dirt. The doctor could fight with them,

14

could argue with them—an educated man, an outsider, a representative of the Shah's army—but how could she, a young woman related to half the village? Of course, with some of the doctor's ideas she was at odds herself; how, for example, was a baby to be kept warm if it was not swaddled?

"There she goes," said Perijan's sister-in-law, the one with the fast tongue, "a nice fat salary for her, and the work and the headache for Perijan."

"Work? What work?" said Perijan's sister. "Now that we have progress and a midwife, you just lie down and take a rest, it's fun."

"Ah, it's wonderful now, you'd want to do it every day . . . "

"You should get pregnant just to try it!"

"And how would the doctor love to give birth just once . . . "

But Perijan's older sister Maryam had practical matters in mind. "Hand me the butter and the herbs, somebody. Perijan, where do you keep it?"

The baby got its spoonful of butterfat and herbs, and sugar candy in water, and soot around its eyes, and an amulet was pinned on the outmost layer of the bundle, for protection. The room got hot and stuffy now that the door stayed shut. Quilts were taken down from the big pile of household goods stored along one wall. Perijan would not sleep alone that night. It was a dangerous time, with evil spirits on the loose and a new mother and her child so vulnerable.

Perijan was relieved, even happy, but still embarrassed. The baby, whom Perijan's sons and older daughters called Shala—a modern, pretty name, one Perijan would not have thought of herself—Shala, then, was doing very well, thanks be to God. Perijan did not take her places, not even to her brother's son's wedding, partly because she was afraid that the evil eye might strike her despite the amulets and the weekly fumigation with the smoke of seeds of the wild rue—beautiful, fat children were especially vulnerable in this regard—or that she would inhale some powerfully harmful scent among the people, like strong perfume or cooking odor, or a whiff of another sick child, but mostly (and she did not kid herself about it) because she did not want to appear parading with her baby like a young woman, showing herself in a prime she had negated and no longer felt. She was ashamed to admit publicly that she was still sleeping with her husband. But despite her caution there were, of course, little jokes from the other women, goodnatured mostly but unpleasant nevertheless. The baby, whom everybody knew she had, belied her dark clothes. Perijan realized that to prevent further embarrassment she had to resort to the drastic measures of the young. She asked the midwife for contraceptive pills.

Like all other women she knew that the pills were bad for a woman's health, that they all but dried up the flow of purifying blood that cleanses the body monthly from within. Women on the pill got sick, weak, their wombs clogged, their hearts weakened. But anything, Perijan said, was better than another pregnancy.

This she said and believed at first. But within less than a year her body was bloated, her breasts twice their normal size, her arms sore and her legs weak. The pills made her faint and sick; they were killing her. On top of this, under the new revolutionary regime the midwife no longer was allowed to dispense the pills. To get them a woman had to take herself to the clinic in the next village and wait hours to see the doctor for a month's supply, at best. So she stopped taking them and felt better almost overnight, strong enough to take her calves out to pasture among the sun-torched scrub way above the cemetery all by herself and to climb the steep stairs to their rooms with heavy buckets full of water, without missing a beat of her heart.

And she became pregnant again.

This time, with Shala nearly four, both older daughters mothers themselves, two sons in school—the oldest engaged to be married as soon as he had the money for the bride price and the second working in the city, grownup youths doting on their aging parents— this time she was too ashamed to tell anybody. Demonstratively she washed her skirts and performed the ablutions in the bathhouse to suggest she had had her period at the proper time. After that, avoiding the public bathhouse, the place where pregnancies unfailingly were noticed first, she took to using her sister's shower, a lean-to adjoining their adobe house, heated laboriously from below once a week, at some cost to Perijan's dignity and highly valued self-reliance. The debt she was incurring required unspoken assurance of later compensation, and an explanation. Hiding behind Shala, she said—and quite plausibly so, after hints of the evil eye and foul spells by an unfortunate mother whose infant had died shortly after being taken to the bathhouse—that she had grave fears about the safety of her child (round, rosy, pretty as a picture for everyone to see) in a place where the admiring and envious talk of so many tongues could do so much harm. The sister's shower was dark and narrow and Perijan tried to come late in order to be alone in it, even if that meant only a short wash with unpleasantly cool water instead of the comfortably hot, long soak in the saunalike atmosphere of a wholesome bath. There was even some danger from malevolent spirits, the *djenn*, known to linger around lonely bathhouses, but Perijan decided to take her chances.

Perijan told her husband. She told Ahmad not because she expected counsel or comfort (she got neither) but because it was a sin to refuse him to sleep with her, yet also a little bit of a sin to sleep with him while pregnant. As usual, he said nothing more than "it does not matter." Another child was all right with him; no more children was all right, too. He had no say in it either way, he felt. It was the will of God if his aging wife still brought children while his younger brother's wife had stopped at only three, many years ago. Without hesitation he assured Perijan he would not tell anybody. It was none of his business to talk about pregnancies. Squarely and entirely it was Perijan's business, unless— God forbid—she became sick and had to be taken to the doctor. Even then her older brother Kerim, the school principal, would take care of her; he was so much better at dealing with city folks, he had money, he liked his sister, and Ahmad chopped his firewood. A pregnancy was a woman's problem, if it was a problem at all.

For Perijan it was a problem, and she did not know how to deal with it. Her children would be embarrassed. Her older brother, the school principal, would scold her. Her husband's brother's wife, who had only one son and two daughters, poor soul, would never stop asking jealously and piquedly how many more sons Perijan wanted. Even before Shala was born, her cousin had joked— what jokes!— that Ahmad surely was getting rich, or else he would not have so many children. Kiddingly people would say that she was very "Islamic," heeding Khomeini's wish for more soldiers. Maybe she would get a letter of thanks from the old geezer? Or at least a blessing?

Her only hope to deter the sarcasm, the criticism, the pity, was concealment. Once the child was born all they could say was, "thanks be to God." It would be easier then. But how long would she be able to hide her condition, even given the wide skirts, the loose tunic, her self-imposed seclusion?

The way to sustain this camouflage suggested itself unexpectedly and exceedingly painfully towards the end of her fourth month. It was a Thursday evening, the time to remember the dead by giving alms to the poor. Not that Ahmad's family had much to give, but Perijan was particular about the sacrifice being proper. Her sons had bought a little meat that day. It was very little, and goat meat—full of rheumatism even in its best parts, but this was only fat held together by strings of skin. Perijan was annoyed at having to give this away. At supper, when the whole family was sitting on the kitchen floor around the tray with food, there was a dispute between her and her oldest son. "I'd rather give Mahmad the Cripple an honest bowl of rice," she said, "than this."

"No," said her son, "I have already told his son to come get the meat."

"Meat? What meat?" Perijan complained. "They can't even make decent cracklings of this."

"Be quiet," said Ahmad, "don't pick a fight."

Perijan, hurt and troubled, turned away from the copper tray with rice and lentils on the tablecloth spread out among them on the floor. "You eat," she said, "I am not hungry."

"Suit yourself," said her son.

Perijan moved over to the milkpot on a tripod in the open fireplace, added another log, blew the coals to red-hot flames, and stirred the milk. It took a while to get it boiling. Mahmad the Cripple's little son came, got the meat, and left. Perijan said nothing. Morosely she stayed with the milk outside the circle of light from the pressure lamp, outside the circle of food and talk, alone with her misgivings and her discomfort. Wordlessly she poured tea and pushed the tray over to her family. When the milk began to rise she expertly lifted the heavy pot from the tripod and set it in front of her on the packed gypsum floor. The lid lay to her left, a little outside her reach. Bending backwards and sideways she got hold of it, and as she jerked it towards her the pot, for no reason at all, she many times said later, tipped over, and the boiling milk cascaded over her feet, all of a gallon.

Perijan screamed. There was yelling and shouting and hustling;

18

children were sent to fetch water, relatives, a car; neighbors came running.

An hour later she was still screaming, hoarsely by then, when her sister-in-law and her oldest son carried her into the doctor's office. Luckily the doctor, a Pakistani, was at home and could be persuaded to attend. Of his ministrations Perijan noticed little. He gave her an injection in her bottom, put a thick salve on her scalded feet, and padded and bandaged them into two huge, white, useless bundles sticking out incongruously from under her long, dark skirts. She was taken back in her nephew's car as far up the narrow lane as it would go, and from there her brother's strong young wife carried her—a helpless, whimpering load awkward to hold—up to the house, through the wide, wooden gate and across the littered yard, up the narrow stairway to the living quarters above the barn and the wood-shed, into the good room, and then lowered her onto her quilt-mat bed on the floor. Moaning, lamenting, invoking the saints, oblivi-ous to the world around her, she lay covered by a blanket from her head to the white fire of what had been her feet, in her little hell.

But worse was to come.

At her next visit to the clinic (on her sister-in-law's strong back and in her nephew's car) the doctor cleansed the wounds and cut off the skin that hung like rags from her toes. He spoke little, and that in almost unintelligible Persian. If it had not been for her brother Kerim, the principal, answering for her, she would have panicked every time the doctor murmured. The salve he put on was sooth-ing, though; she could feel relief, and the new bandages smelled nice and clean. She would be feeling better soon, her brother trans-lated. "With God's will," she said.

The third time her people took her down to the clinic, only the doctor's assistant was there, a bearded young man from the town who thought much of himself and little of the villagers. He was unfriendly and hurt her when he took the bandages off. After what she had seen of her mutilated feet at her last visit, Perijan did not want to look. Burying her head in her sister's skirts, she waited for the smooth coolness of the ointment. Instead what touched her was pure fire: red-hot, live coals pressed into her wounds. She screamed again and blacked out.

What a time they had with her! They yelled and scurried, sprinkled her with water, soaked her feet, slapped her face; her sister cried, her brother's wife wailed. When she came to she was hooked to an intravenous drip, and the doctor's assistant and the lad from the dispensary were busy with her feet, which looked white and dead.

By sheer carelessness and indolence, the wooly-headed, useless assistant, the bearded revolutionary good-for-nothing, may God punish him, had put on the ointment one rubs onto a rheumatic limb, the kind that burns inside and makes the skin glow pleasantly— healthy skin, that is. But Perijan's feet had no skin; her flesh had been burned again. That night, at home, all her neighbors came, her sisters, even her very old, deaf mother; they thought she would die. As for herself, she would rather have died that night, but this was not her fate.

The wounds became infected, especially on the right foot. Her family talked of complaints, of letters to be written to the doctor, the district health office, the revolutionary mayor. Although formal protests would involve only outsiders, her sons and her brother Kerim were against them; theirs was an honorable, quiet family, and what would be gained by such a show of indignity? Instead, because the family stayed perfectly courteous, the foreign doctor and his luckless assistant were forced into care and attention heightened by their own remorse. Again and again Perijan was lifted and carried, given injections against pain, against pus, for her heart, for strength, for blood—so many injections and pills and capsules! At home her husband had amulets made for her; she promised a sheep to the shrine of a holy Imam in the next valley, a pilgrimage there, a long and arduous journey, if only she would get well. She could not walk. She could not work. Her youngest sisters and her nieces baked bread for her; her older sister Maryam, the widow, stayed nights; her daughters cooked; all her sisters and nieces and brothers' wives and her husband's younger brother's wife—she not gladly, though—pitched in, day and night. And nobody noticed that she was pregnant.

After a while the goodwilled help of her people settled into a burdensome routine. Sensing the discomfort she caused them, Perijan refused to be carried to the clinic any more. She would take care of her feet at home. The doctor's medicines did not work anyway. It seemed he didn't have the right ones— everything was scarce nowadays, even drugs. Both her feet were swollen, covered with blisters. With some assistance from her mother and Maryam she took to self-help. Maryam got her some seasoned cow dung and sprinkled it over a tray with live coals, and Perijan bathed her feet in the powerful purifying smoke. She had Maryam boil common yarrow in water and drop some heated pebbles into it so that it bubbled and hissed, and then she put her feet over the hot steam and covered it all with a veil—how nice it felt! It felt so good, she often made it three times a day. And all the while no one had the faintest idea that she was pregnant.

Despite all the care and attention lavished on her, the wounds were healing very slowly. Propped and steadied by a cane, she started to hobble around on one leg. The right leg withered and dried like a twig in winter, and she was afraid she would never be able to use it again. But when Maryam rubbed it with a paste of henna and olive resin and with the fat from the tail of a sheep it became soft again and stronger. By then Perijan could have walked and worked more than she did, but she kept her bent-over, immobilized posture as a convenient (and wholly effective) way to distract attention from her growing belly. "Perijan is getting fat and lazy," her sisters joked, and Perijan played along.

"Just like a khan's wife," she self-mockingly said to her visitors, twitching her face pitiably to belie the levity of such remarks.

The sympathy she elicited was holding up. Her feet, healed over now with a new, taut, shiny-red and tender skin, looked strange and horrible enough to dispel any doubt about the severity of her predicament. The sisters served dutifully. A steady stream of visitors ebbed in and out of her room. Ahmad had to ask the shopkeeper for a loan to keep his house in tea and sugar. The free-market prices were exorbitant, and his government allotment and the gifts from relatives were soon exhausted. Welcome as the visitors were as a source of comfort and of news, and cherished as a sign of the strength of Perijan's own social web, they did pose a threat to her pregnancy. One of the pregnant women sitting near her could be carrying a potent amulet, a rock, an herb, its powers harnessed for her own protection, and dangerous to others. A strong odor exuding from the folds of the many skirts around her, the evil eye, some magical device knotted in the end of the short, kerchieflike veil, inadvertently could cause her great harm, unprotected and unprotectable as she was in her pretentious posture. She could not see to any of the precautionary rituals a careful pregnant woman should observe. But Perijan said nothing and threw herself at the mercy of God, at the pity of the saints. She was not even greatly worried. This pregnancy was so unusual any way you looked at it. The child, it seemed to her, must be especially protected. How else could it simply go on growing inside her, an old woman, despite her infirmity, her pain, the fever, the many powerful medicines upsetting the delicate balance of the hot and cold temperaments of her body, heating her liver, burdening her heart? Praise the Lord, His works were truly inscrutable.

In the few moments when she was alone she furtively rummaged in the bundles of clothes, in the suitcases and few boxes that held most of their earthly belongings, to find a few rags, bits and ends of fabric suitable for the swaddling diapers necessary for the first few days. Very little was really needed. Even the rocking cradle could wait, would have to wait. After Shala had outgrown it Perijan had lent it to her niece. The niece's child was big now, so Perijan could claim the cradle back easily when her time came.

Towards the end of her eighth month, she hobbled around a little more—bent double, to be sure—and assured her people that she was up to taking care of her family again. The visitors thinned, and Maryam no longer spent the nights with her. When somebody came (it was a good thing she could spot visitors, long before she could be seen, when they announced themselves by passing through the creaky wooden gate) she would huddle in the darkest corner of the kitchen at the fire even on the very hot days of late summer, and she made sure always to have the teapot and sugar handy so she would not need to get up for anything. Her distraction strategy, miraculously, still worked.

Her time came one evening, when her water broke. "Pure water," she would recount later, "lots of water, clear as can be, which shows how little blood I had in my veins." She was outside on the verandah then, and none of her children noticed. The water was soaked up by her wide cotton skirts. Later, her husband and Shala and Perijan went to bed in the kitchen, as always. Her boys slept in the other room, for propriety's sake. After all, having two rooms, they could afford this refinement. The labor pains started before midnight. She paced up and down the narrow verandah, in and out of the kitchen, faintly illuminated by the little lantern she had lighted, clutching the banister, not uttering a sound so as not to wake anybody. She spread an old sheet of plastic on the gypsum floor right inside the kitchen door, silently retrieved the little bundle of rags from its hiding place behind the flour sack, took off the topmost good skirt, got a piece of string and scissors, and was ready. Mild and pleasant as the night was, it was a dangerous time to be alone for a woman about to give birth, the time of the spirit-beings, the *djenn*—one wouldn't say their name aloud, hardly think of them, for fear it might attract their attention—the time of cats, of beings that creep, whistle, and flutter. She would not dare to give birth out on the verandah. Whenever the pains seemed unbearable, Perijan bit into the wooden banisters and clicked the scissors—this relieved the pain. After what seemed many long, dark, and lonely hours in the warm breeze between the kitchen and the porch, with nothing around her but a little puddle of light, the sounds of sleep and the noises of the night—a braying donkey, the shuffling of cows in the barn under her feet, the coughing of a sheep, a bark here and an answer there from the neighbor's beast, the wind banging an empty tin can in the rubble in the yard below—the child came with a last tremendous push, just as the first early rooster tried his voice. It was a girl, smaller than Shala, with a shock of black hair and a red and wrinkled face, chirping like a little bird. Perijan did not wait for the afterbirth before she bound and cut the umbilical cord, but she tied a long, iron spit used to turn flatbreads on the griddle onto the end to prevent it from slipping inside and wiped the baby down. She wrapped her in the rags, tied the little thing into a bundle, and only then leaned back and waited for the afterbirth. When it was expelled, she took it downstairs and buried it in the loose dirt in the barn. Back in the kitchen, by the orange flickers of the lantern, she rummaged for a little piece of sugar candy, dissolved it in water in a tea glass, and fed the child its first spoonful of medicine—protective cleansing, the first and only one Perijan would do of the whole array of protective acts which were thought indispensable for the well-being of a newborn. "This child," Perijan said to herself as she had often before, "this child is different. God personally will have to take care of her, all by Himself."

Ahmad woke when Perijan stepped on him as she returned the

water kettle to the tripod in the dead fireplace. "Why didn't you say anything?" he murmured. It was four in the morning by then. A hint of early gray hung in the still air.

"A girl," Perijan said. "Praise be to God."

She sat up the rest of the night and watched the brilliant yellow morning rise over her neighbor's roof. When her sons got up, she had tea and bread ready for them. No one asked about the bundle in the corner. Shala left to play. Ahmad left for the fields. "It's all right," he said, "thanks be to God, it does not matter."

Then Perijan took care of herself. She washed her soiled skirt and the sheet of plastic and put a pot with milk rice on the fire. She was hungry now and milk rice was the traditional food for a new mother, as it was for sick people. Just as she was ladling it out onto a little platter to cool faster her sister's son came by on an errand. "Aunt," he said, "why in the world do you eat milk rice now?"

"I have a headache," she lied in a low voice, "but there is enough for both of us, sit down and eat." She got him a spoon, and he, too young to be polite enough to refuse, sat down and ate, and all the while she hoped fervently the bundle in the corner would not squawk. The boy ate fast—one does not dawdle over a windfall goody—leaving her just a little, and was gone before the baby gave herself and her mother away. At home, the boy told his mother that Aunt Perijan had a very bad headache, and she was eating milk rice and speaking so faintly he could hardly understand her. The woman dropped what she was doing and ran. Inspired by this success, the boy spread the news of Perijan's bad health (which rapidly deteriorated with each encounter) to another of Perijan's sisters, a cousin, and her older daughter. They arrived in close succession to find Perijan sitting by the kitchen door in the rising sun, rocking her child. "This is my headache," she said, and smiled.

Her sons named the new sister Fatima, after the Prophet's daughter. One no longer used names like Shala now. Ringingly religious names were the fashion, and little Fatimas and Sarahs were born all over the village. Perijan did not care much. She kept to herself, smiled to herself, and told no one that she had been alone that night. She lied through her teeth, in her soft and meek voice, claiming so many different companions and so many different visitors that in the ensuing confusion everybody was sure somebody had delivered the baby, but no one knew exactly who. It did not matter. As Perijan had figured, the surprise all but canceled the objections of the others, and the success of her plot canceled her own misgivings. The only one to raise the issue was her oldest daughter. "Now, mother, finally will you stop having children?"

"What am I to say?" said Perijan. "We'll see what God wants."

2

About Space and How Maryam Got Back a Verandah

Like many of the twenty-odd thousand villages in Iran, Deh Koh has grown rapidly and steadily over the last fifty years. The one-story houses of rocks, oak beams, and mud of the handful of original settlers, built close together for reasons of terrain and defense, have grown sideways and up the rocky slope into crowded, two-story adobe compounds as sons have taken wives and as herds and children have multiplied. Within the tumbled village no space is unoccupied, no matter how small, crooked, or seemingly inaccessible. A maze of alleys, tunnels, and stairways between adjacent compounds intersects the cramped village huddled against the flanks of the mountain. Vineyards are planted on the steep and sunny slopes above the village, and higher up still the pastures begin. In the hills on both sides orchards alternate with small fields among glittering irrigation channels lined with poplar trees; these tree-studded hills pan out into larger fields that curve down to the stream dividing Deh Koh land from the neighboring village.

There is a sharp contrast between the overcrowded mud village—with its narrow paths winding between thick, windowless walls that shield dirty yards and cramped living quarters atop dark barns, sheds, and stables; with its dust and odors and noises of too many living things cooped up in too tight a space—and the surrounding expanse of green hills, wooded valleys, and hazy blue mountains, silent save for the wind and an occasional bird. Yet for all its hot dust and dirt, until less than a generation ago the village was a haven of security against a multitude of enemies, almost a fort, guarded by tall fronts of blind, inhospitable house walls. At various times, on the short notice of a mere warning shout, the villagers had to be able to defend their brittle lives and few belongings against neighboring feuding villagers, marauding tribesmen, a khan's or shah's soldiers, swindling itinerant peddlers and dervishes, shrewd gypsies, thieves who drove off one's sheep at night, corrupt gendarmes, and officials. The farther one ventured from the village, the more endangered one felt. Until a decade ago nobody was foolhardy enough even to dream of leaving the confines of the village to build a lonely house out in the open, where the air was clean and the water clear. One did not dare be alone, at least not at night.

During the long, sun-filled days between the first of spring and the middle of fall, many families left the village together to set up camps in the high pastures with their animals. Of those who stayed behind, the men were out in their fields from dawn to dusk, and there were several occasions for the women, especially the young ones, to go out in small groups to gather wild vegetables and almonds by themselves, largely free of the tight responsibilities and restraints that ruled in the village. These were golden days of picnics and laughter, of playing pranks, of exchanging news with other women one didn't see much in the confined circles of movement at home. But such occasions were few, even before the zeal of revolutionary morality curbed even the most innocent ventures of the women. The women had to make do with what air and space and freedom there was among the sun-baked bricks and patches of shade in their own courtyards, whether their father's or their husband's.

Upon marriage a son would move into a room of his own, no matter how tiny, either a new one built onto those already there, or one evacuated by the death of an old relative or the emigration of a young one. The room was his and his wife's and their children's; the barns under it and the courtyard itself were held in common; the open space in front of the living rooms was part of the living space—small and enclosed in some houses, wide and open in others, depending on the layout of the barns below and how crowded the compound was. The flat, earth-packed roof of the houses—the third floor, in effect—also was used: children played up there, and hay, fruits, and vegetables were dried on it all summer long. Each room had a fireplace with a smoke hole, as did each verandah in front of the room. In summer all cooking was done outdoors. In fact, in summer the rooms themselves were used almost exclusively for storage and sleeping, while the activities of everyday life took place elsewhere for men, and for women on the verandah or in the courtyard: cooking and eating, baking bread, visiting, sewing, weaving, washing, mending, spinning, milking, buttering, making cheese, cleaning wheat for the mill, pounding rice in a wooden mortar, nursing children, arguing, looking out over the village, dreaming, keeping tabs on the neighbors' movements. On the verandah one was out in the open yet entirely at home; able to talk and listen and learn, yet safely sheltered inside one's walls; able to look and see yet by dint of a linguistic convention properly secluded, even without a veil.

For men and boys, who had the run of the village by virtue of their gender (and even were encouraged to be out—a man or boy who preferred sitting at home to sharing the company of others in the open fields or in the village lanes was labeled a sissy), the house and the verandah were places of rest and of the chores of upkeep, such as squeezing the excess water out of the flat roof during a rain to prevent it from seeping through the ceiling, or clearing the snow off for the same reasons. On the verandah, men ate and drank and waited for night to fall; one entertained a guest there or talked over the affairs of the day. For the women and girls the verandah was the place to live one's life, no less, within the confines of a horizon marked by the distant blue hills beyond the ochre haze of Deh Koh and the watchful eyes of the other women in one's own courtyard, and the next, and the one above. The fact that a woman was hardly ever alone was reassuring for matters of security, but it was a heavy emotional burden nevertheless. Indeed, it was said, nothing made brothers split up faster than their wives fighting each other at home.

But times have changed. Over the past two decades khans have been divested of power, robbers have been disarmed, prosperity has slowly crept up into the forgotten valleys, and roads have widened the world of Deh Koh. An increasing number of young families have decided to leave the old quarters and to build new houses out in the fields, city style, each with its own patch of garden around it and sheltered by a wall not so much against enemies as against the inquisitive eyes of strangers. Those who remained could take over the vacated rooms in their compounds and breathe easier, or else let the unused buildings be washed down by the rains into the mud from which they were built. The beams were salvaged and reused in the new houses and the rest was melted into heaps of dirt, to be raked a bit and planted with some herbs or sunflowers—tiny patches of color in the mottled brown adobe.

Khorshid's father had started his own courtyard with a small barn and one room above in the back of his father's north wall, through which a tunnel provided passage between the two yards. To the east the corner of a cousin's house together with a short wall connecting this corner with the western front corner of another relative's house provided a safeguard against trespassers, and the back wall allowed for adding more barns and living rooms. To the north there was a little open space with two walnut trees and another wall beyond, running at a southwestern angle, forming a narrow alley along Khorshid's father's wall. This alley opened into one of the main lanes—hardly wide enough for two donkeys passing each other— along an arm of the water channel. In fact, the alley was blocked by an old willow tree, and after regularly cursing it twice a day whenever the sheep and goats would balk at squeezing by it, Khorshid's father finally felled it and made of it a sturdy bridge over the channel.

Khorshid's father had three sons, all of whom built next to him, filling the many-angled space with three barns and living rooms, each at slightly different planes from the other, so that the respective verandahs were not quite level and had to be connected by steps of varying height. Khorshid and his brothers and all their wives proved amiable enough not to split up as long as they lived. Khorshid's first wife died young and childless. His second wife, Maryam—a cousin who had lived in a room backing Khorshid's and only had to move through the tunnel and up Khorshid's stairway into her new home when she got married—was much younger than Khorshid and bore only one child, who died. Khorshid's two other brothers, both older than he, each had two sons who survived a whooping-cough epidemic that had killed a quarter of the young children one winter. The four sons eventually cut down the walnut trees, starting a dispute over ownership that lasted into the next generation, and built this space up to the north wall, adding slanted verandahs and crooked stairways. At one time fifteen adults and twelve children were living in the compound together with some eighty sheep and goats, five cows, six donkeys, and about three dozen chickens, on a piece of land measuring about sixty by seventy feet.

Khorshid's nieces were married off in good time and moved out, as did his four nephews' daughters. With four childbearing women in the courtyard there was always a girl old enough to fill the important role of little servant, of fetcher and bringer and minder of babies and chickens and milkpots, to take the place of the older sister or cousin who got married and was lost to her mother's house. Three children fell off the open verandah—a common enough happening but shocking nevertheless. One of them, a girl, broke her leg and limped badly from then on; another, a toddler not yet walking, fell on a heap of hay, unharmed, by the providence of God; and one, a boy just about to cut his second front teeth, unruly, wild, and moving fast like any healthy boy of that age, tripped and fell down while chasing another at high speed over the whole length of the semicircle of verandahs, watched by his helpless relatives. He was dead when they got down to him. But otherwise the children did well. Whooping cough and measles had lost their scare, thanks to the doctor in the next village and the health teams from the city that passed through and coaxed reluctant mothers into vaccinating their babies. Once a baby had survived the never-ending diarrheas and colds of the first two years, there was a good chance it would survive.

Year after year one of the women was pregnant. Although Khorshid's parents and brothers had died, space became scarce and the fragmented fields no longer yielded enough food for the large families. One by one Khorshid's nephews found seasonal work in the city. One even sold all his animals and went to Kuwait for two years, to come back a rich man. He was the first of his brothers to build a house out in the fields—a big, roomy one with a bath and a kitchen such as he had seen used abroad, a house with a cement floor, a slanted tin roof, large grated windows, and a solid stone wall around the garden. Proudly they left, leaving the others to fight over their vacated room.

Then Khorshid died all of a sudden in his sleep.

Maryam, by far the youngest of the older generation, and by far the brightest and most energetic of all the women in the courtyard, had been the dominant figure even while her mother-in-law, too old and worn out to be of much use or importance, was still alive. Backed by her brothers in the adjacent compound, and just as alert and assertive as they were, she had diminished her handicap of lack of children very cleverly. She built up her position of power by the sheer dominance of her personality and the clever manipulation of her brothers and cousins. None of the younger women ever brought up the topic in her presence, no matter how tempted they surely felt to do so during the infrequent but high-pitched arguments with her. Maryam was strong in will and body. While the other women around her withered quickly into middle age, depleted from childbearing and child rearing, malnourished and anemic, only too glad to delegate work and responsibilities to their daughters, daughters-in-law and sons, Maryam stood straight backed, small, with head held high, and her quick, dark eyes watched her own and Khorshid's interests with undivided alertness. While Khorshid's brothers' land, equal to Khorshid's in size, was too little for the mouths it was supposed to feed, Khorshid's was yielding a surplus. Paying some relatives with his wheat, he had planted one of the finest vineyards in the village with their help and later, when the Shah's government provided apple trees, one of the largest orchards. He was in partnerships— organized by Maryam—with a great many of his poorer relatives, providing land and water against their good labor and successfully keeping a watchful eye on their honesty. Although neither was generous by nature, Maryam realized very early that acts of largesse on their part yielded far more than their initial cost in the compensations to come. Maryam was the master-mind behind all their successful endeavors, and Khorshid and every-body else knew it.

At home, unencumbered by children, she had time to see to the affairs of the whole courtyard. All the children had a healthy respect for her, and none ever disobeyed her orders (although they became experts at dodging them). The verandahs were always swept, even that of her youngest nephew's wife, who was sick a lot. Even the yard below, the barnyard for all practical purposes, was cleaner than most others. All the children in her compound were sent to school, boys and girls alike. Wasn't her brother the school principal? Were not two of her own nieces teachers? Although she never went out to pick berries or gather wild vegetables, more blackberries and wild spinach and wild onions were drying on their roofs than on anybody else's. Wherever she went — to a funeral, a sick relative, a wedding—she came with her entourage of sisters-in-law and nephews' wives, respected and honored if not liked.

After Khorshid died Maryam had to make some choices. Customarily at her age her sons would have taken care of her, but she had no sons. If she were younger, one of Khorshid's brothers would have to take her on as a second wife. But Khorshid's brothers were dead anyway. One possibility was to go and live with her brothers, but this Maryam found unappealing. By now two of her three brothers had moved out of their old courtyard, and she would have had to make a choice among the three of them and their wives. For Maryam it would have meant moving from a position of dominance and control into one of subordination— becoming, in her eyes, a servant. She did not want to be a servant for any of her sisters-in-law. And there was yet another possibility: remarriage.

Maryam considered it with realistic circumspection. Her age, she knew, was not an encumbrance in itself. Although older in years than her wrinkled sisters with their grownup children around them, Maryam looked and felt much younger. There was not a gray hair under her scarf; her arms were round, her breasts firm; and she could climb stairs without wheezing. She had been around a long time, yet she was not old. There were several middle-aged widowers in the village, a couple of them even eligible relatives. But perceptive as she was, she appreciated their problems very well. For a man who still wanted children she was a bad risk, even if there was a tacit understanding that her barrenness probably had been due to Khorshid's inadequacy and not hers. For a man with grown sons, on the other hand, she was not old enough; there was still just a chance that she might have children, which would obviously not be in the interest of the older children. Against the opposition of his sons an older man had little chance to take a youngish wife. Also, there was the matter of Khorshid's property. She was certain that as long as she had her strength and faculties none of her husband's nephews would press her to relinquish what, by rights, could be seen as their due inheritance. In any case she would fight back ably, and they knew it. But if she were to get married again she would either have to sell whatever she could (which undoubtedly would cause bad fights she did not particularly care for), only to have to give the money to her new husband, or else the vineyards and orchards and the fields of wheat and clover would be claimed successfully by Khorshid's nephews, especially those who already had worked the land for many years. She would be mistress in a new house again instead of a widow living all by herself, but the price was very high. Maryam decided on the last choice, namely, to wait and see, and to hold onto the bird in hand.

This was not easy. Khorshid had not actually worked much on his land, but he had watched that none of his partners cheated him, and he had gone out at nights to guard his share of water as it came down the channels to make sure no one else drained it into other fields. He had hustled at the agricultural office for his share of insecticides; he had struck deals with a distant cousin who co-owned a tractor; he was there when the fruit dealer from the city came up to weigh the apples. None of these chores Maryam felt she could possibly do herself, being a woman. Neither could she procure hay for the cow or take the sheep out to pasture when it was her turn in the cooperative herd. She sold the cow, the donkey, the sheep and goats. Instead of using the money to buy more apple trees or another piece of land, as she would have advised Khorshid to do, she lent it for interest. Although she was illiterate and had to do all her bookkeeping in her head, this enterprise was successful. At the next opportunity she sold one of the apple orchards, a small one which Khorshid had been working himself, so there was not much objection from the nephews. Then one of Khorshid's partners got an offer from somebody for a field right outside the old village, by now prime development land, and Maryam agreed to sell and split the profit. Although she lost out on this deal, she knew very well that in a few years the former partner would consider the land his own and his sons would simply take it, on the grounds that they had worked it for so many years. It was standard practice in the village, even if it caused endless disputes and drawn-out court cases. Some weeks later, when the school administration was looking for a piece of land to build a new boys' school, Maryam worked on her brother, the principal, to get the administration to buy the one vineyard that was so conveniently located only a little way off the main road. He succeeded; the nephew who had been in charge of it protested loudly, but his sons were too young to back him up and the deal was put through too swiftly for him to prevent it. Again, Maryam split the profit to keep him quiet, but she knew the others were on guard now and it probably was the last transaction she would be able to pull off. She was right, except for some poplar trees she managed to pass on to Ali, Ahmad and Perijan's son-in-law, when he was building his house on Ahmad's land. As she expected, the returns from the orchards and fields diminished as the partners came to view them as their own and began to regard the tribute they paid to Maryam as charitable gifts rather than her right. Luckily, by then, Maryam had enough money lent out to make a small income, large enough for her few needs and steady enough to make her totally independent.

But fate overtook her in other ways. In the back of her compound all her brothers had moved out into new houses at the outskirts of the village in opposite directions. Gone were the days of just slipping through the tunnel for a quick chat, counsel, news, to borrow or lend something, to keep up. Never too fond of her, and too conscious of their own importance to compromise it by walking through the village and paying her an official visit, her sisters-in-law stayed home, just as Maryam did for the same reasons. (Her youngest nephew's wife she did not see for almost two years after the move.) Half of her own father's courtyard fell to ruin, and the other half was transiently occupied by newlywed nephews and cousins' children before they had enough money to build their own houses elsewhere. The tunnel collapsed. To go to her father's old courtyard now Maryam had to climb two ladders over a high roof. It was not worth the effort. But in her own courtyard the same exodus happened. Both of Khorshid's remaining nephews (her own cousins' sons as well) started to make sun-baked bricks of mud and straw, and cement blocks. They could not afford the heavy stone and cement structures of the *nouveau riche* like their younger brother who had worked in Kuwait, but their own savings allowed them to put up at least a traditional house, modified and enlarged to include a separate kitchen and a "good" room, surrounded by its own private wall. Illiterate and unskilled as they were, the economic stagnation following the revolution had diminished their opportunities for outside work during the agricultural off-season. Money was very scarce and building material was expensive and in short supply, but the prevailing feeling was nevertheless to build now rather than later, because there might not be much of a later.

Within a few months Maryam had the courtyard to herself. The far northern rooms had been taken down by their owner so he could use the old poplar beams for the roof of his new house. His own few poplar trees around one of his gardens were not thick enough yet for the purpose, and, like so much else, lumber was priced beyond his means. For a while the second nephew still used his barns for his two donkeys and hay, and his old living quarters to store wheat behind heavy padlocks until he could build stables in his new courtyard. But except for his infrequent short stops, for the first time in her life Maryam was totally alone.

Beyond the heap of rubble that remained of the northern buildings, Maryam, sitting in the bright sun outside her own room, now had an unobstructed view to the high southern front of her neighbors—people she never had had much to do with and who were even less appealing now because one of their sons had become a revolutionary guard. Once in a while he would mount a loudspeaker on the corner of their high roof and blast revolutionary march music over the village (totally alien in style and intonation to any music Maryam was used to), or announcements, or some preacher's canned, unintelligible sermon. There was nothing now, not even a tree, to shield Maryam from this piercing noise. Yet she could not complain about it, either. It was, after all, a form of governmental action, and one did not criticize the government. Besides, she rarely saw the young man himself, and what good would it do to complain, however carefully couched in sarcasm or a joke, to his parents who suffered under it just as she did and were just as paralyzed to resist it? As long as she had had company in her courtyard and her brothers' courtyard in the back, the women had talked freely about the loudspeaker and the young man and made fun of both, saying things like, "who wants to go to heaven if this is all one hears there?" Or, "you know why the saints in heaven don't answer our pleas any more? Because they are all deaf from this music and can't hear us." Now Maryam had no one to talk to but herself, a condition she found boring and unsatisfactory, even if her own replies to herself never led to the arguments and fights of normal human conversation. Maryam also acutely felt that she was not keeping up with news, not even in her own family. Once a week she would go to the bathhouse (their own bath was a rather makeshift affair her nephew had built and then ruined when he went after his house beams). This she did more for the company than for cleanliness, but the clientele of the bathhouse was dwindling as people built their own shower stalls into or onto the new houses. Even Perijan, Maryam's youngest sister, had taken to frequenting the bath in her sister's house, for fear, she said, that little Shala would somehow come to harm in the public bath, and Maryam did not see either of them for several months, until the second sister fell sick and Maryam had a valid reason to go and visit her without losing face.

Indeed, there were so few legitimate opportunities for a woman to go out now. As a widow without sons she had to do her shopping herself, but how much shopping does one woman need? A little meat once in a long while, some fruits, a spool of thread, a box of cookies for the rare visitor. . . . Sitting on an old rug at the edge of the verandah, she could see a few yards of the road outside her alley and the people walking by just long enough to recognize them. If Maryam saw a particular woman she liked to talk to approach the water faucet by her bridge, just outside her field of vision, sometimes she would grab one of her own big plastic bottles and empty it, if need be—water got warm and stagnant in them soon anyway, in contrast to the old goatskin bags that had held the water in pre-plastic times—and saunter down to the water spout a few steps to the right outside her alley. But how often and for how long could a self-respecting woman linger at the water? Besides, more and more often she was asked there how much longer she would stay here alone, and whether she wasn't afraid to live by herself, and what if a thief would come? More disturbingly, there were also veiled remarks by her closest relatives to the effect that her independence gave the embarrassing impression in public that she had no one to go to, and that this opinion was unfounded and resented by her family. These insinuations were another reason for her to limit her contacts, especially with her brothers and their wives.

Maryam found herself not only alone in a lot of empty space but also with a lot of empty time on hand. Until a few years back Maryam could have taken her spindle and joined the other women on one of her neighbors' porches, keeping busy while visiting, any time. But she had no more fleece to spin. Her sheep were long gone, as were her nephews' sheep—sold, most of them. Her two rooms were immaculate and stayed so day after day. Once she had swept the yard below, it stayed clean. Cleaning the handful of rice for her evening meal was a matter of minutes. The bread she baked lasted and lasted. Lately, young women had taken up needlework. Indeed, her niece Golgol could draw a wonderful pattern of flowers and vases onto a piece of white fabric—the girls in school all had her do it— but Maryam, almost an old woman by any standard, felt she could not very well amuse herself with a pastime of the young. Her routine chores, a little mending and sewing, and her waterpipe were all she had to fill the long hours of the day.

In a corner of the deserted courtyard Maryam planted a few cucumbers and tomatoes and the pits of some peaches and sunflowers. Although the sparrows got most of the seeds, a little garden was sprouting—green, easy on her eyes, a patch of life, and one more good reason to haul water from the water faucet. The nephew, however, was fidgety when he saw the little plants. "Not that I want to suggest anything, Aunt Maryam," he said. "No harm done, for sure, by holy Abbas, but just to keep the record straight: this is my land, it was my barn that stood here, and my house, all along here to the corner over there, and you know it. No, don't say anything, don't fret, just eat your cucumbers, God bless them, but I just want to say that maybe one of my sons will want to come back up here one day, one never knows, and this is our land, not yours, not my brothers, not Uncle Khorshid's, as you know."

Although taken aback, Maryam was not really surprised at that speech. Three of her nephews were fighting with a cousin in their deserted courtyard over a few fruit trees he had planted there, on their land. They argued with him but also with each other, as each claimed the very spot on which the little trees stood. Disputes over a few feet of soil were happening all over the village. "Don't you worry," Maryam said with dignity and contempt, "you will get your share of the sunflowers like any landlord, for sure. Just send one of your kids, I won't cheat you!" But she was so upset about it that later in the afternoon, spotting her brother walking by on the road from school, she took her veil and followed him to his house and there complained bitterly to him and his wife.

"Sister," said Kerim, "my house is your house. The lad is a scoundrel. But why are you staying there? It is not good for you to live alone. Here is room enough for you."

"Yes, indeed, by holy Abbas, we are devoted to you," said his wife, half-heartedly and with a stony face.

"I appreciate your devotion," murmured Maryam, and fled.

At home, she did some hard thinking. Kerim's suggestion that she should give up her place lately had become his standard reply to all of her complaints. In one form or another everybody urged her to leave, even Perijan, who knew very well that Maryam did not really get along with any of her sisters-in-law. They had been close neighbors for too many years not to know this; they all realized how fragile was the heavy mask of familial politeness, how easily it cracked in the shuffle of everyday life. Kerim would probably insist that Maryam move in with his household, since by virtue of his education and his position in the village he was the head of the whole family, and he had the means to support her easily. If Maryam were to go to Kerim's he would make her divest herself of all the property Khorshid's nephews could possibly lay a claim to in order to prevent disputes with them and probably give up her own money, too. She could not imagine him allowing her to have her own business deals in his house. If, on the other hand, she would choose to live with any of her other brothers—her youngest, for example, whose wife, easygoing and much younger than Maryam, had always been devoted to her with great respect and only such a faint hint of insubordination that Maryam was sure she could squelch it easily—there would be different problems. This brother was so poor that he would see to it that she got the lion's share of Khorshid's land (for him to use), even if it meant a distasteful fight with his cousins. Without illusion Maryam appreciated his position and her own in this arrangement. He had a house full of young children and very little land. With her money he would build onto the already overcrowded new house ("for your comfort," he would tell her); his life would ease a little; and in no time she would share his poverty, unequally though, because in a few years she would be old and useless, a burden no one would feel the familial obligation to carry with grace.

She would stay and fight.

No suitor had come. Another husband quite clearly was not her fate. After Khorshid's death she had donned the darker colors fitting for a widow, and she kept to them. For one thing, after the revolution even the young women dressed themselves in the purples and dark greens that formerly had been signs of old age and mourning, but also she felt she could move more easily through the public places outside her own house if she projected the image of an old woman. Although unlike most of her peers she was in excellent health and did not huff and puff on the steep slopes, like most women she walked slowly through the lanes, stopping here and there to exchange a few words, to listen to news. A few years back she would have considered this not quite proper. When she still was in charge of her courtyard she ushered her young women through the village at a dignified good pace and did not encourage them to linger. But now, she figured, a little laxness in this regard was the smaller of two evils. She started to seize every decent opportunity to visit a wide circle of relatives, to sit at sickbeds, to help out at weddings, to mourn untiringly any death. She even joined the groups of women who, after the revolution, had adopted the urban custom of visiting the graveyards on Thursday afternoons to mourn the dead—to sit among the ornate new graves, to wail, to exchange sweets and fruits they brought along for sacrifice, to remind those who had lost a son or a brother in the war of their misery and to remind those who hadn't of their luck, to gossip a little, to sing a few mourning songs with high-pitched voices. Maryam had Khorshid to mourn, as well as the fact that she had no children living and none to lose. But mainly, Maryam went there for the same reason she sought out the company of people other than her brothers and sisters, namely, to bolster her claim to independence, to persuade everyone that she was able and determined to stay on in her place, to ensure herself of their support. She used the others—the distant cousins, the aunts, the cousins' children, the wide network of her family—as moral support and to put pressure on her own brothers if the need should arise.

All this happened over one long summer and fall. Maryam bought a small kerosene heater and a gas cooking burner to avoid most of the cumbersome necessity of getting firewood. Long before the first rains of early winter, with the help of Perijan's son she had her own two rooms waterproofed by spreading tar-soaked sacking on the flat roof. This did away with having to climb up onto the roof during a rain to press the water out of the soaked earth with a heavy oak roller so that the rain wouldn't seep through the roof. As this was a man's job and the oak roller was heavy, the chore had been one of her brothers' more powerful arguments against her staying in her house alone. She paid for this job herself, and none of her brothers could say anything. The verandah, as important a space to live in as her rooms, she could take care of herself; it was not as big as the roof and was right outside her door.

But her two nephews' barns and storage rooms adjacent to hers, unprotected and uncared for, started to melt and crumble under the heavy rains and the snow of that winter. In her own interest Maryam urged and argued that the men attend to their property, but to no avail. Instead, when the first warm and dry breezes of spring blew in from the south, one morning the two men and three of their sons, without any warning that would have given Maryam time to prevent them, stood there with their pickaxes and shovels and started to take the buildings down to get to the beams. There was nothing Maryam could do. The houses were theirs to do with as they pleased; so were the barns underneath. She gathered all her belongings from the porch and locked them into her rooms to get them out of the dust, and then climbed onto her roof to escape the clouds of dust enveloping the scene of destruction. Her house would stand alone now, surrounded by rubble, leaning against the back wall of the house still standing in her brothers' old courtyard. It was not considerate of the nephews to claim those beams now—in a few years she would be dead anyway—but beams were good money. She knew this all too well. Annoying as the affair was, it was not alarming, she thought.

Maryam was in for a surprise. The settling dust revealed a catastrophe: Maryam, perched on her roof with her headscarf drawn half across her face, looked down not onto her verandah but into an abyss. The roofs of the barns that had formed part of her porch had overlapped, and with the collapse of the supporting barn structures almost all of her verandah had been ripped off. Her fireplace was gone; so was the little branch hut shading the water containers and the edge jutting out far enough to give her a lookout into the alley. Her stairway leading up from the alley was broken, one-half gone, the other hanging crookedly and raggedly on the remainder of its support of branches and short beams. To get down from her rooms to level ground Maryam would have to climb onto her roof—where she now sat, rigid with consternation—then up another ladder onto her brother's higher roof, and from there down into their courtyard and out another alley and through a half-tumbled tunnel to the road.

Maryam was perched high up on dusty beams with nowhere to go.

The two nephews and their sons were just as bewildered. No one had realized that the barn roofs had been so interconnected that most of them would come down if only a part was taken away. The men had suspected (in shrewd silence) that a corner of Maryam's porch would go, but not this much. As soon as she had back her voice, Maryam jumped up and, arms flailing, started to give a long, drawn-out wail, the most powerful signal of distress in public. "Woe to me," she shouted in between the shrill screams, "the heathens are destroying me, an old woman, woe to me!"

The youngest of the nephews' sons, an optimistic lad of about fourteen, was the fastest to respond. "It doesn't matter," he yelled. "We'll fix it, shut up." But Maryam took this assurance for what it was: the standard noncommittal reaction to most calamities involving other people's property.

"People, come here," she shouted, louder still, to the figures emerging on the rooftops around her. "People, God is my witness, my own relatives, my own cousin's sons are robbing me, are violating my rights!"

Meanwhile her younger nephew, Faraj, and two of the boys had heaved themselves up onto what was left of the porch, balancing precariously on the wobbly beams, and were gesticulating with great animation up to Maryam. "Be quiet," they bellowed. "Come down, shut up, no one is harming you, do you understand? Shut up!" And then the younger nephew scuttled up the ladder to her and grabbed her. "We'll repair it," he said, to no one in particular, but loud enough for all the neighbors to hear. "It was an accident; we will get it together right away; come down and tell us what you want. We didn't mean any harm, we will set it right right away." At this public proclamation Maryam let herself be persuaded to climb down, which was not without danger, since the ladder was very close to the sagging edge of the mutilated verandah.

As long as there was light enough they were as good as their word. While the boys shored up the pitiable rest of the porch with beams they dug out of the adobe ruins, the two older men tried to restore the stairs to at least temporary usefulness. But night was falling fast, and they had neither hammers nor nails with them. "Don't fall," they said to Maryam when they left. "Be careful, don't go down without a lantern. We will be back tomorrow and do it right."

"What about the porch?" Maryam asked with justified suspicion.

"The porch too, of course," said the older nephew, "by holy Abbas."

"Yes, yes," said Maryam, "Saint Abbas is a very busy man with you. Don't trouble him, just come yourself."

The next day, a Saturday, all the boys were in school until afternoon. It was Faraj's turn to take the cooperatively herded cows out to pasture, so he was out the whole day. The older nephew, Ezad, and his son had promised to work on somebody's house, for a wage. They sent word that they would come in the evening. Another piece of the porch fell while Maryam was climbing the wobbly stairs with a heavy pail of water. The worst was that her toilet, an outhouse built onto a corner of the barn, was inaccessible, possibly even destroyed, and she had quite a walk to get to the one in her brother's yard. She had meant to bake bread that day but was too hot, cramped, and upset to start making dough. Instead she walked all the way out to Perijan to borrow a few flatbreads from her. Perijan was ready to commiserate, but also full of the tiresome advice to go where she belonged, namely, to her brothers.

In the evening, an hour or so before it would be dark, Ezad, his long, skinny frame stooping after a long day's labor, came with his son and his tools. They were annoyed when they saw that no one from the other party had shown up, and Ezad sent his son to fetch at least the young cousins. This took another good while, which Ezad and Maryam used to argue about what should be done. She said she needed the outhouse dug out and repaired, and she needed her own barn back in usable shape, all of it, and the verandah rebuilt, and the stairs fixed. Ezad reduced these demands to their more essential meaning: Maryam needed some sort of outhouse, some porch (which automatically would provide a woodshed underneath), and some sort of stairs. Even scaled down the restoration would be a lot of work they could ill afford now. The boys would have to salvage adobe bricks; old beams would have to be cut to size; and the sump of the outhouse was probably filled with debris and would have to be emptied. "The black death," Ezad said over and over, with great feeling, by way of a curse.

That evening, after the party finally had assembled (minus Faraj, who had sprained an ankle), the boys stacked a small pile of reusable bricks and Ezad shored up the stairs a little more, and together they cleared a path to the barn below Maryam's house so that she could use the barn as an outhouse, they said. Maryam refused to use it, though, not so much for hygienic reasons (in the past barns were used as toilets) but because she suspected that once she started using it the restoration of her outhouse would lose urgency and she might end up having none for good. Instead, ostentatiously swinging the long-spouted water can used for the necessary ablutions and stopping to exchange words here and there with passersby, she would slowly walk around to her brother's dilapidated outhouse or to that of Begom and Akbar, her neighbors across the lane, which was, however, rather dirty and not much better than the barns of old.

The next day Maryam was at a mourning party at a neighboring village all day long. When she came back at night the brick pile was a little higher, but nothing else had changed. The following morning Ezad came bright and early, poked around in the vicinity of the outhouse and found its roof collapsed, and left with many exclamations of "Black death." Maryam asked her neighbor Akbar to help her take down the ladder to her roof for her to use instead of the increasingly unsteady ruins of the stairs. The next day the sky was cloudy. The first rains would start soon and wash away the rest of the porch. When only two of the boys came in the afternoon to find more bricks, Maryam became so annoyed that she walked out to Ezad to remind him of his promise. He was not at home, however, and his wife told Maryam that she was inconveniencing Ezad beyond reason and that she should go and live with her brothers as was only right and proper. After telling her in no uncertain words how little she thought of this advice, Maryam marched back to the southern edge of the village to complain to Faraj about the unfinished work and Ezad's wife's insolence. Faraj was at home and promised to be there the next day. His ankle was still swollen; Maryam could see it herself.

After a week or so, Maryam had become rather dextrous in hauling pails of water up and down the ladder, wide skirts notwithstanding. She had baked bread indoors, which was very hot and uncomfortable, and had watched, practically from her doorsill, the few half-hearted attempts of the boys and the nephews to tackle the job. The progress was nil.

With a heavy heart she went to Kerim and to her second brother, and to her youngest. Each told her that he would do what he could, little as it might be considering that Ezad and Faraj were not their own sons, and that she should probably give up the house altogether. But the unenthusiastic reactions of her brothers' wives provided some consolation: the women did not cherish the prospect of joint housekeeping any more than Maryam did and therefore were her allies. So stubbornly and determinedly Maryam fought for her cause, lobbying with all her accessible neighbors and relatives and preparing the scene for the showdown she knew she would have to precipitate.

Midmorning right after the first slight rain, which had flushed holes out of the remainder of her unprotected and unprotectable porch, she dressed herself in a black skirt, took a black veil out of her bundle of clothes, pulled her hair out to give herself a disheveled look, took in a deep breath and let out a scream that lasted until she was in the main alley. By then she had an audience lined up on verandahs and in doorways. Recounting at the top of her lungs in telegraphic simplicity the highlights of the insults and broken promises of her relatives, without mentioning names, she stormed down through the village towards the main crossroads, shouting her intention to go to the police to complain publicly and without reservations—she, an old woman, who was being done in by her own family.

In no time the children brought the bad news to Kerim in school around the corner, to her brothers and cousins, and eventually to Faraj and Ezad in the fields. A first-rate scandal was in progress, and Kerim, as the head of the family and warden of his sister, felt acutely distressed. He was furious with Faraj and Ezad; he was equally furious with Maryam, whom he saw as the ultimate cause of the trouble; and he was furious with his own wife, who had made it clear that she did not much care to live under one roof with his sister. He knew it was no different in his second brother's house. Now he and his brothers would have to deal with this private family matter, which had transformed itself through the stupidity of some stubborn and quarrelsome women and the irresponsibility of some young good-for-nothing male relatives into a public show of indignation; it left him looking incapable of managing his family with providence and dignity.

By the time Kerim arrived at the spectacle in the village's main crossroads Maryam had worked herself into a fine state of fury. She was disheveled, her hair had long escaped the scarf, the veil had fallen to her shoulders, and she was trembling as she screamed her protests and violently announced her firm intention to complain to the police, the revolutionary guards, the governor, the Imam Khomeini himself, about the injustice she suffered from her own kinsmen. A few of the men, beholden to Kerim by kinship or other allegiances, had blocked her progress towards the police further down the road, but Maryam had reckoned on this, indeed had hoped for it. She had no intention of lodging an official complaint, which would have brought disgrace on all her family, including herself, and would have alienated them from her. She had counted on the matter being resolved right there in the square. However, at this point she was ruled by genuine fury and it was just as well that these men were there to restrain her until one of her brothers would deal with her. Kerim and his son-in-law pounced on her and held her firmly, calming her down with assurances that they would set everything right, with explanations to the spectators, with curses on Faraj and Ezad (four of their children were in the crowd), with solemn oaths that Kerim personally would see to the restoration of her house, with pleas to the more esteemed among the bystanders to bear witness to the promises. In the end, Maryam let herself be led away to her sister Perijan's house, which was the closest to the scene, where she was given tea and showered with soothing noises of sympathy.

Maryam spent the night there. Kerim routed out Faraj and Ezad and hired a young lad to work full time on the outhouse and the barn walls. He decided on the size of the porch and how it would be supported, and he himself, together with his and Maryam's youngest brother, built a new staircase, much narrower than the old one had been but with real cement holding together the flat rocks. The job was done within two days. Maryam was not entirely happy with the small porch but knew better than to complain. She built herself a new fireplace in one corner, a semicircle of a mud wall some fifteen inches high, which would support the convex iron griddle on which the flatbreads were baked, and she even built herself a little henhouse with the mud that now was so abundantly heaped up in the courtyard. She had enough grain to feed a few chickens. For the time being she was content. Her brothers were mad at her, just as a father would be angry with a misbehaving child, but she knew that their wives were relieved and that, therefore, their anger would dissipate quickly. She had come so perilously close to losing her porch and her house and, with them, her independence, that now she felt almost elated, looking down over her cucumbers and out towards the street from her quiet perch, her small window to the shrunken world. Listening to the gurgling of her waterpipe, to the faint noises of distant life, she watched the slow hours of the day pass from dusk to sun to shadows, one after the other, lined up like the beads around her neck. As long as God would give her the use of her limbs, a little food for her belly, and enough strength in her bones to move, she would say, "Thanks be to God" a thousand times a day.

3

About Barrenness and
What Tala Did about It

Bad luck and ill fate are one's most reliable companions in life, the people say in Deh Koh. Sometimes, bad things happen to bad people, and this is as it should be: God's retribution, just punishment. But much more often things just as bad or worse happen to good people. They just happen according to God's inscrutable design we call life on earth, beyond justice, and are seen as punishment only by the odd neighbor who has a little personal grudge and who argues that no one can really know about the secret sins of others, or of anyone's ancestors (for, like other property, sins too are inheritable).

Of all misfortunes, having no children probably is the most exasperating because it is the most durable. It lasts through one's adulthood and old age, unalterable, unforgettable. Without children one is alone in this world. Without children, it is said, one is nothing, of no importance in the eyes of the people; there is no support to back up one's voice, to watch out for one's advantage, to help, to hustle, to speak up, to take care. Only the cynical will say that without a son one doesn't have to put up with a daughter-in-law; that without a daughter there never will be a dispute with her husband's family; that without children there won't ever be a bad word said about land division, water rights, the use of poplar trees, or sheep. This all is quite true, and it is equally true (and just as useless to point out) that childless couples are economically much better off than their neighbors who are blessed with children and don't seem to be any more discontent and unhappy, ill, or wanting in their old age. These factors are not weighed by the public. Large fields undivided and uncontested over by a horde of sons, money in the bank, good food, and neat clothes cannot fill an empty house.

There aren't many childless couples in Deh Koh, and of the few not one ever split up, and no husband ever took a second wife because of his first wife's barrenness. Indeed, after the first few rough years of crushed expectations, attempted cures, amulets and accusations, pilgrimages, travels to doctors, fights, sneers, and humiliating pity, and after hope has dimmed to a faint flicker deep in the couple's hearts, they tune in to each other as companions in misery and live much more peacefully and leisurely than most of their neighbors harassed by large families. As time goes on there is always a nephew or a favorite niece among the many to talk to and be close to; with time and resources on hand, help can be distributed like a valuable commodity, like a loan, to be paid back with interest.

But the first years are tough. Fierce hope and defiance rule the day and every month's bloody purge may push a woman toward hysterics and despair.

Tall and heavy, round-faced and round-hipped, full-breasted and bursting with energy, Tala was the darling in a large, boisterous family, one of four daughters with high, black eyebrows and sparkling white teeth. Like most girls in their early teens she dismissed marriage summarily as useless, unwelcome, disgusting, and altogether worthy of a girl's suicide. In public she wore her veil-wrap pulled tightly around her, covering half of her face even before the revolution, at a time when light, airy wraps were used more as adornment than concealment. But from under her veil she kept track of the young men around her with quick eyes. Once she even was beaten up by one of her fierce-tempered brothers because he had seen her look at and greet (though she denied it) a lad in front of the school—a cousin, true enough, but in public. The brother felt both shamed and called upon to teach his sister proper behavior. Her only satisfaction in remembering this humiliation was that she had given her brother a black eye in the shuffle. She was strong, and the brother was two years younger.

Tala would have liked one of her cousins on her mother's side to ask for her, and so she sent out as many hints as she dared to. They were understood, and Khanom, her mother, started a delicate inquiry without being too obvious, so that if nothing would come of the match one could always deny any previous interest. This maneuver involved several unnecessary trips by Khanom to the doctor, whose office in the next village was one house down from her cousin, the mother of the young man in question, and a most natural place for Khanom to rest her tired feet. But the young man's older brother had married one of his mother's brothers' daughters, much to everybody's regrets, including the young woman herself— she proved incompatible with just about everybody in the house, even the dog, which bit her twice. Quite reasonably, but to Tala's great sorrow, her cousin said he would rather stay unmarried than take a wife from that part of his family. Instead he went to town and a friend found him a wife there, and he didn't come back home, not even for the New Year's celebrations, for five years.

Tala was disappointed and getting impatient, despite her loud exclamations about the rottenness of men and the undesirability of marriage. When one of their relatives told them about an unlucky man in a village a little farther down, a very remote kinsman of Tala's father, who had lost his wife and his only child recently in an accident and was looking for a wife—a good man, with land and a nice vineyard—she considered taking him sight unseen, although it would have meant leaving Deh Koh. Her mother was against the match, but before a decision had to be made the man himself died and the matter was thereby settled. The next suitor, a local man of middling circumstances, got into a prolonged dispute over water rights with one of Tala's uncles, and at the same time his old and widowed father announced lustily that he was looking for a wife himself because his daughters-in-law didn't care for him properly. The young man and his two brothers were busy trying to keep the old man from getting anywhere with his wooings; they did not welcome the prospect of having to take care of, and later divide the inheritance with, another set of brothers the sprightly old man still might sire. Meanwhile one of Tala's father's brother's sons, Yusuf—strong and big like all the members of this family—had tried to get another girl and, angered over the refusal, told his mother to find him a wife, he didn't care whom. Any one of the four sisters in Khanom's house were marriageable by now, and negotiations started between the two houses. Khanom wanted to marry her daughters off according to age, one by one. Yusuf, however, recovering from his morose indifference, decided he wanted Tala. Discord threatened to erupt over the issue until, unexpectedly, a teacher from a village rather far to the south, who was stationed in Deh Koh, came for Tala's older sister, his former pupil, and the situation was resolved.

Tala moved into an empty room in the large courtyard of Aligorg and Hava, Yusuf's parents. Their living quarters and storage rooms were lined up in a semicircle atop the barns and sheds, whose flat, earthen roofs also provided generous verandahs in front of each of the living rooms. Two brothers and their wives and a band of little children lived there in adjacent rooms, as did two unmarried daughters and Yusuf's youngest, unmarried brother. Like Tala's own, this too was a noisy family, in which opinions were expressed freely without regard for decorum and consequences. Neither bashful nor short of breath, and with the advantage of long practice, Tala joined in the chorus with passion. A fast worker, strong as an ox, and generous, she was nobody's fool and nobody's servant. Her husband, so his mother said, was intoxicated with her, like a drunk, and Tala liked him too. The giggling from their room at night was an embarrassment for the children, her sister-in-law Kerima said. Even if Yusuf sometimes beat up Tala a little after an especially galling show of insubordination—like the time she went home to her folks without telling him and then stayed there for two days because, she said, her mother-in-law had insulted her—she was tolerated by all, even liked, in their loud and harsh fashion.

Tala's mother Khanom bore fourteen children, seven of whom survived; Yusuf's mother Hava bore nine, of whom seven also survived. Tala's sisters had gotten pregnant within weeks if not days of getting married. But month after month Tala kept washing her soiled, old, innermost skirt, made of some twelve yards of sturdy cotton which soaked up her heavy flow of dark blood. Every month she noticed with rising anxious hopes her breasts harden and her belly swell, only to wake up one morning with the sickly smell of blood exuding from the heavy folds between her knees, crushing all anticipation. "I can't understand this," said Kerima, her sister-in-law and next-door neighbor. "From the nightly thumping in your house, one would think you'd get pregnant every week." And if there was an audience like Hava or one of the other women, she would go on describing the kinds of noises she claimed didn't let her sleep a wink: thrashing, groaning, moaning, shrieking, gurgling, deep grunting in imitation of Yusuf, until Tala was red with embarrassment and in turn, and with just as much talent, would give them a performance of Kerima and her husband's nightly activities. This was, they all agreed, in very bad taste, sinful even, considering that Yusuf's unmarried young sisters were listening, giggling into their hands, but the occasion was just too tempting for Kerima's boisterous sense of fun.

After a few months of no news, Hava made a special fumigation with seeds of wild rue against the evil eye right in Tala's room. Maybe the evil eye had made Tala slow in conceiving. With so many people (strangers among them) attending the wedding feasts and the dances, such harm easily could have been done despite the precautions Hava was sure Khanom had taken, including keeping Tala properly secluded for that time. Tala's mother, however, thought Tala must have chilled her womb by washing too many clothes in cold water and made her take a sort of steam bath. Khanom seated Tala on a big basket that was set upside down over a pot in which an herb had been boiled in water and three very hot stones had been dropped. Tala had to drink the same herb, brewed like tea, while she sat on the basket like a hen, with steam rising around her. This, too, had no effect.

By now the jokes had given way to embarrassment, irritation, and concern. Tala broached the subject with Yusuf, who was flushed with discomfort and only said not to worry. She complained about pointed remarks and sideways looks by his mother and sisters and brothers' wives, but he ordered her to ignore them.

Secretly (that is, without telling anybody, but this did not mean nobody knew about it) Tala went to see Mashhadi Janjan, the herbalist-doctor. An old, tall, skinny widow, Janjan was living alone by herself in a bare, clean-swept room barely big enough to stretch out to sleep in behind her sons' courtyard, facing a lone willow tree, an alley, and the blind back wall of her neighbor's home. In this way she did not have to look at her sons, whom she called heathens who didn't pay her the slightest respect. Liberated from most of the social restraints of younger women, knowledgeable and wise, she made a living of sorts from collecting herbs and dealing in medicines and powerful rocks and minerals. As her honorific title implied, Mashhadi Janjan had made the pilgrimage to Mashhad, to the tomb of the Imam Reza (and also to every shrine in the area). Wisely she had brought back blessed water from each of the holy places; herbs from every bazaar; and handfuls of wheat scooped up from the ground in front of the magnificent shrines in Mashhad and Isfahan and Shiraz, thrown there by pilgrims for the pigeons. As a sacrifice for the saint, the seeds had absorbed some of the saint's power, Janjan said. They certainly were good for something or the other; she would find out what for. In the pile of household goods where other women kept the sugar, the sweets for guests, the raisins and walnuts and almonds, trinkets, little gifts received or to be given at an occasion, Mashhadi Janjan had a regular pharmacy. In small, dusty bags tightly wrapped with string she kept dried leaves and roots (whole or crushed or pounded to powder in a mortar), mallow and chamomile, olive leaves and black pepper, gunpowder, yarrow, fenugreek, juniper, nightshade, coriander, cinnamon, worseed, wild rue, henna, acorn meal, dandelion, dung from a female donkey, sugar candy, mint, bone meal from a sheep, dill, cow dung, a few beads of opium, mulberries, blackberries, the dried galls of a mountain goat and a cow, charcoal of a willow bark, plantain, filings of iron, bear grease in a plastic bag, the fangs of some bird, the teeth of a wolf, the dried testicles of a wild buck, licorice, wild rhubarb, lovage and ligusticum, borage, maidenhair and camel's thorn, drug fumitory, London rocket, safflower, birthwort, senna, indigo, and more, some of which she didn't quite know what it was, only what it was good for or against. There were bottles and tins and crinkled paper sacks, stained and smelling strong and powerful; and there was a little red velvet pouch with dozens of beads, some loose, some strung on a tightly spun thin cord of wool: amber, glass, jade, blue ceramic beads, shells, fossils from the mountains, rocks and pebbles in all shapes and colors, a few tiny corals, a precious turquoise, mother-of-pearl, agates, cherry pits dyed red and green, and beads made of fragrant woods. Mashhadi Janjan knew all the blacksmiths who passed through Deh Koh, and they brought her fresh chamomile in the spring from the lowlands, and they peddled the most powerful of all medicines, like the black or red child-stone, God knew where from. Janjan knew exactly what she needed and paid promptly in rice and sugar, poor as she was, just as she was always paid promptly by her customers, in kind, or, more recently, in money. She never named a price, though, and never asked for any payment, and never refused a request, unless it was for a medicine to harm somebody. She would not be caught going to hell for having helped people do wicked things, she said.

Janjan knew about Tala's problem, like most women in the village. She started on her with mild remedies first: more of the bitter herb infusion, more sitting over steam on a basket, and, after Tala's next period, for three mornings on an empty stomach, Janjan made her swallow a spoonful of a concoction of ten ingredients, including dandelion roots, pepper, roasted wheat flour, olive oil, and grape syrup. This would clean her womb, said Janjan, and her child would have a beautiful, light skin. But nothing happened.

Scared but determined, with her husband's permission and accompanied by her mother, Tala went to the doctor. Janjan had advised her to go: the more wisdom brought to bear on the problem, the better, she said. The doctor, a fat young man from Tehran who called Tala "Madam," which she had never been called before in her life, asked her how long she had been married, whether she had any pains ("in all my limbs," she said, "and sometimes in my head"—a kind of safe, standard reply, because who really knew what the doctor was after?), and how often her period came. Then he measured her blood pressure and sent her home, saying it was all in her head and there was nothing wrong with her, she shouldn't worry. Bewildered, she felt acutely that she must have said something wrong for the doctor to come to such a nonsensical conclusion, because, after all, she didn't get pregnant, and this surely was wrong, wasn't it? So what was this man talking about, not to worry? She was disappointed. He hadn't given her one single pill, not even one single aspirin, not to speak of a shot.

At home, efforts were increased. Janjan gave her her most precious remedy, a dab of cotton wool into which she had scratched a few specks of powder from forty different beads, to wear like an amulet. Hava took a chicken to Master Hosein, a literate, semiretired builder and sought-after amulet writer, who wrote something from the Koran onto three tiny pieces of paper—one to be burnt over a candle, one to be swallowed with tea, and one to be sewn into a little bag and worn around the neck. But neither had the hoped-for result. Khanom suggested a pilgrimage to Bibi Masume, a most wonderful woman-saint whose shrine at a mighty spring amidst a waste of tumbled rocks was venerated for hundreds of miles around; it was said that she worked miraculous cures for the faithful where doctors, amulets and other human efforts had failed. As a woman, she was especially sympathetic towards the worries and ailments of her sisters, and the people said that no one who approached her with humbleness and pious ardor had ever left her tomb without a feeling of calm and comfort. Not having had many worries to cope with, like most young people, Tala had felt lukewarm towards saints but now was most enthusiastic about a pilgrimage. There was a hitch, though: she could not go without a male relative on her side or Yusuf's. Not only would it be improper for a woman to travel unaccompanied, but also the journey was long and rough: the roads were bumpy and rutted at best and became impassable with mud for long stretches after any rain, and the trip required at least three days, with overnight stays in strange, and, God knew, dangerous places. It was the end of spring, a busy season for men, and no one could be persuaded to leave his fields to take Tala there. Yusuf, Tala was sure, was glad he could plead urgent work; he was not a pious man and didn't pray, unlike Tala herself, who had taken to praying regularly recently. He also used to make disparaging remarks about the groups of pilgrims who left the village now and then, or who came back, telling the most wonderful stories of joy and healing— all lies, Yusuf said, but Tala wasn't so sure. All she could get Yusuf to agree to was a promise of a pilgrimage at some more opportune time, and a promise of a sacrifice to the saint, offered with a plea for help. But no help was forthcoming.

By now, gloom and anger had settled on the courtyard. Gone were the light-hearted banter, the ribald jokes, the laughter. Differences that before had been handled stormily but settled with a dollop of goodwill and humor now were thrashed about like clubs over days on end. The men, coming home to angry wives, spoke loud and final words and thus were dragged into the fights. One day, when she learned in a roundabout way involving a neighbor that Kerima was pregnant again—her fourth pregnancy in six years—Tala, in a fit of rage and despair, tore the amulets from her neck and flung them down into the yard, ripped the design of wild rue seeds off her wall and trampled on it, and yanked off her headscarf and threw it into the fire; in high-pitched screams of frenzy she accused Yusuf's people of conspiring against her, of black magic, of evil intentions, of hostility, of being heathens who basked in her misery, the whole lot of them.

With this, Tala had transformed herself from a young daughter-in-law to be handled circumspectly, watched carefully, and trusted tentatively into a hostile, insubordinate, wholly unreasonable, and spiteful enemy. She alternated between self-imposed seclusion in her dark room, where she would sit like a spider for hours on end, and angry bursts of impatience at the slightest disturbance, such as a child running across her verandah—which the children couldn't avoid, because the more convenient staircase down to the water faucet was at the other side of Yusuf's house. Or else Tala would cry. Her current needlework—a stitchery of convoluted garlands with large, red blossoms marching around a central, huge, violet vase with more large, red blossoms (a cover for the skirts and pants hanging on nails on the wall)—was blotched in green where her tears had dissolved the color of the green floss. She put the stitchery aside and stuck it deep into her household pile, because the very fact that she had time to do stitchery reminded her as well as everybody else that she didn't have the more important of a grown woman's chores to do. She wouldn't leave her house, wouldn't even visit her mother after her brother's wife there had had her baby. She felt ostracized. People looked at her with pity and whispered; she was poor Tala, who didn't have any children. As the closest neighbor, Kerima bore the brunt of Tala's ill temper and had her husband put up a wall between their respective parts of the verandah, whereupon Yusuf beat up Tala, reluctantly, more out of his own unhappiness than anger, although by all standards Tala behaved like an especially recalcitrant and unmannered child and not like a woman, who should bear both joys and misery gracefully and quietly.

The revolution brought a new physician to the village, a young man from the north, with a pleasant face and an unhurried, polite manner such as the villagers had rarely seen in a stranger. Everybody spoke highly of him. Tala went to him all by herself and told him of her plight. The new doctor asked her the same questions the other one had asked, and many more, like, whether she had any discharge (she didn't), whether she had cramps (she didn't), and then how often her husband slept with her, and whether he left much or little fluid in her. This was hard for Tala to answer because of her utter embarrassment about talking about such matters at all, and to a stranger, and to a man, but also because she didn't know the answer; how should she know how much of his fluid there should be? But the doctor was patient, and in his detached and polite way he put her at ease enough so she could describe the situation in her own way. (It was rather little, she concluded—sometimes she didn't even feel the need for an ablution afterwards.) The doctor did not examine her, for which she was glad. She thought if one ever did, she would surely die on the spot of embarrassment and fright. In the end the doctor said that he would give her a letter to a doctor in the city, a specialist, who would examine her, and that she should go there with her husband because he, too, should be examined.

Now Tala had something to work on. It was not easy to convince Yusuf to take her to the city and to have himself examined, too. Hesitant to be drawn into a matter that, for him as generally for all men, was purely a woman's affair, Yusuf by now felt enough pressure around him and was sufficiently alarmed at the prospect that he really wouldn't have any children, any sons, to consent to go to the city with Tala and the doctor's letter. Thus a few months after she had seen the good doctor from the north, Tala found herself on the bus in her best skirts and tunic, covered demurely from her eyebrows to her toes with a long, dark, cloaklike veil. Tala had been in the city twice before with her father, but not since she was married and not since the revolution. Yusuf had been there many times. He knew his way around, at least around the places that mattered to people like him: the guest house right outside the northern end of the covered bazaar, with rooms (bare save for several beds) opening to a courtyard with a little pool and a fountain in the center; a common toilet (filthy, by Tala's standards, but what could one expect in a city?); and a foul-smelling shower in one corner. There was also the room of the proprietor himself, who was rich and known by everybody as "Haji" because he had made the pilgrimage to Mecca, and there was a dark and greasy kitchen where tea could be bought, and bread. In the evening the Haji's servant sometimes cooked a big pot of rice for those who wanted to eat a cheap, simple meal of rice and onions, greens, bread, and tea, in the privacy of their own room, rather than fancy pilaf in the expensive restaurants or dusty food from one of the street vendors. Yusuf knew the Haji. He also knew the bazaar well enough to find anything he might need or might be able to afford, from shoes to shampoo, from a new cooking pot to nails, from a bird cage (not that Yusuf had ever needed one) to rugs of any size and quality, from aspirin to buttons to a golden bracelet, from used keys to a bottle of perfume. Yusuf also knew how to hail a taxi and shout, while it was slowing down a bit, where he wanted to go—a special vocabulary consisting of road names, names of squares, names of houses or gardens or buildings that no longer existed—and that way he could get to a certain lawyer, a couple of money lenders, a tea merchant, the hospital where his mother had been operated on for ulcers, several doctors and clinics, a garage that sold spare parts for Mercedes trucks (he co-owned one with his brother and two cousins), and some other places of interest and significance for him. The big shrine, with its splendor of gold and tiles and mirrors and roses, was within walking distance of the bazaar. He had gone there often. Although he was not a pious man and had never felt a personal need to prostrate himself before the saint, he was dazzled by the sheer luxury of the place, and he savored the feeling of power, almost of exhilaration, that hung over the vast courtyard and the glittering rooms, floating upwards like whiffs of perfume from the throngs of pilgrims flowing in and out and around the place.

Tala, wrapped in her veil, followed a few steps behind Yusuf wherever he took her. Although the places she saw now were by and large the same places her father had taken her several years ago, the city looked very different. Gone from the streets were the women. The few she did meet (there were still plenty at the shrine, though) were clad in black, indistinguishable from one another except by the quality of the veil's fabric. The few who were not enveloped in yards and yards of dark cotton, muslin, or stiff and shiny synthetics wore pants and tunics, uniformlike in dark blues and browns with wide headscarves to match, like those worn by more and more teachers back in the village and by most of the schoolgirls. The people now looked drab to Tala, and she felt conspicuous for being a woman, a villager, and for being dressed in colors—muted, darkish colors, but colors nevertheless. So she wrapped herself into her veil tighter and took smaller steps to prevent the many folds of her skirts from escaping the veil. There were beggars in the streets, throngs of them, women, children, cripples, more filth and misery than she had ever seen back home. Long streets were lined with vendors squatting on the sidewalks, their wares spread out in front of them on plastic or paper sheets: soap, razors, socks, watches, films, detergent, cigarettes, pocket knives, lemonade, books, sandals, tapes with sermons and revolutionary music. The vendors were forever wiping their goods in an unwinnable race against the pungent dust that enveloped the city. And there were banners and posters and graffiti everywhere there was any space to be filled. She had never seen the face of Khomeini, the old man, so many times, in so many colors. Row after row of photographs of young men, martyrs of the war, hung on lines high across the vaulted ceiling of the bazaar; long banners of white cloth with holes in them (to let the wind through without tearing them, Yusuf explained, but to her they seemed riddled with bullets) hung across the streets with slogans she knew from the radio, from television, from the chants of the school children back home, from the loudspeakers. There were murals with figures so huge, so colorful, that one couldn't even take in their meaning standing directly in front of them: a giant monster clad in the American flag, with bombs as arms and legs and a head like that of a tremendous insect, and with a vulture on its shoulder that had the flag of Israel painted on its feathers; the monster with its fiery feet was trampling on a destroyed city, but it was held in check by a group of small people, a mullah with a white turban and brown cloak, some men dressed like workers and soldiers, a black-wrapped woman without a face, warding off the monster with a white flag. "We will destroy our enemies with the power of our faith," the caption read. Some pictures had fancy writing that Tala, having gone to school for only four years, could not decipher. The throngs of people, the pictures, the loudspeakers, together with the noise, the heat, and the heavily armed soldiers and revolutionary guards she saw everywhere (back in the village there were only three of them, and she hardly ever saw them, and she never had had the feeling that they were in any way dangerous) gave Tala a sense of urgency, of being driven somewhere against her will, and not even knowing where or for what purpose. She became very tired.

It was one thing for Yusuf to find his tea merchant or the contractor who used to find work for many of the villagers in the winter, when fields could be left for a while (now there was no work to
be had), but quite another to find a doctor whom none of his acquain-
tances around the bazaar had ever heard of and whose address, written on a smudged envelope, suggested a quarter none of them had
ever been to. With the help of the Haji and several of his friends,
the address was finally determined to be in a wealthy neighborhood
to the north, one that recently had been hit by squads of revolutionary guards purging the city of enemies of the Islamic Republic. There
was some debate about whether Yusuf should go there at all, but
on Tala's insistence the quarter was described with city landmarks
Yusuf and the taxi driver knew, and so, on the second day of their
journey, Yusuf and Tala went to see the doctor.

They found the address in a tree-lined, graceful street that looked
deserted. It was a big house with a gray marble facade rising above a
few pomegranate trees behind a wall. The wall was covered with
graffiti and posters; the wide, ornate iron gate was scratched and
gray with dust. The doctor's nameplate was on the door, but it was
dulled with dirt and almost covered by a picture of the president,
whose eyes had been scratched out. Yusuf pressed the bell, but there
was no sound. He pressed it again, harder, but again there was nothing. Now he knocked on the metal door, and the rattling noise rose
loud in the still air of the quiet neighborhood. But nothing stirred.
Again Yusuf banged on the door, this time with a pebble. The door
to the neighbor's yard opened a little, and an old woman in baggy
pants and plastic sandals peered out. "Go away," she said, "nobody
lives there."

"Madam," Yusuf said, "Sister, I am looking for Doctor Yamani. I
have a letter for him, this is his address, a friend sent me here, it is
for my wife; tell me, for the sake of God, where can I find him?"

"Go away," the old woman said again, retreating even further
into her yard and closing the door to a narrow slit. "The doctor has
left. He was a Bahai, a heathen; he left, they all have left. Don't
hang around here, it is not good for you. He is in America or maybe
Turkey, what do I know? Go away." She shut the door in their faces.

This was in the morning. In the afternoon Yusuf took Tala, who
was crying out of disappointment and exhaustion, to the doctor
whom half the village went to if their maladies were too serious or

too urgent for the facilities and abilities of the local government physician. He was an elderly gentleman, a general practitioner and surgeon who specialized in ulcer operations. His office, in one of the busier streets of the city near the big hospital, was mobbed with patients. His assistant sent Yusuf away, telling him to come the next day or next week or in a year, or, better, not at all. Very early the next morning, Tala and Yusuf sat on the sidewalk outside the building. When the office was opened at around eight, just as the heat of the day was breaking into the cool shades of the early morning, there were already two dozen patients waiting along with them. It was well into midmorning when Tala and Yusuf were finally admitted, paid their fee, and could see the doctor, an old, white-haired man with tired lines in his meticulously shaven, wrinkled face. He fumbled impatiently with his glasses and drummed on his desk while Yusuf, interrupted by Tala, explained their situation. "I will have to examine you," the doctor said to Tala, and told her to lie down on a high table behind a curtain. Tala was rigid with fright. But then a woman came in wearing a white coat and a blue headscarf pulled far down over her forehead. With a plastic glove over her right hand she inserted something into Tala and squeezed here and there, all the while speaking in a loud and clear voice to the doctor, who stood outside the curtain and asked questions. (Tala understood neither the questions nor the answers.) When it was all over Tala summoned up her courage and asked the woman whether she was a doctor, too. "No," the woman said, "I am the doctor's assistant. I tell him what I find, because our Prophet has ordered that a man should not touch a strange woman." Tala had never heard of such an arrangement, but she thought it very clever. Hadn't the last doctor in the village been imprisoned or fired or, in any case, removed after charges of dealing improperly with women patients? A good Muslim, the old doctor, and clever. Yet he, too, said there wasn't much wrong with her, other than maybe some minor infection, some inflammation, some pus which needed to be dried up, and he would give her a prescription. He would also give her a very good medicine, a hormone—expensive, but powerful—which should take care of her problem, God willing. Then they were dismissed. Tala was furious because Yusuf had not asked to be examined, too, although they had paid for both of them. She hissed at him and tugged at his coat to make him turn back, but he told her to shut up, and so they left.

The antibiotics were available at the small pharmacy around the corner, but for the other pills, the powerful ones that would make her pregnant, God willing, Tala and Yusuf unsuccessfully tried six more pharmacies, and in the end needed the good services of the Haji from the guest house to get them at all. Like almost everything else, drugs had become scarce in Iran. The package Yusuf procured with so much trouble cost him the equivalent of three days' wages and it was outdated, but Tala and Yusuf didn't know that. The label on the package was in German.

The trip to the city had been costly and unsuccessful, but it was not the last effort. In the months that followed there were more doctors, in the village, in town, in the city; there were pills and bottles and injections; there was a pilgrimage; there were sacrifices and more amulets; and there was talk of divorce (by Tala's people) and fights between Tala's people and Yusuf's, the former charging the latter with mistreating Tala, conducting black magic, and not giving her proper medical care. All of this was interspersed with threats of suicide by Tala alternating with violent cursing of Yusuf's people and appeals to Yusuf to take her away and to go to a doctor. If only she would be pregnant once, and even if the child was only a girl, and even if it would die after a few months—as long as she could prove that she was a woman, so she could shut up her mother-in-law's malicious barbs, the spiteful gossip of Yusuf's sisters, the mock pity of Yusuf's brothers' wives, the whispering of her neighbors, of the whole village. . . . A dead child all would mourn, all would help her forget; a barren womb only she mourned and everybody made sure she wouldn't forget.

Things came to a head when Yusuf's youngest brother's new wife, a meek little speck of a girl who had married quietly after the rules of the day, had her first child. Tala had not been a guest at their wedding (whether by choice or because she was not invited was another matter of contention between the families), and either she had not been told about the pregnancy, which meant that she was slighted, or else she had been told right away, and in a fashion designed to make her unhappy. Both versions were asserted at times. After the baby was born, a boy to boot, Yusuf's brother and father slaughtered a ram—a sacrifice to their joy and a sign of their satisfaction, visible to everybody who got a piece of the meat. For whatever unfortunate reasons, Hava decided to bring Yusuf's share personally to Tala. To do so she had to climb over the wall Kerima had put up between their parts of the verandah and Yusuf's, thus appearing suddenly at the threshold of Yusuf's room. It was midafternoon and Yusuf was at home, drinking a glass of tea. Tala, irritated and hurt by the sounds of festivity issuing from her youngest sister-in-law's room further down the semicircle, was complaining bitterly to Yusuf. "They rub it in, they are just rubbing it in," she said. "They dance around a ram, they do; may its blood turn to flames in hell where they surely will go. When my brother's wife didn't get pregnant for ten years, my own mother forbade all her other daughters-in-law, and my sister, to say anything at all when they were pregnant, so as not to make her sad. But these heathens . . . every time one of your sisters has something in her belly, they let the world know from the mountaintop to the river, just to spite me. Today all day long your sister with her wretched kid on her arm is parading up and down the alley here, and whatever donkey she sees she says, 'Oh, Tala is so unhappy, she is crying for a child!' You think I don't see her? You think she doesn't want me to see her? If you had any courage in your bones you would silence her, you would tell her to go and crow on her own pile of dung."

Yusuf kept muttering that she should shut up, that it was none of her business, but Tala paid no attention. So when Hava suddenly entered through the curtain that hung in the doorway, Tala was in full swing and was taken by surprise. Hava hadn't been here for several weeks. Tala jumped up and held her breath. Hava extended her hand with the small parcel of meat wrapped in a piece of plastic. "Here," she said, "this is your share."

Tala crossed her arms on her back and tossed her head. "I don't want your meat," she hissed through clenched teeth. "Take it away, I don't want it, do you hear? I don't want your meat, eat it yourself and choke on it!" She was shouting now. Hava continued to talk about it being Tala and Yusuf's right and proper share, good meat; she put the small package on the window sill and, uncomfortable and strained, slipped out. Shouting abuses, Tala dashed across the room, snatched the parcel from the window sill, and threw it at Hava through the curtain. At that, both Tala and Hava, each from their vantage point on either side of the curtain, unleashed tirades of name calling and curses on their respective mothers. Tala, seizing the advantage of a youthful volume of voice, got her points across the whole courtyard to any neighbor who cared to listen. "Who am I," she cried, "to be treated like this by my sisters-in-law? Shouldn't your new daughter-in-law have come and kissed my hands and kissed my face when she came here as a bride? Isn't she much younger than I? And what does she do instead, encouraged by you all? She treats me as if I didn't exist; she looks the other way when she sees me, not one word of greeting for me. And why weren't we invited to the wedding, ha? Why not? And now I should eat her ram, which you bring here only to rub it in again that I don't have a child? Or do you maybe want me to go and wash her brat's diapers? Is this what you want?" Yusuf had not moved from his corner and had said nothing for a while, but as his mother's voice retreated he told Tala, getting louder and angrier as she paid no attention to him, to close her dirty mouth, to shut up, or else. And he grabbed her arm and yanked her down. But now Tala's fury was turned on him full blast. "You aren't better than they are," she shouted, flailing her arms, "you aren't, or else you would stand up for me! You would tell them to leave me alone, but you are afraid of them and you let them abuse me, your own wife! But if you don't want me, go look for another one, I don't care. I'll gladly go back to my father; there they like me, all of them, not like here."

Yusuf tried to be reasonable. "If you don't like the meat, take it and then give it to somebody at night, to Mahmad the Cripple, to the poor," he said. "The way you carried on with my mother, you destroy your honor and mine, too. A guest is a guest. You don't abuse a guest, no matter how little you think of him. After a guest has left, you can say what you want, but not in his face. Curse the meat after she is gone, if you feel like it, but you have no sense, no shame."

"Ah, but when they fight and quarrel in their house with me, then it is all right, isn't it? If Kerima throws a log of firewood at me—and here I still have the lump on my head—you say nothing of honor, and when your own brother—may God blacken his face—beats me black and blue, and when your sister throws me down the ladder, oh, no, you won't lift a finger, you won't talk about honor then. They want to destroy me, they want to silence me, and you let them. Where were you when they troubled me so much the other day that I took the hot iron spit out of the fire and pressed it onto my own forearm? Here, look again, a blister the size of a saucer it was, to show them I meant it, to show them how sick and tired I was. But I tell you, only when I am stretched out and the earth is on my eyes, only then will I have peace, and only then I won't see and hear any more, and only then I won't answer their vileness. But that's what you all are waiting for: for me to kill myself, to poison myself. Don't think I don't know where you keep your herbicides, but I'll eat your father's poison, it will kill me faster!"

"No one was mean to you today, no one harmed you, my own mother herself came up here, gave you honors, did what was right and proper, brought you her own meat to make peace between us and them . . . "

"Meat from the ram for that wretched woman's child! This is supposed to make me happy? I tell you what it is: They are making fun of me with their meat. Why didn't they give us any the other day, when your father had to slaughter the sheep the wolf had attacked? A few days ago when I got out of the shower at the bathhouse, your sister was sitting on that wretched woman's clothes, and when Leila asked why, the snake said, 'so that Yusuf's wife can't do anything with them to harm her.' So she said, ask Leila. And now they send me their butchered ram! Or did maybe you tell her to come?"

"I didn't know of anything. My mother came herself to honor you . . . "

"Honor, ha! When your cousin was killed in the war, I, I of all people, put on a black veil and black shirt, and a black skirt, to honor your family, to show everybody my respect for you all. This was half a year ago. And when two weeks ago my own aunt died, not one of the women in your family came for the mourning ceremonies, not one! This you call honor and respect?"

"An old woman . . . you can't compare the martyrdom of a young soldier with the death of a sick old woman . . . "

"One-half of my old aunt is better than three of your cousins, and don't you forget what your own 'honorable' cousin called you the other day, in public! How he shouted after you that you were a nobody, a nothing, that you couldn't even do you know what to your own wife!"

At this point, livid with rage, Yusuf jumped up and slashed Tala across the face. Tala flung herself on the floor, crying. Yusuf stomped out, sending an elaborate curse over the wall before turning towards the stairs. Tala, hoarse and choked with tears, huddled in a corner, whimpering, and rocked herself back and forth, lamenting in a high-pitched sing-song: "Woe to me, my life is gone, I am a bundle of misery, the spark of life has left me, woe to me, I want nothing any more" long after Yusuf had left.

The same day late in the evening, Yusuf and Tala moved their belongings down the stairs, bundle for bundle, box for box, through the alley, past the water fountain, into the two vacant rooms in the courtyard of their neighbor. Yusuf had negotiated the move, and Tala agreed to it immediately. The neighbor was a distant cousin of hers and his wife was sympathetic. Tala would look at other faces, hear other voices, be left alone. And thus Yusuf and Tala embarked on the long journey of reconciliation with what seemed, for now at least, the will of God.

4

On Wealth and Poverty and How Gouhar and Aftab Had a Falling-out

Between the courtyards of Begom and Maryam (or, more appropriately, of Akbar and the late Khorshid) lay, on Akbar's side of the water channel, the walled-in house of Haji Reza Ali, a prosperous trader and entrepreneur from a small city near Shiraz; and, on Maryam's side, the ruins of Akbar's cousins' place, a corner of which had been kept alive in the form of one room atop a barn, presently rented to Bandar, a young have-not from Deh Rud. Thus, one of the richest and one of the poorest men in the village were facing each other across a narrow water channel and decaying mud walls. Beyond Haji Reza Ali's high solid walls, broken only by a huge wooden gate painted blue and studded with iron, the tips of some poplar trees swaying above the wide roof of the second floor bespoke the gracious comforts of life in the house. In his small courtyard, Haji Reza Ali—or Mister Hoseini, as he liked to be called, in the fashion of the city—grew some apple trees and vines around a small, tiled fountain, bordered by a medley of marigolds, dahlias, roses, windflowers and geraniums in beds and pots. To anyone who entered it or could steal a glimpse through the half-open gate, it was a garden worthy of a rich man: green, shady, cool, and fragrant with blossoms and lush grass, and only negligibly marred by the occasional strong whiffs of outhouse rushing through the leaves from a southwestern breeze. The Haji, middle-aged and prosperously rotund, had come to Deh Koh some thirty years earlier, equipped with the fine-honed business skills of a trader's son and enough money in his pocket and credit to his name to set up a store and money-lending business, which soon spread healthy runners far beyond the village. Using his resources cleverly, not only did he eventually buy into several local businesses and partnerships in buildings leased to government agencies and a bank, but also early on he managed to marry a woman from one of the most respected local families. This tie proved more advantageous for him than them, except for Gouhar, his wife, who never had to worry about her daily bread from then on and became a lady altogether.

Bandar, a stone's throw from splendor, had an unobstructed view of wealth well kept and well displayed, while he himself provided the Haji with only the cheerless spectacle of gray and dusty poverty. Illiterate, without family connections or land, and limping from a crookedly healed fracture, Bandar had lived a hand-to-mouth life since he had come to Deh Koh as an orphan some ten years before. He worked as a cowherd, a jack-of-all-trades, a laborer with wages negotiable in cash or kind. A few of his masters had paid him with kids and lambs, which had grown into a small herd over the years, providing him with milk and wool. One of his patrons, who owed him remuneration for many years of occasional work, canceled his accumulated debts by finding him a wife, a young girl faintly related to Bandar and just as poor as he. Aftab, riding on her father's only donkey, came from Deh Rud freshly scrubbed, wearing mascara under her eyes, crookedly cut bangs, and henna-red palms and toting one new skirt and a new tunic shirt of cheap red polyester, a cooking pot and a ladle, a breadboard, a lumpy mattress, a blanket and a pillow roll, a small mat of cotton for a floor covering, and sundry little odds and ends tied in a bundle. This was all her father could afford with the meager bride price he had gotten from Bandar and his benefactor, her stepmother said. Akbar's cousin, also as payment for services rendered and thinking about the prospect of a small rent in the future, let Bandar use his recently vacated room in his old courtyard. Bandar hauled buckets with dirt up onto the leaky roof to repair it and made a new door out of tin and lumber scraps. Aftab planted some cucumbers and tomatoes in the ruins, but they did not do well because she was not equal to the task of carrying enough water up to keep them alive. For hours on end she squatted on the narrow ledge of the barn roof in front of her door, a spindle resting in her lap, watching people and animals move up and down the lane in the dusty haze of the mellow afternoon sun. Gouhar, always short of servants, since no woman in Deh Koh felt low enough to hire herself out (and no man felt low enough to allow his wife or daughter to be in somebody else's service), had tried in vain to inveigle Aftab, a true pauper who should be humble, into doing chores for her.

"Aftab is proud and plain lazy," said the neighbors.

Aftab was very young when she came to Deh Koh, with the delicate, thin limbs of an underfed child; an oval face with large, wide-set eyes; and a small, round mouth. Bandar was content with his wife, and she was glad to be out of her father's poor, crowded house where she had been everybody's servant—too old to be treated with any indulgence, yet too young to be granted any privileges or to assert even the most innocent claims. In Bandar's house no one scolded her, no one argued with her. They owned little, so there was little to take care of; little work meant long hours of leisure on the porch. Her neighbors were reserved but not unkind; they talked to her politely and let her borrow things she needed but did not own. Maryam even gave her a plastic pitcher (scratched and wobbly, but still serviceable) after Aftab had borrowed it for the umpteenth time. Aftab took it with some embarrassment and brought Maryam a bowl of yogurt later.

In Bandar's house there was enough food for her. She milked their few goats, made yogurt, baked bread, and ate as much and whenever she wanted. Her cheeks and her arms filled out. She put mascara of oil and soot under her eyes, trimmed her bangs carefully, and took to swinging her hips when she walked. Bandar thought she was very pretty. Begom and her daughter Mehri, however, said that Aftab was lazy and flighty. Maryam, in the spirit of charitable neighborliness, told Aftab not to walk around with painted eyes and henna on her hands like a young bride. It was vulgar, she said; it was conspicuous; people would talk. She should do it at home, for her husband—they were both young, after all—but not for other men to see. Aftab looked her straight in the eye and told her to mind her own business.

"Aftab is lazy and flighty and flippant," Maryam said.

One day Bandar brought home a small rug, good enough for them, even if it was old and worn in spots. He told her to wash it but she demurred, and then Bandar hit her. Aftab cursed him, and there ensued a long, loud argument, which ended when she took the rug down to the water. This was their first fight, soon resolved, but now the neighbors said that Aftab was lazy and flighty, had a big mouth, and was disobedient, and when she came to borrow something, they would whisper "beggar" behind her back.

At first Aftab did not like it at all when Bandar slept with her. He was clumsy, and what he did to her hurt. Later she got used to it, taking this discomfort as a small price to pay for the freedom she had otherwise. In time she got pregnant, which was as it should be. When her time came, Bandar fetched the midwife, who came dutifully, as she was paid by the government to do, and delivered a son, but there was no one else with Aftab—no mother to help her do chores, no sister-in-law to wash the baby's soiled rags, no cousin or sister to milk her goats, no mother-in-law to feed her or fetch water, and no visitors either. This, she learned, was the real hardship of poverty and of being a stranger: the loneliness born of the indifference towards those who don't really belong. Aftab cried a little, but there was no one to hear her. Later she painted her eyes again and, wrapped in her one and only veil, she sat on the ledge with her son in her lap, looking down on her world defiantly. And when the incessant boom-boom of the big drum echoed throughout the village at the wedding of Tamas's daughter (another neighbor), shortly after Aftab had made the customary ablutions in the public bathhouse forty days after having given birth, Aftab locked her door behind the baby sleeping strapped to the cradle and went to dance.

"Aftab is plain foolish," said the neighbors.

A few months later, in early fall, the rumblings of the revolution started to roll over the village, and Aftab got a most exciting spectacle. For a long time, rumors had been going around in the village about secret service agents. Aftab was not quite sure what the secret service meant, except that it was bad and that Tamas's son Rahmat and a few other schoolboys kept saying that once the Shah and his secret police and his thieving servants were gone, everybody in Iran would get seventy Toman a day forever. Like all her neighbors, including Rahmat's own mother, Aftab wisely reserved judgment about this. Begom even told the lad that as long as she had her lentils (which she was washing at the time) she would be content, and he could, with all due respect, feed his seventy Toman to his donkey. But then the news spread that a teacher in Deh Rud had been accused of being a secret service informer and then was beaten up and dragged away, thrown into prison, or maybe even killed, who was to know, and people everywhere put their heads together, whispering. A few days later five or six bearded young men in blue jeans and green jackets came storming up the lane, shouting something about the glories of the revolution and the destruction of the country's enemies; they burst through the Haji's wooden gate, and a great tumult arose in the courtyard. Aftab left her cradle and the tray with rice she was just cleaning and flew down her steep stairs and across the lane and the water channel to be where the action was.

The open gate was clogged with people. Inside there was shouting and banging about, topped by the Haji's staccato shouts and Gouhar's shrill wailing. People appeared on rooftops, in the lane, in doorways. Aftab was pushed back out into the lane by a dense pack of human bodies squeezing a struggling and flailing Haji through the gate. His hat was gone, his face scratched, his pyjama-pants torn. "It's a lie, all lies!" he shouted. Gouhar, in the rear, was thrashing around with a broomstick, and the Haji's daughter was screeching and throwing things at the young men. On the Haji's bridge, right outside the door, the struggle intensified; the pushing and shoving mass swayed and teetered, lost its collective balance, and stumbled into the shallow, muddy bed of the water channel. Aftab got a close view of the rumpled, mud-smeared Haji clambering to his feet and of Gouhar swinging a copper toilet can by its spout onto some broad padded shoulders at her feet. The Haji's son was pelting the group with rocks from the roof. As the men were climbing out of the slimy channel, the flabbergasted spectators retreated behind the safety of their own walls. The dense group slowly moved down the lane in a cloud of dust and noise, followed at a safe distance by the Haji's son hurling rocks. Gouhar collapsed on Aftab's shoulder. "He isn't a secret service agent, it is a lie," she wailed. When the dark cluster with the hapless Haji was out of sight, the women reappeared. Aftab led Gouhar back into her house, followed by the neighbors, who talked, consoled, and tried to get the story. So it was true that the Haji was a paid agent? So that was how he got rich? But what in the world did he report on—how many sheep Akbar had, maybe? How much bread Maryam ate? How often Tamas and Hakime fought? Who had debts? (A lot to report on that topic, Hakime said.) Or who still used the barn as an outhouse although the doctor and the Shah had forbidden it? Gleefully they winked at each other. The learned, literate Reza Ali, the Haji, Mister Hoseini himself, bless or curse him, was in trouble. Aftab, listening and talking at the same time like everybody else with great animation, had forgotten all about her own duties, when a boy got hold of her and told her that her baby was howling. "Oh, holy Abbas, dear me," she cried, and with billowing skirts ran home to find that her baby had cried himself blue in the face, the chickens had eaten the rice on the tray, and the rug was full of chicken poop.

"Tsk, tsk, tsk, what a bad mother she is," the neighbors said.

As had been the custom until then, Gouhar went to the gendarmerie to complain about her husband's abduction. She even took a gold coin with her, a very small one, to give her claim more persuasive force if need be. The gendarmerie post lay a little ways outside the village, a fortlike building commanding the only road into the village. Recently the gendarmes had kept close to their stronghold behind locked doors and had begun to steal dogs. Clearly afraid of the world outside, they kept them as watchdogs in their walled yard, a dozen or so fierce and hungry beasts. The gendarme at the gate turned Gouhar away, saying that these matters were none of their business and that she should go elsewhere to complain, to town or to the prison or to the governor. Gouhar went to her brothers for help, but none of them was eager to get involved in what was clearly a touchy situation in most opaque circumstances. They all told her to wait a few days. Sure enough, after three days the Haji came home as a passenger on his own minibus, dirty and unshaven, with a bare head and black smudges under his eyes. Shoulders bent and limping slightly, he hurried up the lane accompanied by stares and whispers. Fortunately for his pride, he met no men, only a few boys he could as easily ignore as the nosy women.

Time and money quickly heal the wounds of pride. While the unmasked Mister Hoseini had lost some of his dignity, he had lost none of his wealth. Neither had Gouhar, even if she no longer wore her golden necklace and her heavy earrings and the wide bracelet with the huge red gemstone. Such ostentatious display had become unfashionable, together with bright clothes and bead-embroidered velvet caps. Much afraid of thieves and robbers, she locked her jewelry away in one of her many trunks and hid the keys in one of her many bundles.

Aftab had no such worries. She had never owned a piece of gold in her life. Her bracelets, peddled by blacksmiths, were of iron and cheap, dull yellow metal that bent easily. They were not pretty, and the twisted iron band even was old-fashioned, but it was, together with a few beads and an amulet around her neck, all the protection she thought she needed, and all the jewelry she thought she probably would ever have. Bandar, working day after day from sunup to sundown, earned just enough to keep them fed and clothed. The only luxury in their room was a small gas range, two burners hooked onto a gas bottle, which Bandar had bought second-hand when one of his patrons had made up his debts in one lump sum. Although gas wasn't always available and cost money, the burner spared him several arduous trips to the far-off woods for firewood, a job which was especially taxing for his lame leg. Aftab liked the burner. She would also have liked an oil stove for the winter, a television set, or at least a radio, and a refrigerator. All her neighbors had them, even Maryam, who lived alone by herself, and Gouhar had two refrigerators and a washing machine. A few times Gouhar had given Aftab some ice cubes for their supper's buttermilk, but Bandar forbade her to take anything from that house after he and the Haji had started a running dispute about a few goats Bandar kept for him in his herd in a fifty-fifty arrangement, in which Bandar could keep half of all the proceeds from the goats, including their sale price. Haji Reza Ali, as he liked to be called again now that the country had returned to religious symbols, eventually accused Bandar of cheating him, whereupon Bandar drove the goats across the street into the Haji's yard, thus severing his business ties with him, and instead took on a few animals of Nur Ahmad, a distant relative and competitor of the Haji. Matters now were strained between the two houses. Aftab, pregnant again and as cocky as ever, told her neighbors at the water faucet that the Haji could take his goats out to pasture himself, and

Gouhar could as well sit down in the dirt and milk them herself; she, Aftab, did not need the milk.

"Aftab is getting big-headed and ungrateful," the women said.

In fact, Aftab started to make some money now selling milk and yogurt. Things were becoming scarcer and more expensive month after month. "It is because of the war," said the people, echoing the radio and television. They sighed and grumbled although the mullahs in their television sermons told them that the Islamic Revolution was not meant to make more watermelons but to spread the true faith. Aftab, who did not own a watermelon patch or a television set, did not feel her faith becoming any truer than before. Like Begom, and Maryam, and Hakime, and Gouhar, she said so, only a little more often and louder, until one day, when she and a few other neighbors were talking around the water faucet, Rahmat happened to come their way. Young as he was, he had become a revolutionary guard, sporting an unshaven look and a gun, much to his father's bewilderment and his mother's misgivings. Although usually he never as much as looked at any of the women when passing through the lane, today he stopped in front of Aftab and, steadfastly looking sideways and far over Aftab's head (she was much shorter than he), addressed her with visible embarrassment. "Sister," he said hurriedly, "with your talk you show great ignorance of the important matters of the revolution. You should come to the sermons, you should better yourself." So he said and disappeared. The women were stunned for a few moments.

"Impudent ass," someone in the group said after him, and Aftab, recovered, even shouted an obscenity. But Maryam hissed, "Shut up," and Gouhar shook her head at Aftab and motioned silence. From then on Aftab, like the other women, looked over her shoulder before she gave her opinion out in the open.

Slowly a new order was creeping into the village. Some women changed the cap and light scarf of the traditional costume for a heavy headscarf pulled way down over the forehead. Whoever needed a new veil-wrap made sure it was of dark fabric. The village was swarming with strangers now: revolutionary guards coming and going, mullahs, Afghani refugees working for cheap wages for a local contractor, a few families from the south displaced by the war, local men returning from the cities after many years because of lack of work there. Self-respecting women wrapped themselves tightly in their long veils when they had to be outside or else stayed home. Gouhar never went out. At most, she would stand in her doorway or squat right outside it, ready to retreat whenever strange men were in sight. She even had a private water faucet in her own court-yard. But Aftab, as usual, sat in full view on the ledge of her barn roof, not even wearing a veil—she was at home, anyway, she said—and the people started to whisper that she was begging for trouble.

The demand for fresh food in the village was rising with the increasing population, so the few men who had not sold their herds to go after more lucrative work in the cities now were besieged with demands for yogurt, milk, and butterfat. Bandar had kept his few sheep and goats, and Aftab started to sell yogurt to the Afghani work-ers who lived seven to a room in a house behind Begom's. The men took turns shopping, cooking, fetching water, washing clothes, and going to various houses for milk and yogurt. (Butterfat they could not afford; like almost everybody else, they had to make do with the small allotments of indefinable, coarse, yellow cooking fat the government sold cheaply on rationing cards.) These raggedy lads, sunburnt, wild-looking, lean strangers, kept mostly to themselves and gave no offense. Begom had been worried on account of her daughter Mehri at first, when the room in the courtyard bordering theirs in the back was rented to a bunch of them, and she forbade Mehri to go up on the roof, where she could be seen. The narrow side of their verandah, visible from the lane, was screened off with a wall of sprigs and twigs, but she need not have worried. The Afghanis never as much as looked her way, and none ever spoke to Mehri. "The Afghanis, poor devils, are good Muslims," Begom said. Maryam, who by then was not on speaking terms with her because of the trouble with her niece Golgol, Begom's daughter-in-law, said that Begom could have spared herself the effort of building a branch screen, because she was sure the Afghanis made a detour around her house anyway in fear of her and Mehri's foul mouth. This, in a moment of unguarded talkativeness, Aftab reported back to Begom, who in turn did not keep her source a secret, whereupon Maryam called Aftab a brainless gossipmonger and some other things and looked through her whenever she met her by chance.

Close neighbors that they were, it was natural for the Afghanis to buy yogurt and buttermilk from Aftab. They paid weekly without remiss and without bargaining, in crisp bills, which Aftab put in a bundle and saved. After a few weeks she went down to the stores in the main street and bought herself three yards of shimmery green fabric criss-crossed with silver thread. Rahmat's sister Banu cut it for her, and Aftab sat on her ledge for a few afternoons, sewing herself a new shirt.

"Spendthrift," said Gouhar.

"Bandar should give her a thrashing," said Maryam. But not even Mehri or Gouhar, both at vantage points for observation, could find any fault in the transactions themselves. Rotating their chores, the Afghani men took turns fetching the yogurt at night, and Aftab learned to know them by sight and by clothes, if not by name. Rarely did one speak to her any more than a perfunctory greeting; rarely did one stay for more than a minute, just long enough for Aftab to fetch the bowl with new yogurt from under the rags where it had jelled and hand it down to the man waiting on the stairs. This pattern changed, however, one day, after one of the young men broke his leg stacking sacks of cement. Now the contractor had no use for him. He had to stay home and assume the duty of housekeeper for his comrades. From then on it was he of the faded green sweater who filled big plastic bottles at the water faucet; washed clothes, awkwardly stooping and pitied by all; hobbled through the village on various errands; borrowed Akbar's donkey to fetch their allotted sack of rice; with the help of many little boys rolled an empty gas bottle down to where it would be filled eventually; and who, all alone, came to Bandar's house twice a day for Aftab's buttermilk and yogurt. His name, the neighbors found out, was Heidar Khan, which they amended by adding "Afghani" for exact identification. Communication with him was neither fluent nor easy, given the restraints of propriety and the strange way he pronounced words, but good will and curiosity went a long way to overcome these difficulties. Besides, Heidar Khan Afghani with the broad shoulders and slanted eyes was the only young man around during the day, impaired by a homemade cast of wood and straps and rags, but ablebodied otherwise and friendly in a shy and proper way. One afternoon, when a lost and frenzied goat sailed into Begom's verandah and out through the branch screen with one big jump, the Afghani offered his help to mend it. (Begom accepted it and got a reprimand later from her son, who said that it made it look as if he and his

75

father did not do what was necessary around the house. "You don't," said Begom, "everybody knows it anyway.") Another day, he caught Gouhar's new cow as she tried to trot off towards her old quarters, and one sad afternoon he carried home Maryam's nephew's son bleeding from a rock-inflicted wound on the head. In turn, when the bakery in the next village—the only one for miles around, the one where the Afghanis got their bread—was shut down by the revolutionary committee for reasons of unsanitary conditions (there were charges of flies in the dough, which the baker denied), and the Afghani lads had no way to get bread, the neighbors helped out for the sake of the religious merits to be obtained by such acts of pity with strangers. And Aftab even was persuaded by Heidar Khan to bake them a batch with flour he had bought with some difficulty at the mill. This, in the eyes of the neighbors, was stretching Muslim charity quite a bit.

"Rash women and hail make a lot of trouble in the world," Begom said.

Heidar Khan, who actually had had a very hard time keeping his comrades fed during the baker's shutdown, was grateful to Aftab. She, a stranger like himself, was not quite as coldly reserved towards him as the other women who, in the beginning, turned their backs when they saw him coming to the water faucet, covered their faces, and did not even want to sell him any milk. When he had a question, like where to get laundry soap from, he asked Aftab, because she would answer him without ado. Thus, when one day Aftab asked him to get her an iron spindle-spit from the blacksmiths who camped along the roadside in the next village for their annual few weeks' stay in the area, whom he was about to visit anyway, he was glad to do it for her. And when one evening, at the customary yogurt time, he saw Aftab still milking her goats because she had no one to help her fetch and hold the animals, he pitched in without waiting to be asked. Bandar, who usually helped her, had not come back yet from a job in Deh Rud, she said. The milking was finished quickly, the animals were driven into the small corral Bandar had made for them in the courtyard, and the yogurt was handed to Heidar and he promptly departed. But the whole scene had been observed by Gouhar's youngest son, who was washing his dirt-caked feet in the channel, and he told the story to his mother and siblings a little later. "Heidar Afghani was holding goats for Aftab, and they talked,

and then Heidar Afghani and Aftab drove the goats into the courtyard, and then the Afghani went up the staircase and Aftab gave
him something, and then they talked some more," he said.

"Is he there still?" asked a scandalized Gouhar.

"No, he left," said her son, regretfully, because for him as well
as his elders Aftab was surrounded by an air of scandal, and Heidar
Khan Afghani entering her house at night would fit nicely, he felt.
In the spirit of educating the young in proper moral attitudes, Gouhar
said something about impudent strangers and bad women and filed
the information away for further use sometime. Right now, she felt,
she had more pressing worries than Aftab's conduct.

Despite the many rumors and promises by revolutionary sym-
pathizers, the poor in the village had not gotten any richer since
the revolution, nor had teachers or other government employees.
Everybody was urged constantly to work hard, to be patient, to pray,
to donate money to the war chest, to help the soldiers, to volunteer
for front service (if a man) and to rejoice over the martyred (if a
woman). Everybody was in debt. But while the war and the difficult
economic conditions put a heavy burden on the have-nots, it was
generally felt that the rich—the merchants, those with access to
capital and to the black market, those who managed in a thousand
ways to profit from the wants and needs of the poor now as before,
those who could buy their way through this world and, people like
Begom suspected, into heaven as well—did not suffer at all. A feeling of prevailing injustice and resentment was growing everywhere.
Speeches and homilies extolled the virtues of poverty and chastised
greed and avarice. In the cities, in exemplary fashion, many of the
houses of old wealth were destroyed by revolutionary guards, valu-
ables confiscated, owners killed as enemies of the state. The old
moneyed elite fled, and those who stayed behind took on a crum-
pled, unshaven demeanor and kept a very low profile while trying
to send abroad as many of their assets as possible.

The Haji, well connected in the city, became rather nervous at
this news. He was a good Muslim and not an infidel Bahai, who got
hit the hardest by the zealotic wrath of the new regime, but he did
have to bear the stigma of being a former agent and he was, by local
standards at least, a rich man. What prevented one of the revolutionary hotheads, one of the misguided robbers, to close in on him
again and loot his house and destroy his wealth, which, small as it

was, he had scratched together by the efforts of his own hands and his own head over decades with the help of God? To Gouhar, with whom he discussed his fears, the issue was just as burning: a good deal of the Haji's assets was in gold coins, and, gratifying for her, in the form of her jewelry. Both, she knew, were much more vulnerable to theft or looting or confiscation than shares in sheep or houses or a tractor. Finding a safe hiding place for their treasure became a concern of great moment. To safeguard the money outside their house was next to impossible, they realized. Her people, Gouhar knew, either would refuse the thankless burden of guarding her gold with a thousand polite reasons and excuses, or, if pressed, would expect a very heavy cut which the Haji, even if he promised it in the clutches of pressing necessity, would hotly contend later. The Haji himself had no trustworthy relative close by. His only kinsman, Nur Ahmad, a distant nephew, was his most successful and bitter competitor, not an ally. There were no faithful servants, no beholden retainers. Times had changed: everybody was on his own now, even the rich, and one had to pay dearly for help and loyalty.

The Haji and Gouhar decided they had no choice but to find a hiding place inside the house. They went through the whole house, from barn and storage rooms to the roof, from kitchen to guest room, from woodshed to outhouse, both bodily and in their thoughts, many times, in search of a safe hiding place. In their minds they dug holes in the garden and made adobe bricks of mud and straw mixed with gold coins; they hollowed out apple trees and hung boxes in the chimney; they stuck the gold in holes dug into the ceiling above the poplar beams and buried it in the dung in the barn. But each idea soon was discarded as either impractical to carry out (for example, digging the ground unseen), or too unsafe (for example, mixing grain with gold in the hollow wall segments that served as granary in older houses like theirs). So, until a better idea would suggest itself, Gouhar let the gold, tied in innocent-looking bundles of clothing and locked in various little boxes, disappear here and there between the sacks of walnuts and almonds, the boxes of candy, the bags of fleece, the bundles of clothes, spindles, needlework, red velvet, blankets, pillows, schoolbooks, and the colorful odds and ends of a long-established household, stacked on a wooden platform against the far wall of their utility-living-lounging-dining room, where the beams were dark with soot, the walls gray and fly specked, and the gypsum floor covered with the oldest and least valuable of the Haji's many good rugs. The Haji was not in the least convinced of the effectiveness of this arrangement. On her part, Gouhar did not even dare to think of the systematic searching and looting the Haji was afraid of. Rather, she acted on the model of the predicament of one of her sisters' daughters, who was married to a township employee in the next town and lost all her jewelry to a burglar because she had kept it (very conveniently for the thief) all together in a locked metal box. Gouhar's conclusion drawn from this episode was to disperse the jewelry or, even better, to pretend it wasn't there. This she told the Haji, and it got them thinking along a very different line.

Begom's long-suffering sister finally had died. Although she came from only a small family and had been old and sick for quite some time, as the widow and mother of successful and well-regarded men she was mourned in style by her people. In small groups of neighbors and relatives, half the village was flowing in and out of the mourning sessions in Begom's sister's house, men and women separately. For three days, from morning until deep into the night, the porch and living room were crowded with dark-clad women and little children sitting on rugs along the walls, drinking tea, talking in hushed tones, and sobbing in refrain to the songs one or another of the women would sing in a shrill falsetto, veil drawn across half her face. From time to time also Begom or one of the dead woman's other sisters or one of her daughters would work herself up into a frenzy of grief and throw herself into the circle of squatting women, wailing loudly, writhing in the pain of loss, and bemoaning, in a sob-choked sing-song, her own great sorrow, the dead woman's virtues, her last days, the moments of her death. The performance over, she would collect herself and then go back to brewing more tea or directing the preparation of meals for those mourners who had come a long way.

As Begom's neighbor, Aftab went to the mourning session with her son and her baby, bringing along a little bag of sugar as a gift to help defray expenses. She slipped into the house almost unnoticed. Gouhar, as both Begom's neighbor and a relative of the dead woman's husband, went there with her daughters and her neighbor Maryam and her own sister from a little further up the lane, who in turn brought her daughters and daughters-in-law, taking along tobacco, tea, and sugar; all were greeted with the prolonged wailing trills with which every esteemed party was announced. The porch was crowded. Aftab was astounded when Gouhar squeezed into an already tight spot next to her, apart from Gouhar's own group, and gave her a friendly nod. And even more astounded was she when Gouhar started to inquire after her health and the little son's health and the baby's health, and how things were going, in endless rounds of polished phrases. Aftab had no choice but to answer in kind and with as much politeness. Aftab was suspicious, but she had no idea what Gouhar was up to. Her suspicion deepened when tea was served and Gouhar offered her, the no-account Aftab, the first glass with considerable insistence, which led to more exchanges of polite expressions of humbleness, worth, esteem, and self-deprecation, before Gouhar finally gave in and took the first glass, unquestionably due her superior rank anyway. The dead woman's daughter came in from the courtyard with a waterpipe for Gouhar, who offered it all around and, appropriately finding no takers, smoked a little and then passed it on. Three little boys escaped their mothers' folds and advanced stealthily towards the sugar bowl on the forgotten tea tray. Aftab pulled her son back by his leg and planted him firmly in front of her. Perijan closed her eyes and started to rock herself, humming. The crowd fell silent. A red-eyed woman next to Perijan drew her veil across her eyes and cried softly while Perijan, with a screechy head-voice, sang, "Get up, sweet flower. The morning star is driving off the herds, and it is prayer time. Your prayer rug is a bed of rose petals on which you lie stretched out." Loud sobbing accompanied the last words and filled the pause Perijan took to recover from the exertion. Cries and sobs ebbing away, she took a deep breath and started another verse: "I went to the flower's house, but the flower was not home. She had left to wash her fine skirt at the faraway spring." Again, the last words were drowned in noises of grief and exclamations of pain. Aftab, who had barely known the woman, wailed vigorously. The mood of loss and despair was catching. She felt a profound misery welling up inside her; deep pity for the baby sleeping in her arms through the noise; pity for herself, for the sick, for the martyred, for the soldiers, for the poor. She cried for the misery of the world, moved by the songs, even if she could not understand the words, which were stretched beyond recovery into shrill

80

modulations and chopped by sobs beyond recognition. A few verses later the group recuperated somewhat and the dead woman's daughter sat down inside the circle, threw herself flat on the floor with her hands up, pulled her hair out from under her already crooked headscarf, let out a few piercing screams, and then recounted her mother's last day: she asked for water; her son went to the doctor and returned with the best medicine; they prepared the finest kebab for her, the sweetest, coolest drink; they sprinkled rose water on her bed, held her head and stroked her hands; and then finally . . . Again there was a burst of loud commiseration. The daughter composed herself, dried her tears, and murmured that they had loved their mother, she had been the finest woman, pious and industrious, the best mother, the truest wife. The group nodded their assent, with many sighs. Then in solemn, measured tones the daughter thanked the assembled party for their great sacrifice of taking the time and effort to join the family in their mourning and prayed that God might pay them back their kindness. Everybody murmured that it was not worth mentioning, and then the party broke up and talk resumed about matters in general.

At this point, just when another tray with tea glasses was handed in to make the round, Gouhar leaned over to Aftab and said, "There is a favor I have to ask of you, if it is not too much trouble for you." To which Aftab, greatly alarmed but also curious, mumbled a string of expected pleasantries—that Aftab was her servant, that Aftab entreated her to let her know what she could do, that she was ready to be her sacrifice. Gouhar replied, "I would be very much obliged if you could come by tomorrow at your convenience, maybe in the morning sometime if it was possible at all and you are not too busy, while the children are in school."

"Certainly, certainly," said Aftab, by now consumed with curiosity. "It is no trouble at all, it is my pleasure, by the light of my eyes."

A party of women who had been there since early morning rose to get home in time for lunch, when the children would come home from school. The waterpipe appeared again with fresh coals. Gouhar was entreated to stay for lunch but refused, which caused another lengthy exchange of politenesses. An old woman from another village, tired from the long walk and the exhausting mourning, stretched out in a corner, pulled her long veil-wrap over herself and fell asleep instantly amidst the hum and commotion of the coming and going. Gouhar collected her people—except Maryam, who stayed to have a long and hot talk with her sister Perijan—and left. Aftab went with them, but no more was spoken between her and Gouhar.

The next day, at midmorning Aftab picked up her baby, locked her room and walked into the deep shades of the Haji's garden to see Gouhar. The Haji, she knew, was away on business. Gouhar expressed gratitude at Aftab's taking the trouble of coming over and ushered her into one of the good rooms. Many thick cushions with gigantic flowers stitched on white covers lay along the walls on a thick rug, portraits of the Imam Khomeini and other dignitaries on one blue wall serenely looked across to posters of fat cows in lush meadows and a boat sailing on a lake of uncommonly vivid blue, and the window was graced with a curtain displaying rows of bleating roebucks with bloated red heads. In a niche stood a big gilded vase with dusty plastic roses on a purple doily. It was a room Aftab had never been led into before. She took it all in and was impressed. Gouhar sat down next to her on the rug, inquired about her health and the baby's health and the health of her little son, in a duet with Aftab, who asked the same of Gouhar, and then suddenly and wholly unexpectedly Gouhar heaved a huge sigh and burst into tears. Aftab, horror struck, rapidly scanned her store of information for any misfortune in Gouhar's family that might account for these tears. Was anything wrong with the Haji? An accident? But news of such calamities would spread through the village long before they were broken gently to the family. One of Gouhar's nephews, a teacher, had been accused of being a Communist and had lost his job—a common enough occurrence these days. Gouhar's brother's wife was sick in the hospital in Shiraz but was due to come home any day, and besides, there was not much love lost between them. "What is the matter?" she asked at length.

Gouhar, still sobbing, got up and went to the niche with the plastic flower vase and took a book out from under the purple crocheted doily. Aftab felt a cold shower along her spine. She knew that it was a Koran, and that whatever Gouhar was about to do would be frightening. Gouhar kissed the book and put it into a horrified Aftab's lap. "Why? What?" Aftab stammered. She took up the

Koran hastily, kissed it, and put it between herself and Gouhar on the floor. "What is the matter?" she cried. "What do I have to do with the Koran?" She was trembling with agitation.

"Aftab," said Gouhar, with a deep sigh, "my jewelry was stolen, all of it, down to the last little gold coin I had saved to sew on my daughter's cap when she would get married." (Here Gouhar cried again.) "A thief," she sobbed, "at night, a misguided man. Aftab, I want to ask you by the Koran, by Abbas, by Saint Sarah and Saint Mary, in the name of Ali and Hassan: haven't you maybe seen it somewhere around your house, somewhere in the ruins of your court- yard, hidden somewhere, maybe, by your husband?"

Aftab was speechless. She pushed the Koran away a little fur- ther, clutched her baby and looked around herself wildly.

"Or maybe Bandar gave it to Nur Ahmad? Maybe Nur Ahmad wanted the gold because of the troubles over the inheritance with the Haji? Or maybe just to harm the Haji? Maybe just out of spite, because surely, Nur Mahmad does not need my jewelry, surely his wife has more gold than I do? Maybe Bandar is just helping Nur Ahmad in this. Speak up, my dear, I beg of you, I will make it worth- while for you: a hundred Toman, a thousand Toman I will give you right now if you will testify against Nur Mahmad. You see," she continued, when a very white-faced Aftab still made no sign to reply, "you see, the Haji has been away now for four days, and he knows nothing about it yet, and he will surely kill me and cut me to pieces when I tell him. Out of pity for me I entreat you to tell me where Bandar has hidden it, so that I can get it back before the Haji comes back, before I have to tell everybody what calamity has befallen me."

At length, Aftab found her faculties again. She jumped up and said, with a dense calmness close to hysteria, that no, she knew of nothing, she had seen nothing, and she had never heard such vileness, such slander, such godless lies in all her life; Gouhar should be ashamed of herself, she would roast in hell for this lie, together with the Haji and her jewelry; and she, Aftab, had no more to say and was through with her life. Aftab stomped out of the room, sent a bloodcurdling curse up to Gouhar as she was running down the stairs, and was gone.

Aftab ruminated on this insult all day long. She did not even cook any rice for dinner, so worked up was she. In the evening she told Bandar. Bandar scolded her for getting involved in gossip and for entering the house of strangers, and then said he would break the Haji's back. As the Haji had not yet returned, however, he instead went to Nur Ahmad, his business partner and moneylender, and told him. Nur Ahmad said not to worry, he would go to the village council with a complaint against the Haji. And so when the Haji returned from his business trip two days later, he was faced with an invitation to appear before the revolutionary village court, elected from a roster of righteous and ideologically sound citizens, to answer formal charges of libel. The Haji was furious. Although he claimed not to know anything about what was going on, having just come back from a week-long absence, Nur Ahmad produced a witness who testified that the Haji had talked to him about the theft on the bus ride to the city, which shed a very unpleasant light on the Haji and made the council very sympathetic towards Nur Ahmad's claim that it was all contrived by the Haji for the sole purpose of injuring him. The council members, all of them young people who did not quite know what they were supposed to do, suggested that Nur Ahmad should make peace or take his case to court in town. Nur Ahmad gravely announced he would do so, whereupon the Haji said that all he knew was that the jewelry was stolen, and maybe somebody else was the thief—maybe one of the Communists in the village, all of whom the regime had proclaimed villains and criminal elements anyway. The council members, who all knew their Communists and very much doubted that any one of them would be fool enough to embark on such a risky undertaking, if for no other reason than to remain as inconspicuous as possible these days, assured the Haji that it was entirely possible and that the jewelry also could have been stolen by the gypsies, a stranger, a basket peddler, or for that matter just about anybody. The case was dismissed. The Haji was fuming. At home, he had a terrific row with Gouhar, whom he blamed for messing up the whole situation. By now, he had been made such a fool of that he did not even dare to go to the gendarmerie or the revolutionary guards to report the theft. Bandar made the measure of the Haji's trials full by storming into his house the same evening and abusing him heartily and mercilessly with strong language, until Gouhar drove him out with a heavy poker. After this, and Gouhar's help notwithstanding, the Haji's patience was broken, and he beat up Gouhar and yelled at his children.

Gouhar, full of misgivings of the most varied kinds, was brooding on the next step of action. In the evening she sent her little son with the sharp eyes out to hide somewhere convenient, together with his little friend, a nephew of Rahmat, the revolutionary guard, to observe Heidar Khan getting yogurt from Aftab and to listen to every word that was said. Under the pretense of shooting sparrows with a sling, the boys loitered under the trees around Aftab's ruined courtyard. As chance had it, that evening Heider Khan brought Aftab a sack of rice which he had borrowed a couple of weeks before, when the Afghanis had run out of their staple and had been unable to get their share at the village cooperative store. Instead of receiving his customary bowl by waiting somewhere on the stairs outside the house, that day he stepped inside and waited until Aftab had emptied the sack; then he stayed a few moments longer to tally up milk and yogurt for the past week and to pay her, and to wait for the change that Aftab had to rummage for in the stack of goods heaped untidily on the rack. Gouhar's little spies by then were sitting in a willow tree right outside Aftab's verandah. They could not hear anything spoken, but they thought they heard somebody laugh. And when Gouhar's son told the story to his mother, he enlarged a little on the "gift" Heidar Khan had brought Aftab, on the welcome Aftab had given him, on the laughter he had heard through the curtain across the open door, and on the overall length of the visit. Upon this, Gouhar gave her son a huge cookie with pink cream in it, the kind one usually only could steal while they were being served to a visitor, and called him "my dear" and "my life."

Rahmat's young nephew meanwhile told the same story with similar enlargements at his home to an audience composed of his mother; his grandmother Hakime; his grandfather Tamas; his half-deaf great-grandmother; an elder brother's wife, who giggled all the while; and his two unmarried sisters, who burst into laughter behind their hands. Hakime was horrified. She forbade him to mention any of this to anybody. She even bribed him with some coins and the promise of a new sling or a plastic toy car if only he would keep quiet, but to no avail. The young man prudently took the money and then told the story to his uncle Rahmat, whom he worshipped, with some more embellishments. The young revolutionary guard had come to take a grave view of the world, especially of its sins, and felt a great responsibility to keep the village on the straight and narrow path of virtue. So he reported the incident to his fellow guards, outsiders all of them, who decided to take action immediately by summoning Heidar Khan Afghani and Aftab and, without listening to any remonstrances, whisked them away to town in two separate vehicles to be questioned and tried before a judge.

Aftab stayed there for three days. Meanwhile the baby, neglected and fed awkwardly and insufficiently by her father, got ill with diarrhea. "It breaks my heart to hear the poor thing cry," said Mehri.

"It has to suffer for the sins of its mother," Gouhar said darkly. "It serves Aftab right. Why did she behave so badly?"

The others kept quiet about it. There was no reason to get mixed up in the affairs of strangers.

Aftab never told anybody what had happened to her in prison. She picked up at home where she had left off, seemingly without having missed a beat. Heidar Khan came back two weeks later, beaten up, with a swollen eye, his cast broken. He had almost been executed, the villagers whispered, although, they said, it had really been Aftab's fault. Isn't it always the woman's fault when such things happen? Isn't it the duty of a woman to guard her reputation? Were not men lustful and immoderate by nature? Heidar left the village shortly afterwards and was never heard of again. Some two months later, Aftab's baby died. It was washed and wrapped hastily in a piece of white cotton, as is the custom with small children, by Tamas's old mother, out of pity, for the sake of God, and was buried by her at the edge of the graveyard in a shallow pit dug by a kind man with a shovel who happened to pass by on the way to his field.

Only a few women came to console Aftab. Mehri sat with her a little while, and Hakime's daughters; and Nur Ahmad's wife sent her a little bag with sugar; and Tala, when she heard Aftab crying while walking down from a visit to her father's house, stopped by a few moments and cried with her.

"You are young," Tamas's mother said. "You will have many more children, God willing. Don't cry, a mother's tears weigh heavily on the soul of a child."

A few days later, eyes painted with mascara, hands clasped over her glittery shirt, Aftab was sitting in her old place on the verandah in the shade of the willow tree, gently rocking herself, and humming quietly the melody of the mourning songs. "You are a wild almond tree, but your roots are in gravel. Your fruits were not ripe yet when your trunk did dry up." So she sang for her dead child.

"Aftab forgets easily," said Gouhar, squatting broadly in the deep shade of her doorway.

"She'll never wise up," said Begom.

5

About Telling It As It Is and How Golgol Left Her Husband and Went Back to Him

Facts and truth are fickle brothers in Deh Koh. Hard to get hold of, hard to pin down, so loosely moored to memory that any whiff of intent, or mere boredom, can blow them loose into the neverland between what was and what could have been, or, probably, what was meant to be, from which they can never be retrieved again.

Of course things do happen in particular factual ways in Deh Koh just as elsewhere. But in Deh Koh, people say, things take on shapes and forms of their own as they are happening; some sparkle, some fade, and none ever stay the same.

There is no word for *fact* in Deh Koh; only one for *truth*, *correct*, or *right*; and one for *lie*. Beyond the truth one witnesses directly (first-person-truth, so to speak) there is no absolute truth, no indisputable fact to be had for love or money, no guarantees, only witness accounts, whatever they are worth. Their worth is calculated from one's assessment of the witness's character and ulterior motives, and how badly one wants to believe what is said. Generally, lies are small change in the give and take of a day, and trust is the luxury of saints and fools.

Of course, some happenings jell into shapes that are so straight, so plain, so tangible, that they remain their dull and heavy selves, impervious to embellishment, elaboration, and interpretation. Only the long shadows of time can blur their outlines. Death is such an occurrence, or the birth of a child. There are also some objects that are, for a while at least (nothing lasts very long in Deh Koh), reliably anchored at certain places, like houses or walls or trees. But such facts are few, and by and large they don't hold much interest. They sink into the routine of everyday life and can be forgotten there until one unexpectedly bumps into them—a child destroys something, a walnut tree is fought over, death reshuffles the members of a household. The much more interesting and important matters, those with elaborate shadings between truth and untruth, have to be argued, discussed, consented upon. They don't present themselves ready made. Indeed, if it were not for the endless possibilities of arguing about the shapes of things that are, or were, or might have been happening, knowledge would be reduced to statements of the obvious—a tree is a tree, a bird flies, grass is green—and the world would be very reliable and just as boring, without spunk, flat as a breadboard and just as colorless.

Not surprisingly, then, the bare and indisputable facts everybody agreed upon regarding Golgol and Ali's marital discord are dry and devoid of drama. Ali, a young man, neither rich nor poor, with a small salary as a clerk in a bank with which he bolstered his status and fully supported his parents and an unmarried sister, asked for, and was promised, Golgol, one of Ahmad and Perijan's daughters. After a lengthy and uneventful betrothal during which Golgol finished high school (this was before the revolution, when girls with a diploma reasonably could hope to find suitable employment), the wedding took place with some suddenness at the end of a mourning period in Perijan's family. The pair went to live in Deh Rud, a village down at the river, where Golgol worked in a little job with a little salary. Ali commuted, and several of his relatives took turns living with them to keep Golgol proper company. After about a year in Deh Rud, Golgol had a miscarriage. Ali started to build a house on his father-in-law's land on the other side of the village from his parents, and Golgol found a job in Deh Koh. Entirely proper and expectable under the circumstances, they shared his parents' crowded two rooms in their old, ramshackle mud-brick house until the new house would be finished. Quite as expectedly, although not quite as properly, there were harsh words and hurt feelings among the women in the house. Eventually Golgol and Ali moved into their new house. A few weeks later Golgol went back to her father. As is customary in such cases—hers was not the first, nor would it be the last—after a while Golgol moved back in with Ali. Here, this story ends and a new one starts, as can be expected, given that all the actors survived and energetically remained their old selves.

These are the facts, undisputed so far, yet undisputably not equal to what people remember as having happened, what brought out the schemers and movers and the gossip, and the tears, and a chuckle for good measure.

The story of Golgol and Ali is largely a story of women. As in most domestic dramas, in this, too, men keep a low profile. They frame the stage, as it were; they do the promptings and set dramatic accents, but it is the women who provide the action, and it is the women who remember the truth: Golgol's aunt Maryam, the widow; Huri, Ali's cousin and older brother's wife; Ali's mother, Begom; Golgol's mother, Perijan; and, in a small way, her cousin Leila.

Begom and Maryam were neighbors, spatially close but unrelated, used to treating each other with great reserve over many years of meeting regularly at the water channel and later at the common water faucet in front of their respective courtyards.

Says Maryam, Golgol's aunt, who, widowed and childless herself, has the welfare of her whole large family at heart, especially that of her favorite niece, Golgol:

"Our family is not really related to Akbar or Begom, only a little bit, far back, so how are we to know them? Begom—well, the whole village knows better than to get in the way of her tongue. Her tongue is longer than a sword and deadlier than a bullet, and a lot faster, too. Her husband hasn't had a day of peace in his life, you only need to look at his skimpy frame to know what is going on. But they are honorable people, sort of, anyway, and we all thought their youngest son, Ali, did turn out rather well, much better than his brother or his sisters with their dirty mouths. Mehri will never get married off if she doesn't shut up and get some sense. Well, Begom was on the lookout for a good match for Ali. She knew of Golgol, of course—she kept track of all the girls in our family, and didn't I know it. So, when Begom started to talk to me nicely-like, and call me 'Aunt Maryam' respectfully, and let me go ahead of her when drawing water, and such things, I should have known what she was after. One afternoon she came up the ladder to my house with her spindle and sat down and smoked a pipe with me, all sweet honey. Was I ever surprised. From then on she came again and again, with a pipe full of tobacco one day, a bowl of yogurt the next, a handful of dried cheese the other, asking my advice on something one day, bringing a bag of blackberries the next. . . . Well, I got the hint. She talked about how good a lad Ali was, and his salary, and their two cows and ten sheep and goats, and their apple orchard (apple orchard indeed, ten measly trees or so in all), and how highly they all thought of Ahmad and Perijan and their sons and daughters. As if I didn't know where the wind was blowing from! I told Perijan. I warned her. 'Peri,' I said, 'they want Golgol. Now, I don't say yes, I don't say no. Begom has a tongue as sharp as a razor, and old Akbar has never amounted to much, and neither has their older son, and there isn't much land or anything else of account, but then again, Ali is a decent fellow, educated too, and he has a salary. So think it over and take your choice.' And finally when Akbar did send for her—that is, Begom did the sending; she got Ali's boss from the bank to go, plied him and his wife with a dinner, she did, and with her bowls of yogurt—so, in the end, Ahmad couldn't say no to a bank gentleman from the town, could he, and Peri, bless her, said, 'It is her fate.' She was right, of course. Had Akbar himself gone, or Ali, or his brother, they would have said no, but Begom is clever.

"Golgol was a student in eighth grade then, and she cried and cried, but the girls all do anyway, so that did not matter. They wanted her to finish school and get a salary, so she studied some more, and then Ahmad's mother died, and of course there couldn't be a wedding, and soon after that our oldest brother—may God have mercy on him—had the awful accident. Although the bride price was settled (and much too low, I said, fifteen thousand Toman, and most of this we pardoned the beggars, not that Ahmad has more than they do, except honor and pride), and although the marriage contract was written, and although brother Kerim and Golgol's brother had done all the shopping in town for the bedding and the kitchen stuff—a gas stove, even—and clothes, and gifts, the best of everything and mostly out of their own pockets, there was no way on earth we could have done a wedding with Golgol's uncle just buried. But then Ahmad himself got so badly sick with his stomach that we had to take him to the hospital. Sure enough, Ali came along and stayed with him day and night; the best doctors, the best medicine, no expense spared, a taxi here, a taxi there, fruits, sweets. After this show of respect, what could Ahmad have said? The wedding was done as soon as it was decently possible, quietly, of course, no music, no dance, although this was before the revolution and the weddings then were big feasts, but such a festive show would have angered Ahmad's relatives. There was a huge dinner, though. I cooked all day and half the night, and we slaughtered three sheep and two goats. Perijan cried all the while. She knew what we didn't. Brother Kerim even scolded her badly for carrying on that way.

"The principal of the girls' school in Deh Rud, down by the river, knew Golgol and wanted her as a secretary. Begom and Ali thought of the salary Golgol would earn and said yes, the heathens. Not a good place, Deh Rud. Heat, flies, dirt; heavy, still air; bad, tepid water; and the people there all know more about everything than is good for others. Ali went back and forth between Deh Rud and Deh Koh, up and down the mountain on his motorbike. We didn't like Golgol to be alone there all day long, it wasn't proper.

"When the people started to talk about this, Begom went and stayed with her for a while, then Ali's sister Mehri went, then his brother Sadrullah (who never seems to find any work) and his wife Huri took turns there and lived out of Ali's pocket. Beggars altogether. Then Golgol got pregnant, but they didn't tell any one of us, not even Golgol's own mother! That's the kind of people they are. Not knowing that she was pregnant, we couldn't do anything for her: no vitamins, no amulet, nothing. And they just let her stay there, alone, unprotected! Of course, Ali and Golgol didn't like it in Deh Rud, either. They wanted to live here in Deh Koh, but Ali knew very well that Begom and Mehri would make life miserable for them, he said so himself to Perijan.

"One early morning Golgol was washing dishes at the water channel (such a primitive place, they don't even have piped water there) when a woman came and sat down next to her with a whole bunch of beads around her neck, one of these necklaces women used to wear here too, with different beads against diseases and pains, and for protection. Huri still has a lot of these beads, but in Deh Koh now we know better than to wear them—such beads are always dangerous, one never knows what powers they might have. Sure enough, Golgol all of a sudden was overcome by such a tremendous pain in her back and belly that she couldn't even get up any more, and a little while later she miscarried. These Deh Rud women! For sure, one of that woman's beads was a child-bead, and of course that's deadly for an unborn child. Here, if a woman has one at all, to protect herself, let say—which isn't so bad an idea, I wish Huri had given Golgol one—she would be ever so careful not to take it close to another pregnant woman. We would think it a sin to do otherwise. But in Deh Rud—damn them all, those women!

"Anyway, after that even Ali's people said that Deh Rud was no place for Golgol. Ahmad in his kindness gave Ali a piece of land so he could start building a house with the savings from Golgol's salary and offered to help him with his work, because Begom didn't want to let go of a piece of their own land for a house, and Akbar is too old and bent to do much work of any kind. But no sooner had Ali started to truck rocks and cement that Begom started to bicker and to nag, because now it hit her that she would have to move to the other end of the village and live among our people. 'I won't go,' she yelled like a child, 'I am staying here!' She got mad when I told her that everybody would thank her if she stayed.

"Eventually Golgol's uncle Kerim found Golgol the job in his school here, so she could leave that dreadful place down at the river. Of course, they had to live with Akbar, where else? A youngest son has to stay with his parents. From the very first day Begom lived up to her reputation: 'Don't eat this, don't do that, don't sit here, don't go there, don't say this, do that, do this,' all day long, and whenever Begom was quiet, Mehri took it up. And those endless hints at the things she and Mehri needed, a skirt here, a trip to the doctor there, this and that, all the time. Begom was into all her things, too, and the tiniest crumb on her rug she made into a heap of dirt, while they sat in their filthy room gossiping. Whenever Golgol as much as passed the time of day with me in the alley they would scold her, and her own mother she didn't see for weeks on end because they didn't let her go there. Ali was unhappy about this, too, but he said he was working on the house as hard as he could, so she should just shut up and not be contrary. Easy said for him who is never home, I say, and also, whenever he was home, they would be very nice to her and pass her the sugar for tea, and give her a cushion to lean on, and Mehri would offer to do the dishes, in his face. Aftab saw it and so did I. Yet, behind his back—one wouldn't believe what schemes they came up with! Begom is so old fashioned she refused to cook on the gas stove. Yet the first time Golgol cooked on it herself, Mehri or Begom—one no better than the other—put a handful of salt into the rice, secretly, so that Ali wouldn't be able to eat her food! She is such a quiet and well brought-up girl, Golgol is, and for the longest time she said nothing, but who can stand this kind of nagging all the time? There she was, working all day, bringing home a good salary for them all to eat—and they had never eaten as well before—respected, honorable, pretty too, one would think they'd like her, but no, only bad words the moment she stepped over the sill. Ali liked her well enough, but his mother and his sister were jealous. They filled him with lies and tales behind her back. And when Golgol finally complained to Ali about them he beat her up, the same Ali who had said that his mother and sister were a bad lot! I myself have seen her with a black eye, her veil drawn half across her face. 'The cow hit me,' she said. The cow indeed. Was she maybe milking the cows for them? Oh, no, we all knew what was going on. I told brother Kerim, but all he said was to leave them alone. Golgol would learn to keep her place. Perijan I didn't tell, she only would have been upset. 'Everything is fine,' I told her.

"But Ali himself had sense enough to move to the new house as soon as the plaster was dry in one room. Now, finally, there would be peace, we thought. But by then Begom had gotten it into her head that she wanted a house on their own land after all, on the heap of rubble behind the village. She kept after Ali to let his house go and to start another, or else she wouldn't move out of the old one, and he would be shamed, because parents ought to be taken care of by their youngest son, and if they didn't live with him it showed that he was a bad son. At home, Golgol showed him how much money they'd lose and how much better it was there instead of on the steep slope of his father's field, but in the end he listened to Begom more than to Golgol—it's always the loudest wheel that gets the grease—and he started to be cross again with Golgol and beat her up.

"And then one day when Ali had gone to town to bring more cement, Mehri was supposed to bring Golgol ice from the refrigerator, which they had left with Begom for their convenience, because Golgol had to make lemonade for the workers. It was a hot day. But no matter how long she waited, Mehri didn't come, and Golgol had to go and borrow some ice from a neighbor, which was sort of disgraceful. When Ali came back the next day, Mehri came, too. Golgol asked her why she had not come the day before, and she just said she hadn't had time. Hadn't had time, my word! So Golgol said it seemed she only had time when Ali was there. Mehri got mad at that and in the evening when Ali went to see his father about something, she bitched. When he got back he beat Golgol up without saying a word.

"By then she had had enough and went to her father with nothing but her clothes on her back—work clothes at that. Who is going to blame her? It served them right, too. Now the whole village knew what was going on. They were shamed. For quite a while they didn't even have the courage to ask anybody to go to Ahmad to ask Golgol back, because they knew they'd be turned down. In the end, Ali had an awful fight with his mother and made her go and beg old Seyed Shansi, a Seyed, a descendant of our Prophet and a relative of Ahmad, and such a respected woman; she scolded them but in the end consented to do it because it has religious merits to make peace among people, especially for a Seyed. Being who she is, there was of course no question of refusing. If anyone else had come we would have held out and bargained really hard. But with her . . . well, she took Golgol back to Ali. Now they'll think twice about making life miserable for her, for sure, and we'll see what God has in store for her."

Says Huri, Ali's brother's wife, a young woman, poor and hard worked, who has kept her beads and has collected insights and wisdom and a bagful of memories far beyond her age:

"Goodness, all that fuss! Who pays any attention when Begom fights with me, or when my husband beats me up? There is a difference, though: Golgol comes from a family with land, on her mother's side at least; her people have gone to school, they have salaries, they are somebody, while all Akbar and my husband Sadrullah have are a few acres on the slopes and a few trees and a few animals, and bent backs from the hard work. Money isn't everything, but no money is nothing, and that's the truth. When Begom let on that Ali wanted one of Ahmad's daughters, I told them there would be trouble. They are a stubborn lot, and proud for no reason—haughty, I would say, looking at them. Sure enough, the trouble started right away with the bride price. They asked the sky for the girl, as if she would bring the Shah's treasury with her. Our mullah had to talk sense into them, but still Ali went into debt over his ears, and I think even Sadrullah helped him, although, by God, we have nothing ourselves. Yet when you look at what they gave her by way of bride wealth, dear me, not much more than I got from my father, who is only an ordinary farmer. Ali was so ashamed of the little rugs she got that he himself went to town and took yet another loan and bought a fine big rug so that people wouldn't say how shabby everything was.

"Well, when this finally was settled, Ahmad's people started a 'not today, maybe tomorrow' game, postponing the wedding from one month to the next, always finding some other threadbare excuse just to show off. Of course, the village is so big by now that it is hard to fit weddings in between the different mournings. Too many people die. It really suited her father, though, because this way he could scratch the expenses for the musicians and the feasting. Even I, coming from an ordinary family, illiterate and uneducated, had a proper wedding people still remember. Golgol got nothing; they fetched her without so much as a song. We did a big dinner, though, and they gave a little one, just for the family, that was all. It's cheaper that way, for sure.

"For the love of God, Sadrullah and I spent many a night with her down in Deh Rud. I didn't sit around with my hands in my lap, either. Even if I wanted to, I don't think I could count all the suppers I cooked for her and all the breads I baked. Nobody has done this for me, ever, except my mother when I was ill. But one could see that Golgol didn't like it much, she didn't really appreciate what we were doing for her. She is nice enough—I always got on well with her, but then I am not one for gossip and fighting anyway—but she always gives one the feeling that she is better than we are. Not a single time has she come here to visit me, although she is much younger than I am, not even when I was sick last year. She doesn't take advice from us either as she should, considering that she is young and inexperienced. These girls out of high school know really nothing about housekeeping, they have no common sense.

For example, I warned her, and Begom did too, and Sadrullah, of the women in Deh Rud, who know all the tricks there are to be known, and black magic, too. One day, when Sadrullah was there, she found a box of sweets on the window sill. Sadrullah took it from her and looked the sweets over carefully. Golgol made fun of him. But sure enough, he found one with a little slip of paper in it. It was clear that somebody had messed with it to harm her. He threw the whole box away. God knows what would have happened to Golgol if Sadrullah hadn't been there to watch out.

"If she really ever was pregnant—as she now says she was—she should have told us. But it would be just like her to keep such news to herself. If we had known we would have given alms and made her an amulet, gotten medicine against fright, would have made a promise of a pilgrimage to a saint. In a strange village one has to be on guard. The day she says she had the miscarriage Ali had gone to town without telling us. Sadrullah was to go there the next day. It was just chance that only the dumb local girl who did chores for her was with her that day when they had the earthquake. Not that anyone can do anything against earthquakes, though. A half-finished stone wall crashed down, and she was frightened and screamed. When Sadrullah got there he offered to find a car and take her to town, but she refused, stubborn as she is. Next day, when Ali came back, she claimed she had lost a child, and he took her to the doctor in town. It so happened that Golgol's younger brother was in town that day, too, and by chance met somebody who told him that she was in the hospital, so her people knew before we did and this again gave a big row. That snot-nosed kid could have told us, too, it would not have hurt him. He did it on purpose, though, I know.

"Then Ali tried very hard to find her a suitable job here. But she said she wouldn't move back here unless he built her a house, because she didn't want to live in Akbar's shabby old house with Begom. I myself have lived there for six years, I did, and never said a word, although Begom is a real devil and doesn't like me at all, while she does like Golgol all right. Golgol is pretty and has a salary, I have a dark face and no salary, and that's the truth. She didn't trouble Golgol half as much as myself, ever. Well, Begom and Akbar too were tired of the old house with its leaky roof and dirty barnyard, and they said they should tear the old place down and build a new house right there, and not in one of the fields, which all are rather out of the way. Now, of course, so many people have built houses out in the fields it is like another village, but back then it was very lonesome. But Golgol didn't like this at all and dinned Ali's ear full about the inconvenience, and how far away from the school it was, and how steep the hill was, and whatnot. Of course, it is all mountains around here. Our place isn't level, either; I wish it was. She even worked on her father and her brothers to sell them a piece of land in the orchard behind their house, which they did. We were all against it because, of course, why should Begom and Akbar move into a part of the village where they don't have any land and no relatives either? But they got Ali all softened up and sweet, and he took out a tremendous loan and started to cart rocks and cement, because his home would not be a simple adobe house like ours. Such houses are old fashioned, not good enough for one with a wife with a salary and a high school diploma. He worked his fingers to the bone, and Sadrullah neglected his own fields and didn't go to town to find a job as he does every winter but stayed right here for weeks and weeks, helping his brother. When they had a lot of workmen, I went and helped Golgol fix dinner, too, for a mere 'Thank you' and 'May God pay you back your kindness,' usually. She is very pious, our deal Golgol is, which comes in very handy now after the revolution.

"The day she ran away they were just doing the barn and had a couple of workmen, when Golgol said she would not cook any dinner after she came home from school in the afternoon. Nice talk that is, indeed. Ali said why not, and she said that since they were building the barn for Begom's cows, Begom and Mehri should do the dinner. As if she would not later eat the yogurt and the butter from the milk of these cows! Well, Ali got mad at her, and she just walked out on him, taking all her jewelry, too, in the middle of the work. Again we all had to pitch in, and it was quite a feeling, looking up over the trees and seeing Perijan and Golgol sitting on their neighbor's roof, looking smug. Ali wanted to go after Golgol right away to beat some sense into her, but we said no, this would look too eager on his part; he should let them stew in their own juices for a while until they would get really anxious and think he would not want her back. It worked, too. They started to drop little hints here and there, and to visit Akbar's relatives, and to ask about Ali and whatnot. They even persuaded Seyed Shansi, who is related to them, to offer to go as a middleman. Not to seem unduly proud in the eyes of the people, Ali in the end said all right and took her back. They were all mighty glad to have her off their hands again. I am sure they have beaten her up at home to teach her how to behave. I think it will be better now, although what will happen once Begom moves there, I don't know. She is a dragon, and Mehri is a snake, and Golgol is a princess. There is no way they can live together in peace."

Says Begom, Ali's belligerent mother, who has lived through more hard times than she cares to recount, cooling and hardening in the process, and now has set the hopes of her waning years on the one son who has made good:

"Ali could have had any girl he wanted. We did a good deed asking for one of Ahmad's daughters, because they have altogether many more than they can handle, Kerim's people do. Maryam played up to me, it was just scandalous the way she carried on, to persuade us to take one of them. They had half a dozen or so between them at that time ready to be married off, and no suitors in sight. One thing I have to credit Maryam with: She worked really hard to find Golgol a good husband, and although I warned Ali that they were a stuck-up lot, and there would be trouble (and, oh, how right I was!), he wanted a wife with an education, himself being such a smart and knowledgeable man, praise be the Lord. Again I warned him. I said he should marry her right away, when a girl should be married, young enough to learn her place in the house, and not after she thinks she knows it all and is stubborn and won't cooperate with her husband's people. Again he didn't listen and let her have her own will, although I warned him: 'Ali,' I said, 'With these salaried women it is always the same: instead of helping their mother-in-law, they play the great lady. For the few hundred Toman they bring home they think they can be insulting and boss everybody around.' And it is true! They can't even cook a decent meal for their husbands. Indeed, what I should have done without Mehri all the time, I don't know. She is a hard-working girl, a good girl; I committed a sin by not letting her get married earlier—it isn't for lack of suitors, but how would I have coped with all the work? Golgol certainly never lifted a finger to do anything around here.

"Kerim did all the bargaining, and shamelessly so. He squeezed Ali dry. Ahmad had his roof waterproofed with tar with the money he got from us, instead of spending it on Golgol's bride wealth. He cheated his own daughter and Kerim gave his blessing. The whole affair wasn't right from the beginning, which just goes to prove that I was right. Deep in my own heart I think that they made some magic to blind Ali, to make him want Golgol against all reason. How else can one explain why he didn't listen to me? Still, the match almost fell through because Golgol got it in her head that she wanted to go to the Teacher Training College and not marry Ali. And those fools paid attention to her! I sure don't know what the world is coming to. Now, of course, I wish we had just let her go then, but poor Ali—he himself admits he must have been under a spell then—he patiently waited until they came to their senses. I mean, she flunked the entrance examination, and now Ali was good enough for her.

"Ali shouldn't have let her go to Deh Rud, but the poor man was blinded by her people. Later, they themselves saw how dangerous it was, and it gave Perijan and Maryam another reason for slandering us by saying we had sent her there because we were greedy for her money. Ali had nothing of it, he said so himself. Down there her salary went up in rent. And whenever one of us went there to be with her we brought them eggs, butter, flour, a chicken. It was a loss, not a profit. But whenever one of us was down there, she would find a thousand reasons why we should go home—it was embarrassing in front of her neighbors. As if it was fun for us to be there, among strangers, working at two places, not to speak of the discomfort of getting there. There was no taxi service then between the two villages. When she had the miscarriage she had sent Mehri and myself away just the day before, so we could visit my sick sister, she said. The miscarriage was her own fault, too, because she is so careless about the evil and dangerous powers we live with—God have mercy—and didn't take any precautions by way of beads or fumigations or amulets. This is another folly of some of those educated women. The whole misfortune was her fault, but of course her people blame it on us. Only then, and not earlier, did they urge her to come back. Ali, with his good connections, found her the job here, because despite all the ruckus her stay in Deh Rud had caused—Ali once half killed himself going back and forth every day— she said she wouldn't come up if she didn't have a job and if Ali wouldn't find her another house. So Ali—he really must have been under a spell, I swear—made another foolish decision against my good counsel and took out a terrible loan and started to build a house on Ahmad's land (on Golgol's insistence!), instead of spending a tiny fraction of the money repairing and building onto this house we have right here, which is conveniently located, close to the water; and we could have gotten Akbar's cousin's buildings in the courtyard very cheaply because they were moving out.

"We moved out of our good room and let Ali and Golgol have it. This was a real sacrifice, because the old room is also the kitchen and storage room, it is old and black with soot, and the roof is leaking. Golgol went so far as to lock their room when she left in the morning, so that I couldn't even use it for a visitor. She said we were snooping around! All that happened was that once a bundle of bedding, which she had carelessly thrown on top of the pile of household goods that should be stacked neatly along one wall and covered with the kelim a bride gets at the wedding—this bundle had fallen down and opened up, and everything was strewn on the floor. She is a bad housekeeper all around. We had heard the thump and Mehri and I were just straightening out the mess when she came in. Instead of kissing our hands in gratitude she yelled at us. She can pick a fight at the drop of a needle, or else she is sulking, sitting in her room by herself, not speaking a word. Instead of making tea for us, her old and worn-out mother-in-law and her old and tired husband's father, cheerfully, she only sits in her room, doing nothing, with a book in front of her face or scribbling, secretly-like, and when I call out and say, 'Dear, come drink your tea,' she will only grumble and mumble. Some politeness she has. And always she was after us, Mehri and myself, for not doing things right: the dishes were not clean, the water was dusty, the rice was too greasy, the green vegetables that go with the bread weren't washed enough, there were too many flies, she even complained about the fleas, by all saints, as if they didn't have any fleas in her father's house! After all, they live above the barn, too, just as we do, and it stands to reason that you can't avoid fleas if you keep a flock of sheep downstairs! And the wash she had! I don't think Mehri and myself had washed that many clothes in a year as we did then in one season. I mean, cleanliness is good, it is prescribed by the religion, but when it means that somebody has to wash her fingers to the bones in cold water in the dead of winter, then I guess something isn't right, and whoever was writing down the religion didn't think it all through.

If they teach girls in school that they should change their shirts every other day, and wash their skirts all the time, and step into the bathhouse every time they pass it, then they should also give them a washing machine when they graduate, because it is just plain unfair to give them such notions if they go off then and get a nice and easy job while their mothers-in-law or their own mothers have to break their backs for them. That's what I said, and she picked another fight. When she bickered about my cooking, I told her to suit herself and cook her own way. She did, but this was even more inconvenient for me because we only have this one kitchen, and Ali didn't like it at all, because his dinner was always late and never the way he is used to it, and so he spoke to her sternly and forbade her to criticize me. She tattled on me and, dear me, did Maryam fly at me next time she saw me! As if I had strangled their precious little bird.

"Golgol was always rather inconsiderate in everything. She is very pious, which is a good thing in itself, all the praying and the ablutions . . . well, we'll see who is going to make it to heaven in the end. But I know she refused Ali his right at night, saying they wouldn't be able to make a proper ablution bath in the morning and therefore he shouldn't do it. If this isn't a sin, I don't know what a sin is. The poor blighter gave in most of the time, too! I really set his mind straight on this issue, though. But it was worst during the month of fasting. Akbar and myself are old and weak, we can't fast. Mehri has an ulcer, she can't fast either. Ali, well, he is a hardworking man, and fasting makes it very tough to fulfill one's duties. Only one who can afford to sleep half the day can afford not to eat and drink, especially during the heat of summer. It was all right for Golgol to fast, her life is easy enough. But it stands to reason that somebody's fasting shouldn't be done in a way that inconveniences the whole house. She would eat her dinner at sundown, because of course she was hungry by then, while we wouldn't eat it until quite a while later. Of course I had to refuse to cook twice. What would she demand next? But even more aggravating was that she would get up long before dawn to have her morning meal: making fire, slushing water, clinking glass, the smell of food cooking, all while we were still asleep, trying to get our strength for the day's troubles and hardships. When I spoke to her about it she called us heathens! Well, Ali had to set her straight on this issue, too, but since then the whole country has gotten this religious madness and I can't say any more what I think.

"I for one was glad when they moved into the new house. There was no question about me moving there—a house in Ahmad's garden, indeed, while we have our own land on the other side of the village, not to speak of the old house site. I told them to go and not mind us, we would scrape by without them. Ali was really upset about this, one could see it plainly. At one point he even said he would divorce her to live in peace, but I talked him out of it. He had married her, and even if she wasn't a good wife she was his wife, and he should shoulder his responsibility like any good man. It would have been easy for him to divorce her, because they didn't even have a child yet. I am sure she did something so she wouldn't get pregnant, just to spite me and Ali. We saw little of her during that time— I didn't go there, of course, and she didn't come here, which was impolite, but that's the way she is. Mehri was there almost every day, though, to help her cook for the workers, to bring them yogurt, butter; I even baked bread for them a few times, but Mehri said Golgol said it was not thin enough and too salty, and so I thought why bother. For all her troubles Mehri got nothing but harsh words. But when Golgol started a rumor that Mehri would come only when they had workmen to make eyes at them, I forbade her to go there at all, and of course I had to tell Ali. Ali got so furious that I had to calm him down before I could let him go back, or else he would have killed her. Whatever he said to her that night, she just turned her back and hollered for her father and got the fool to keep her. Good riddance, I said. She even sneaked back into the house the next day with a suitcase and took all the jewelry and clothes and the pressure cooker and such things that aren't even hers. So what? I said, let her have it. Now Ali was much more reasonable. He decided he would finish the house roughly and then sell it and build a new one on our land. Again he said he would divorce her and look for a better wife, but again I said that this was bad in the eyes of the people—Maryam even hinted that Golgol was pregnant—and he should take in consideration our good name and that it has religious merits to care for a woman, especially such a difficult one, because she wouldn't find another husband easily if it were generally known how hard she was to get along with and how bad a housekeeper she was. In the end he was willing to take her back, but he made it clear to Ahmad and Kerim that he would do so only with the understanding that Golgol and Ali would move over to our side. Perijan didn't like this at all, and Maryam made the worst fuss she had ever made; it was a regular fight down at the water but the people were on our side, naturally, and so they had to agree to this condition. We have already found a good spot near the new lane that is being built off the main road, and then we'll see who is the master in this house."

Says Perijan, Golgol's aging mother, at a time when she is already unhappy about her untimely pregnancy and feels weak and out of control:

"If I had had any idea that it would come to this, I would have let her go only over my dead body. Of all my children, Golgol is the most reasonable, the kindest, the wisest, and we all like her the most. She deserves better than that. My sister Maryam and my brother Kerim are behind this calamity, they are to blame. Maryam should have told us what kind of people Begom and Ali are—one no better than the other. How should we have known, here, at the other end of the village? Now Golgol is reproaching us for putting her into such a disagreeable situation. I am crying my eyes dry, but what does it help? The moment Golgol left the house, I had a feeling as if she had died—which she nearly did, in Deh Rud, for lack of care. They are not even Muslims, the way they treat her. Never should they have made her go down to Deh Rud, or if so, at least Ali's sister should have gone with her and stayed with her, day and night, and not just for a few hours, like a guest, making Golgol wait on her. How sweet they talked about how wonderful Golgol was, and how they would treat her like a princess, while all they really wanted was a servant and her money, and we were too stupid to see this. Now the water is down the river, it is Golgol's fate—who can go against the wish of God? Begom knew very well that they had nothing in the past, have nothing now and would never have anything unless Ali would marry well. She is sharp, she is conniving, she blinded us all. We should have given Golgol to Ahmad's brother's son, as it would have been good custom, even if he only has eight grades of school and is a humble worker. But he is a good lad and his family would have treated her well, salary or no salary. How blind we were! Four or five suitors came, but Maryam and Kerim said that Ali was the best. Now they eat their words, at least Maryam does, apologizing a hundred times a day. Kerim only says that what is going on between Ali and Golgol is just normal for young people, and we shouldn't talk about it. What does he know, even if he is my older brother and well educated.

"It is her fate, for whatever unknown reason—I am sure she does not deserve it. She knows her religion; she is well versed in the scriptures; she is pious; she says her prayers; she even fasts, although she has to work hard at her job and has to work for Ali too. She never was one to let others wait on her. It must be her fate, because how else could one explain that nothing we try to make her lot a little easier works out? When we wanted to wait with the wedding until we could make a big feast for her, Begom and Ali accused us of stalling, and so she didn't even get a proper wedding. And she was so good about it: she didn't mind because music and dancing are forbidden by the religion, she said, even then when there was music and dancing at every wedding. And when we agreed—how reluctantly!—to let Ali take her to Deh Rud, we did so only to give her some peace from Begom. But this crazy old man—a lunatic they let run loose in Deh Rud—appears at her doorway with a heavy club in his hand, and although she said that no one was home and he should go and come back later, he just came in and sat down and wanted cigarettes from her, and she was so frightened that she passed out and eventually lost her child. And when we gave her a sewing machine, Ali's whole lazy family made her sew clothes for them because she is so clever with everything she does—she even made skirts for Huri, what an injustice! And when Begom didn't allow her to visit us for fear we might conspire against them—which we never would do, we are good Muslims—we offered them our garden so that they could move closer to us and I could help Golgol a little with her work, because neither Begom nor Mehri helped her. And how awful *that* turned out for her! At first Ali was all for it because it was closer to the bank, so convenient for his motorbike, and also he said he hoped that among strangers his mother would be more reasonable. But reason doesn't move Begom. She said she would rather live in a stable with her cows and sheep than move over here. Akbar would have liked it here. He even has a sister living just around the bend of the creek. But this is another shortcoming in that family: they don't give proper honors to Akbar, always treat him like a nobody, Begom and Ali, both of them. In the end, Begom got her whole family worked up so that everybody was telling Ali to sell the house. Brother Kerim told us not to get mixed up in this, so we didn't, but I cried a lot, seeing how things were turning. Although Golgol didn't complain—she did not want to embarrass Ali's family—we could see clearly what was going on and hear it, too. Even Akbar's sister, the one who lives so close to them, said that Golgol always was alone with the work, and what work! Tea and dinner and lunch and lemonade for the workers, on top of working in school. Akbar's sister said Golgol didn't have any help with the bread baking, that Ali yelled at her . . . it breaks a mother's heart to hear such news. This flippant Mehri too gave her a lot of troubles. Once she offered to help Golgol wash the tea glasses at the pool in the courtyard, and then she hid them, and Golgol, after hunting for them everywhere, had to borrow some glasses from us or else she couldn't have served tea to their workmen. And when she was late with the tea that afternoon, Mehri even had the nerve to tell Ali that his wife had studied enough to make glasses but hadn't mind enough to remember where she put them.

"We were all so glad when Golgol came back to us. Ali had simply sent her away like a servant because Begom had told him to. And I know why: the wretched woman thought that Golgol's father and her brothers would scold her, would beat her up probably, would send her right back and tell her that a wife has to do whatever her husband wants her to. But she was wrong: we told her to get a divorce; even her brothers said so. What could happen to her, with a salary? She could live with us, with her father, and keep her money instead of having to put up with an unfriendly husband who took all the money and spent it on his greedy mother and sister. But if she wanted to go back to them, we would hold out as long as possible, saying no to anyone they might send to make peace, and in the end we would give in only after they would solemnly promise in front of the mullah not to make her any more troubles. We had it all figured out. How hard they tried to find a go-between; all over the village they went, and everybody turned them down! But in the end those desperate wretches went to Seyed Shansi and gave her God knows how much money, may God punish her, the old devil with her amulets and verses and whatnot, and once this was out, there was of course no bargaining possible for us; we just had to let her go without any additional guarantee. Golgol herself said it would be a sin to bargain with Seyed Shansi or to send her back to Ali empty handed. So Golgol went away again, and I am sitting here, fretting and worrying."

Says Leila, Golgol's spirited cousin, a young, vivacious teacher and mother of three, who unerringly finds the bright spot in just about any situation:

"Golgol is bright and a good woman, pious and all that, but a little dark and dumpy, not really what I would call pretty. I always thought how lucky she was to get such a fine husband. Ali is a handsome lad, although I shouldn't say this about a strange man, and much better than his mother and sisters. There wasn't a day without a row Aunt Maryam could hear over three courtyards when Huri and Sadrullah were living with them. But then it also depends on the daughter-in-law, of course. My own mother-in-law is a mean old hag too, yet what is the use of fighting with her? It is much better to keep quiet and be polite—not that I can do it, though . . . ei, that's life, and why should it be different for Golgol?

"Aunt Perijan always said that it should be written into the marriage contract that Ali's people had no right to make Golgol any troubles whatsoever, and probably even that they should live separate from Akbar and Begom. Everybody else was against it, because such stipulations simply aren't done here; it would have reflected very badly on us for insisting on such unusual demands. On the contrary, because they are poor people, Uncle Kerim said we shouldn't ask a high bride price, and he made up for it. I think he spent more on Golgol than on his own daughter. It was probably stupid that they waived the divorce settlement in the marriage contract. If Ali would divorce Golgol, God forbid, she would not get anything from him but one Toman and a volume of the Koran. When the contract was written, this showed how highly our family thought of Ali, and Akbar was really pleased about it, not to speak of Begom, who strutted around like a young rooster, crowing all the while.

"I tried to get Golgol a job here, but she and Ali both wanted to be elsewhere, unusual as it is, because they were afraid of Begom. That's why Golgol went to Deh Rud, where I wouldn't even want to be buried, and Ali had to dash back and forth on his gleaming motorbike, and of course he had this accident which left him with the long scar on his face. He isn't half as handsome now as he was before. However, the worst was that Golgol had a miscarriage. They say it was because a stranger frightened her—we all know what strange men are after! Well, it certainly was bad that she was alone so much. At night Ali was with her, of course, otherwise she wouldn't have gone there—it would have been outrageously indecent—but still. . . . If somebody had been with her that day she would not have lost the child. It was a boy, too, what a pity. All the while Ali tried to make his mother agree on a site for a new house, but Begom was stubborn. Ali was on very good terms with Ahmad and Aunt Perijan; he spent more time there than at home, which was funny because they didn't let Golgol go there at all yet *he* was there all the time. When Ali saw that Begom was adamant about the new house, Ahmad told him to build one in his orchard. This was really generous of him; my own father would not have done this for any of us sisters, I swear. But now Begom and Mehri and their folks started to wag their tongues. Huri was the worst of them. They told Begom that she would be a stranger in that quarter of the village, that Akbar would have to spend half the day just getting to his own fields, that Golgol and her mother and brothers would stick together like resin on a tree, that she would end up as Aunt Perijan's and Golgol's servant, that she wouldn't find any pastures for her cows, and whatnot, all lies. But Begom sure enough got all worked up about it, and Golgol and Ali didn't have a moment's peace. But here Golgol made a mistake. She behaved very badly because she talked back and fought with Begom, which she shouldn't have done. She was no better than them, really, and my father told Ahmad and Perijan they should keep out of it because it was really Golgol's fault. It doesn't reflect well on a family if one of its young women carries on like this. If Ali beat her up, which people say he did, then probably she deserved it. Every day Golgol had a new story to tell in school although I didn't really listen; Uncle Kerim had very rightly said I shouldn't get mixed up. One thing, however, was clear: Ali and Golgol were crazy about each other, ah, the young people! Lucky Golgol! I was astonished when she walked out on him over a dispute with Mehri, who said she didn't want to be there alone with the workers because it was improper for a young girl, as indeed it is. Men are dirty minded. And so what, if Mehri is a real pain, which she is, a real schemer? Instead of fighting with her and tattling on her to Ali, Golgol and Aunt Perijan should have tried to find her a husband; then Golgol would have been rid of her! Now the whole village knows what a harpy Mehri is, and she'll probably never find a husband. Pretty she isn't, either, poor girl, unlike her brother, and getting on in years; she must be nineteen by now or even twenty.

"Whatever happened, Golgol went back home, but she took all the keys to the house with her. And whenever Ali wanted to get into a cupboard, or a trunk, or the shower, or even into the courtyard, he had to go to Ahmad's house, standing in the yard and yelling up to them like a love-drunk young man who is too bashful to look at his bride! I was there, once, and it was so funny, I died laughing. Golgol made a big scene of it, claiming she didn't have the key, looking everywhere and all the while Ali was standing down below, ankle deep in muck, waiting, with a face like a wet sheep. Ah, one could see how he was longing for her, and Golgol ogled down with sparkling eyes, she couldn't deceive me. Pregnant she was, too—I could spot all the signs, no matter how hard she denied it—so there was not the slightest doubt they would eventually get together again. It does happen, well, not often, but it does happen once in a while that a woman leaves her husband just to drive home a point, and when he had enough troubles finding someone to milk the animals, and to make yogurt, and to feed the children and himself, and to sweep the house, and to fetch water, and all the thousand things a woman does, well, then he appreciates his wife better, and things look up for her. For Golgol, when she went back to him—and sooner than we thought she would; Ali only had to ask once instead of the customary three times—a second bridal chamber was waiting for her! It was just as well that they were living alone then . . . she didn't even come to school the next day, I remember. It makes me wish I would run away from my husband, just to be able to come back and have a good time with him. . . . Ah, the joys of youth!"

6

A Betrothal, a Rape, and a Guess
About Turan's Fate

Animated discussions in Deh Koh are polyphonic and contrapuntal. Everybody talks more or less simultaneously, indeed often seemingly to themselves in monologues interlaced with comments, responses, and questions flying in all directions. Rendering such conversation two-dimensionally in writing gives it a structure and logical sequence it does not really possess. It also levels the tonal quality and the volume—Mehri's screechy soprano and Tala's booming alto are assigned the same value on paper. This is a pity, but what is being said stands out a lot clearer in print than in the chorus, and, besides, what is written cannot be argued away.

This was also Banu's opinion that warm afternoon in May on her shady, narrow verandah.

"A description of Abbas is being sent around in the whole area, a big poster, I know. My mother has seen it because brother Rahmat has one; she told me so herself this morning—all the revolutionary guards have it . . ."

"His photograph too?" Leila was leaning against a wooden pillar, fanning her broad, freckled face with her veil. "I would like to see one; I don't think I have ever seen Abbas."

"So what?" said Mahin, "a scoundrel." She snorted loudly.

There were five of them squatting on an old rug on the verandah of the small house behind Tamas's big courtyard. Notwithstanding appearances of extreme modesty and stone-walled seclusion, the dusty place had been the social center for the younger women of the neighborhood ever since Banu had moved there from her father's house as her cousin's wife. There was not really enough room for them in her uncle's (and father-in-law's) place, next to her own father's house—separated from it by a wall since her grandfather had died—especially after another son got married only a few months later. When their first son was born, her husband had invested his small savings in two adobe rooms surrounded by a wall outside the old house, in a corner left open by the odd angles of the old compound's yard walls. Living in the shadows of both parents had made that move acceptable for Banu although her husband was at home only rarely. At night, a cousin or sister or her grandmother often would keep her company, or else she went home to sleep. During the days neighbors dropped in regularly for no apparent reason. No one could say why it felt so good to sit with Banu on her small verandah, looking at the single scraggly walnut tree next to the barely tray-sized pool, the dusty yard, and the oppressively close walls all around it, but it did. True, hers was a safe place for unmarried girls like Mahin, because Banu's husband was working in town and no other man was living there or was likely to show up unexpectedly. Secluded behind the massive wall, even the most careful woman could let her veil-wrap slide down safely without having to fear embarrassment or rebuke. True also that Banu was easy to look at: small limbed, light skinned, with a broad mouth that smiled easily in a delicate face dominated by large eyes of light brown color under straight black brows. She was well liked by all, respected, lively, full of stories and good sense, a woman who had gone to school for eight years and knew things without being uppity about it. But whatever the reason, there were never any lonely afternoons for her.

That day, Mehri—prim, slow, and tightlipped—had brought her spindle and fleece over from her own house to escape one of Begom's bouts of quarrelsomeness. Leila had dropped in on her way home from school. Mahin, the oldest unmarried girl in the neighborhood—straight backed and with eyebrows perpetually arched, giving her small face an expression of mocking disapproval—was cleaning rice on a tray for the dinner she would cook later. She lived only a small apricot orchard and a bramble hedge away and was a frequent visitor on Banu's porch. Tala, on one of her extended visits at her father's place two courtyards up the hill, was working with fast, big hands embroidering a huge red vase on a pillowcase, and Banu herself was stitching a boldly colored zig-zag pattern on a bag made of a piece of sacking. Presently, work stopped. The topic of conversation was absorbing.

"Turan will have to do something, for sure," Mahin was saying, letting rice idly flow through her fingers.

"Yes, but what? What?" said Tala fiercely. When she spoke, everything on her moved—eyes, head, arms; her whole body was in it, and whiffs of very sweet perfume rose around her.

"Well, she was his fiancée, after all, ever since she was *this* small," said Banu, indicating a midgety size. "She told me herself, in school. We were together in school until I got married."

"She is no longer his fiancée," said Leila. "Her people broke it off when Abbas lost his head over Setara and married her instead of Turan. A lovesick man . . . "

"Scoundrel," Mahin hissed, tossing her head.

" . . . a lovesick man is worse than a drunkard, I say," Leila finished her sentence, throwing up both her arms. Her black veil-wrap slid down into the dirt below the verandah.

"It was Setara's fault," said Mehri. "I know because Huri told us, and Huri knows because she is a neighbor of Setara. Setara made eyes at him. Shameless widows! He never said he did not want to marry Turan. He wanted them both."

"The dirty-eyed bandit! Well, her people said no, and Turan said no, and good for her." Mahin was emphatic. She tossed her head again and plunked the rice tray behind her on the floor. "Even Setara divorced him when he was thrown in jail a year ago because he was in a car-theft gang."

"That's when he went after Turan again, so she told me, although her people returned all the gifts—imagine, everything: clothes, jewelry, rice, butterfat, everything." Banu was shaking her head in wonderment. "They really did it correctly. Our religious law says . . . "

"Even Setara said Turan was lucky not to have married him," said Mahin. "She went to Turan's people and told them herself, and wept."

"They even made a pilgrimage to the shrine in Shiraz. I know, because my mother was on the same bus with them," said Tala.

"He wanted her anyway. Bandar's wife Aftab told me—you know, she is a cousin of Abbas, so she knows—'Mehri,' she said to me, 'they still owe him a refrigerator and a sack of rice.' That's what they are fighting about. But Abbas wanted her anyway, and after Setara divorced him they should have gone through with it." Mehri, screwing up her lips in disapproval, gave her spindle a decisive twirl, threw it down on the ground below the low verandah with an expert flick, and twisted some feet of yarn out of the fleece wrapped around her right arm.

Mahin produced a grand gesture of contempt which scared a loudly protesting chicken right across the abandoned tray with rice. "A thief, a jailbird . . . " she cried.

"People say her brothers said she shouldn't go to school any longer," said Mehri. "It is a long way to school here, all the way from Mahmudabad. Dangerous. An hour at least."

"He should have been kept in jail," said Mahin.

"And they were right, I say, about her walking to school, with him just out of jail. She should have stayed home. Nothing would have happened," said Mehri with conviction. "Now, my own brothers never would have let me . . . "

"She was not alone, though, ever. It was *his* fault," cried Tala. "He is rotten . . . "

"Usually there are four or five girls from Mahmudabad coming to school here. They always walk together. But it was final exam and Turan and this other girl were out later than the others. Just their bad luck," Banu said. She was fanning her baby, who was sleeping next to her on the ample folds of her skirts with her rice-sack bag. The sacking was stamped *Louisiana*. "And our religious law says . . . "

"A girl shouldn't go to school if it is so far away. It just shows," said Mehri. "My brothers . . . "

Mahin snorted twice.

"It is his fault, though," Tala said again. "He followed them."

"They were walking fast too, through that lonely wilderness there," said Leila, with a faraway look on her face.

"He was waiting for them down by the bridge," said Mehri. "Maybe he just wanted to talk to her. She was his fiancée. Maybe . . . "

"But if he wanted no harm, why did he have to crack her head with a rock?" cried Tala.

"I am sure he wanted to kill her," said Mahin darkly, wagging a finger at Mehri.

"He must be a strong fellow," said Leila, dreamy eyed. "I have never seen him, though."

"He didn't crack her head either. He only tied her hands and feet with a rope—and why would he do this if it was not that he wanted her?" Mehri, challenge in her eye, was stabbing the rug with her spindle. "He could have killed her, but he didn't."

"Really strong, a devil . . . "

"Nothing but rocks and trees around there, not a soul, and the brook is so noisy, one can't hear one's own voice . . . " said Banu sadly.

"He jumped out from behind a rock . . . oh, dear me, poor Turan!" Tala shook herself violently, and another cloud of perfume spread around her.

"The people say the girl who was with her—I mean, I would be scared to walk there practically alone, really I would—people say she passed out from shock," said Leila.

"No, no, she ran away . . . "

"It was *her* head he cracked with a rock . . . "

"She hid behind a tree . . . "

"Coward," cried Mahin.

"Anyway," said Leila, "she wasn't there when he bound Turan or whatever, you know. I mean, they say he did it with a finger . . . imagine!" Mahin raised her eyebrows higher yet and turned her face to look up into the walnut tree. Mehri hid a red face behind her veil and giggled. Tala shot Leila a nervous glance.

"The police doctor says she is all right, she is still a virgin," said Banu.

Mahin snorted loudly. "And how does *he* know?"

"It was a woman doctor who examined her," said Banu. She shooed another chicken away from Mahin's rice and spread the end of Mahin's dropped veil over the tray.

"With a finger . . . I mean, the things that happen in this world . . . and she was maybe screaming and yelling all the time," Leila said, her face flushed.

"She was gagged," said Mehri.

"How do you know? Maybe she passed out too. I am sure she did. I would," said Tala.

"The two men who found her had heard her yell. Two men from Mahmudabad. I don't know who. Abbas would have finished his job otherwise, but he had no time," said Leila.

"Maybe he would have killed her," said Tala.

Banu clucked "tsk, tsk, tsk," and shook her head.

"The son of a bitch," Mahin said, with feeling.

"Well, the other girl had left, and he was alone with her . . . " Leila filled a pause with heavy meaning.

"Men are dirty," said Tala.

"When Abbas saw the two other men coming, he took off into the mountains," said Banu, "but they recognized him. He had a gun, too."

"I have never seen him," Leila said again. "He must be awful to look at."

"The whole family is bad," said Mehri, "just like this beggar Aftab and her people. Really lightweight, no honor, no substance." Her long face was pinched with offended righteousness.

"If he is anything like his brother, he has a dark face, huh," said Leila.

"They are all sort of bad in Mahmudabad. Two of his brothers are in jail still because of the stolen cars," Mehri went on.

"No, Yusuf says they broke into a bank or a store or something like this," said Tala. "It was not only cars."

"Cursed semen. All his children will be bad . . . seven generations," said Mahin.

"In the Koran . . . " Banu tried.

"Well, sometimes the children of bad fathers turn out well. So maybe, if Turan would marry him after all, and had children . . . " Tala's loud voice was trailing off. She swatted at some flies with her red vase.

"Setara says he has money stashed away someplace, from his thievery," said Mehri. "It was never found."

"Unlawful money, cursed money," Mahin said.

At this point Leila's little girl appeared in the narrow court gate in dirty cotton pants and a pink shirt too big for her. She ran up to her mother, just about disappeared in the many folds of her wide skirts, and whispered, "Grandmother says—she says come home right away, she has something to tell you."

Leila murmured something like, "The black death on the old woman." Aloud, readjusting her daughter's scarf over her matted hair, she said, "Instantly, my sweetheart, right away—go tell your grandmother I am on my way. Now go, hurry, run, my dear, my life, run, run!" The little girl left reluctantly and slowly. "Old woman!" Leila murmured again, defiantly. Fingers spread, she moved her hand in the direction of her house in a quick gesture of contempt. "Humph," she said.

But the others had gone on. "Abbas isn't poor," Mehri was saying, "and if it is her fate, she'll marry him."

"She'll have to do something," said Mahin. There was a moment of silence. Somebody sighed. Banu unhappily was looking at her sleeping baby under her veil. The sun had gone low enough to illuminate the cooking pots stacked on the rim of the pool. Two shovels appeared above the wall, moving along at a good speed on the shoulders of invisible men in the alley. Leila followed them with her eyes and started to fish for her veil.

"I guess," Banu said at length, "she'll probably have to kill herself . . . although the religion . . . it is a sin . . . but then again . . . "

"Poor thing," Mahin said.

There was more silence. Sparrows were twittering around the glistening water. Tala started to shake her head. "No, no," she said, finally, "no, she is innocent. They'll execute him, for sure. They have to—the revolutionary guards will shoot him. He is guilty . . . "

"They don't even have him," said Banu. "It has been, what? Four days or five now. Who knows where he is? He fled; he has taken to the mountains, maybe he is in Iraq by now or with the rebels in Kurdistan."

"Imagine if he were still around and you would be sitting at home, alone-like, and he would come through the door . . . huh, I would faint right away," said Leila, wide eyed.

"You don't even know what he looks like, you would be very polite to him," said Tala.

"Huh, huh!" cried Leila, shuddering.

"Aftab says Turan's brothers are after him with guns," said Mehri.

"So, big deal. She has only two, and one is not older than twelve or so. A lot of help, this!" said Banu. "Besides, it is a matter for the judge, for the Islamic Court . . . "

"And she says his people and her people have a bitter fight because they blame each other for this mess," said Mehri.

A little boy of about three, dressed in nothing more elaborate than a short, dirty T-shirt and big plastic sandals, was strolling in through the gate. Tala was the first to spot him. "Hamid, Hamid," she shouted at him, "run home quickly or else the rooster will get your little you-know-what!" Banu turned and smiled. It was her nephew. "Look, look, watch out for the rooster, here he comes!" Hamid looked at the rooster and the women, picked up a pebble as a weapon, but then decided it wasn't a good time to visit Aunt Banu after all and ran out. Tala and Leila giggled, Mahin grunted.

"Imagine," said Leila, "imagine if Hamid would have been Abbas . . . terrible!"

"People say somebody saw him in Shiraz . . . "

"I have heard they caught him on the other side of the mountain . . . "

"No, I told you, all the revolutionary guard posts in the area got pictures of him and a description, so they all can look out for him," said Banu. "He has disappeared."

"But if they catch him they'll execute him," said Tala, "for sure!"

"If. . . . " Mahin said, darkly.

Banu's baby stretched. Flies were buzzing. Leila's little daughter reappeared in the doorway. Leaning against the gate, she watched both the women and the lane, blowing huge gum bubbles.

"If she is pregnant she'll kill herself, she'll have to," said Banu. "Although strictly by the rules of our Prophet . . . " Mahin was nodding emphatically.

"But it was only a finger—she is still a virgin, she'll get a husband, for sure," said Leila. "One can't get pregnant with only a . . . well, I mean!"

"No way, never," cried Tala, "She won't get a husband after this. For sure they'll execute him, or at least they'll beat him up awfully. Remember what they did with Heidar Afghani?"

"They'll flog him publicly and then they'll let him go. And then what?" asked Leila.

"Turan should flee, go someplace," Mahin said, but this suggestion was met with noises of doubt.

"You are crazy," said Mehri. "Where can a girl like her go?"

"But what can she do here?" Mahin was passionate. "Just pretend there was nothing? People won't let her. Her people won't even let her finish school after this, I am sure."

"Suicide," Banu murmured, "poison, like my stepmother . . . and last year the miller's wife . . . "

"What does she herself say?" asked Tala.

"She says she won't marry him, no matter what," Mehri said.

"Yes, I know," added Banu. "My brother Rahmat says the judge told her she has to marry Abbas as soon as they catch him. They'll force him, too. She really has no choice but to . . . "

"Force! Brutality! Injustice!" cried Mahin. Banu's baby stirred again and started to whine. Banu patted his back.

"Aftab says his people say they no longer want Turan," said Mehri, "but . . . "

"Rahmat says the judge . . . "

" . . . but anyway, if it is her fate to marry, she'll marry," Mehri continued.

"Besides, they'll make it worth her while, for sure," said Tala. "They'll give her a handsome gift, and a big golden pendant with 'Allah' engraved on it, and a nice wristwatch, and in the end she'll agree; what else can she do?"

"If he is so crazy about her anyway . . . " said Leila.

"They'll beat her up at home until she says yes, just like my folks tried it with me. For a golden 'Allah' and a thousand Toman they are ready to sell a girl!" Mahin's voice was gloomy. She snorted again and picked up her tray.

"Don't snort," said Mehri. "It wasn't your fate yet to get married, and it wasn't mine yet either, and we'll see what Turan's fate will be."

"Ah, fate . . . " said Tala, with a sigh like a sob.

"Fate, ha!" cried Mahin. "You know what I'll do with my fate? I'll pee on it." They all laughed.

Banu's baby started to bawl and Leila's daughter in the doorway got impatient. "Mother," she shouted, "Hey, listen, Mother, Grandmother says . . . "

For the moment, concern for Turan's fate gave way to the demands of a waning afternoon.

7

The Little Changes That Happened When Simin Became Avdal's Wife

One of the more surprising peculiarities of Deh Koh is the transience of its components. Nothing in the village stays the same for long. There is, of course, nothing peculiar about change; finding it remarkable is a reflection of our romantic, far-distance view of country life: small, tucked-away villages are supposed to keep their shape and substance stable over long stretches. Time stands still, we say, where the sun and the seasons set the pace of life. This view is an illusion.

In Deh Koh life generally is but a round of seasons long and rutted with disruptions. Nothing is made to last, and not much is expected to. A grain bin in the wall, full with this year's harvest, will be empty before the next summer; lambs last, as lambs, only from spring to winter, if they don't die before then; on the rocky ground, a pair of shoes is worn through within mere weeks; a road bulldozed through a vineyard will end the vineyard planted only a few years ago, but after a harsh winter the road itself will turn into a dusty line of potholes; shahs and khans, doctors and revolutionary guards last their allotted times and vanish; men grow tall before they wither and die; girls, like flowers, bloom shortly, only to wrinkle and dry up; houses stretch and shrink with the size of families they shelter; and whatever children get their hands on will break or die instantly.

Within any compound, not only do the wheat in the wall, the number of rooms, and the size of the porches change, often from year to year, but also who lives where and stands in what subtle relationship of power and subordination to whom. This is so despite some pious rules about proper living together dear to the people, such as that old people should be honored, husband's mother obeyed, and husband's relatives treated with great respect; and that all brothers' wives are equal except for a slight hierarchy according to age, which for the older one carries the responsibility of care, circumspection, and impartiality and for the younger one the obligations of cheerful cooperation. But life does not really work by "thou shalt" prescriptions, not in Deh Koh anyway. (Nowhere else on earth either, the people of Deh Koh suspect. Otherwise, they argue, we would have paradise here on earth and need not fear hell.)

Blueprints for correct hierarchies and proper etiquette notwithstanding, relationships within each compound are constantly challenged and redefined. Any change in circumstances—the birth of a child, the death of a grandfather, the return of a son from school, the departure of a man for work, a sickness, or even just a new skirt— changes the foundations on which likes and dislikes are based, responsibilities discharged, and duties assumed, and opens them up for renegotiation.

In some rare houses these negotiations are quiet, the changes gentle. These are houses not talked about much—good houses, its women wise, men equanimous, young and old guided by dignity, honor, and wholesome fear and respect. There also are loud houses like that of Yusuf and Tala, where short-tempered men and cantankerous women set the tone. And then there are the many houses in between, whose members try to keep a quiet front and their fights indoors, succeeding sometimes and often not.

When Simin got married to Avdal, the fourth son of Tamas and older brother of Rahmat and Banu, the courtyard of Tamas and his brother Trab was in upheaval. Tamas and Trab were arguing hotly about land they had inherited from their father; Trab's daughter-in-law had hurt her foot on the day of the wedding, tripping over a log of firewood in the dark while tending the huge copper cooking pots in the clean-swept yard; a suitor had come for Perigol, Trab's last unmarried daughter, and she was furious because it seriously undermined her chance to get the high school diploma she had her mind set on; Banu's husband was trying to persuade her to move to the city with him and she was balking; Banu's youngest sister, Golperi, who had completed a government training course in weaving rugs on the large, vertical loom imported from the city, was sulking because no acceptable place could be found to set up the huge contraption in the house; Rahmat had come home with a gun and announced that he had enlisted as a revolutionary guard. Tamas's wife Hakime was upset about all this and also because she knew that her eldest son Aziz, getting impatient with his sickly wife, was looking for a second one. In addition, Avdal had ulcers and could not eat, Tamas had a "prostate" and could not pee, and Trab's youngest grandson had an eye infection and could not see. Of the whole family, only Tamas's father was not hurting, Hakime said with disgust, and he was dead.

None of these calamities were apparent to Simin when she arrived from the other end of the village in a pickup truck piled high with her dowry on the night of the wedding. The pickup truck carefully negotiated the narrow alley between the house wall and the water channel, only to get stuck a few yards ahead because the doorway was too low and narrow to let it pass. Simin, hardly able to see anything from under her all-encompassing veil, climbed out and, only narrowly missing the channel in the process, squeezed between the truck and the door frame into the patchily lit courtyard. As happened so often, the electricity had been cut off (because of the war, it was said). A lone kerosene pressure lamp illuminated a circle of cooking pots on softly glowing embers and a moving crowd around them. Hakime started to ululate in welcome, but Rahmat, from the shadows, yelled at her to shut up and she did. It was non-Islamic, improper noise, he said. Simin was ushered up the wide staircase to the left, leading to the living quarters lined up around two sides of the yard. The bridal chamber was prepared in Aziz's good room, painted blue and bare except for cushions along the wall on a large synthetic rug on the floor. Simin did not know that this was Aziz's room, nor that he had earmarked it for a new wife he hoped to bring soon. As she entered, Hakime held a Koran over her head. Simin kissed Hakime's hand. The room instantly filled with other women and girls, and the stale odor of the little-used "good" room mixed with lamp smoke and perfume. Simin sat where she was pushed down, on the rug, against a cushion, head bent under her veil, motionless. This was how she had seen many brides sit on their wedding nights when she was a spectator like the girls squatting around her now, whispering, pushing. She knew she would be urged to eat and would refuse, although she had not eaten anything since morning. She would be urged to drink tea and would refuse that too. It was proper to do so. Her brother's bride had not eaten anything for two days and this showed modesty and respect. (In her, it had also shown stubbornness.) Simin did not think she could refuse food for two days. She was hungry already. Hakime came in with a tray of sweets and urged them on her. "Dear," she said, "you must eat something, you'll feel weak if you don't eat."

"I can't eat," Simin murmured so faintly that Hakime had to bend down low to understand her, "I am not hungry."

Her bundle of bedding was brought in from the truck and the girls giggled, and one woman patted it and said something about a new bride and new bedding being extra soft, which made everybody laugh behind their veils. Most of the women and girls were strangers to Simin. It was hot, her henna-colored hands felt moist, sweat was trickling down between her breasts. Her hair, cut a few hours earlier in bridal fashion left and right to ear length, was tickling her cheeks, the braids in back were tight. The pressure lamp in front of her was losing pressure rapidly, but nobody seemed to notice until the red flames of a dying light shot up and somebody started to pump fresh life into it. Women came and went. She did not stir. The night was long.

When the women finally had scrambled outside and Avdal had been pushed into the room, Hakime came in once more and pressed a piece of white cloth into Simin's lap. "You know what for," she said. Hakime rolled out the mattress, white and new, and the shiny new quilt. Simin felt sick to her stomach. Why did she have to be here instead of sleeping peacefully with her sister at home? Hakime left, closing the door behind her.

Against her will, Simin started to sob. Avdal sat next to her. "You don't need to cry," he said. "Don't." They sat for a while in silence until Avdal got up. "I am going to sleep," he said. "You come too." She shook her head, but he took her arm and pulled her towards the bed. So she lay down at the edge of the mattress, facing the wall, and Avdal lay down on the other side, facing her. She was at a loss about the proper ways of a bride now. They lay in the near dark, and neither spoke and neither moved. Simin fell asleep.

A little later Simin was awakened by Avdal, who had moved close to her and was fumbling under the quilt to get inside her skirts. She threw herself around and hissed, and he grabbed her really hard, and she wriggled a bit and hissed, and her headscarf came off and her cap, and she heard a piece of fabric tear in her back. He pinned her down with one hand, hurting her, and she wanted to scream but did not dare to. He lay on top of her, pulling up yards and yards of fabric from her five skirts, and panting, and grunting, and no matter how hard she strained and bit she could not get free, and he shoved himself closer and closer, pushing into her with great force, until a sharp pain shot up between her thighs and inside her. Now Avdal let go of her and turned over and jumped up and ran outside. A commotion arose there, women's voices, and somebody started to ululate but was hushed. Simin groped for the cloth Hakime had given her and stuffed it between her legs. There was blood there, she knew. Then Hakime came in and Simin handed it to her. Important proof of her virginity and Avdal's manliness, it would be shown around outside among the women of her and Avdal's family. Hakime made soothing noises. "God bless you," she said, "our dear bride, the light of my eyes, I'll be your sacrifice, you are the light of our house . . . " Simin said nothing. She wondered where Avdal was. Her brother had stayed with his bride the whole night, almost until morning. But anyway, she was Avdal's wife now, a woman; he would come back. Simin fell asleep, alone for the first time in her life, and did not notice when Avdal, a long time later, crept under the quilt next to her.

The next few days Simin had ample time to ponder her situation. She had nothing to do, absolutely nothing. Steadfastly she refused breakfast the next morning, but by noon she was so hungry that her modesty broke down and she ate what Hakime urged on her, just enough so that she would not be said to be either timid or haughty, and little enough so that her husband's people could not regard her either as shameless or as easy to subordinate.

Sitting in her room, she received visitors—mostly the women in Avdal's family. Simin had seen most of them at one time or another. This had not been easy, as she lived in a different neighborhood and was only distantly related to Tamas's family. But she had made an effort to see everybody, ever since she found out she would be Avdal's wife, a year ago, when she was thirteen. Avdal himself was not much to look at, she had decided after she had watched him unobtrusively from her grandmother's doorway while he was unloading goods in front of his store. He was rather small and thin, with a worried look on his pale face and close-knit, bushy brows, but he was a shopkeeper and not a mere worker like her own brothers and cousins. Simin was glad that it was not her fate to marry one of her cousins. She found them poor and ugly and did not like them. Nevertheless, she had protested tearfully and sworn passionately never to marry, and then had mumbled "yes" when she was asked in earnest, just like all the other girls did, except bad and unreasonable ones like Mahin and Avdal's own cousin, Perigol. For whispering her "yes" Banu had hung a golden chain with a round golden pendant carrying the name of Allah around Simin's neck and had slid a watch on her wrist. Both were gifts from Avdal, and admired duly. Banu herself gave her a golden wedding band. Wedding bands were a new custom, and Simin was gratified to get one.

Simin was glad Banu was living in the same compound. Everybody seemed to like her. She was not sure about the other women, though. Hakime seemed nice enough. She always called her "dear" and said, "I'll be your sacrifice," and "just tell me what you want, I'll bring it for you," which, of course, could be ever so many lies. Her lined face looked worried, and she moved slowly, as if she was rather weak, but with mothers-in-law one could only find out by experience. The old, bent grandmother was of no account, Simin decided, as she took stock of her visitors. She was quite deaf and obviously no longer did much work. Her demands, Simin felt, could easily be ignored. Avdal's youngest sister, Golperi, was plain in face and dress. Her front teeth were rotten black, and she tried to conceal them behind her hands and her veil. She was older than Simin, had gone to school for only three years as compared to Simin's five, and had no fiancé, so Simin figured she might be jealous of her. Simin wondered what the loom Golperi kept mumbling about was like. Behjad, Aziz's wife, very pale with bloodless lips and beads of perspiration on her forehead, clearly was sick. Simin noticed through her door that when climbing up the staircase, Behjad had to sit down and rest, and her large sad eyes were red as if she was crying a lot. Her three children were wild and unruly. She told Simin that the doctor said she would probably die if she got pregnant again. Simin felt sorry for her. Perigol, Trab's daughter, plump and with pimply skin and very white teeth, was someone Simin had never much cared for. In school, she had found her a schemer and teacher's pet and stuck up because she got the highest grades. She put on airs even now, although Simin was married and she was not. There was also Negin, Trab's daughter-in-law, who had to work for the whole family since Trab's wife had killed herself over nothing (Trab had beaten her up, it was said) three years ago. But as Negin was in the hospital in the city with a broken leg, Perigol had to work hard, and Simin could hear her barking irritably at Negin's children outside.

She did not see much of the men in the house. Tamas, her father-in-law, shriveled, bent, and coughing a lot, had greeted her through the door, friendly-like. Avdal's oldest brother was in Shiraz. Aziz was not home much; neither was Banu's husband. Rahmat never as much as looked at her. Avdal slept next to her but had not touched her again by the third day, when her people came, as was the custom, to take her to her father's house for a few days as a visitor and pampered guest, no longer theirs. Another big meal was cooked, the pact between the two families sealed. Simin's father asked Avdal to accompany him to the bank in town because he needed a loan, and Avdal, a businessman, could help him in the negotiations with the bank officials, who otherwise would be rude to him, a villager who could not read and write. Avdal agreed politely—as a son-in-law he had to be at his wife's father's service.

Back at Tamas's house Simin found herself and Avdal the center of an argument. Aziz wanted the good room back. Behjad suspiciously asked, what for? They did not need it. Aziz said his father needed it, and anyway, there must be one good room for visitors. Simin said any visitor could come into her room, she was a good housekeeper, or what did he mean? Avdal murmured that he had as much a right to his father's house as Aziz had and would keep the room. Tamas said he had done well enough all his life without a good room, and he thought his own room was still good enough for anybody who came to see him. And besides, there was no other room. Tamas's mother should move in with Uncle Trab, said Aziz; he did not have a wife and could put her up easily, and Avdal and Simin could move into her room. The old woman said she was not moving, no way, and Trab said that since Tamas was the younger son he had gotten the lion's share of their father's inheritance in order to take care of their mother. She had to stay with Tamas. Golperi mumbled behind her hand that they should build a little room in the corner of the porch for Avdal, then she could put the loom up in the good room. Hakime made soothing noises. Vali, Banu's husband, said that he and Banu were going to Shiraz, and Avdal could have his room. At this Banu firmly and repeatedly declared that she was not going anywhere, he could kill her or divorce her, she would stay. Trab said good riddance—to his son, not to Banu. Simin already had realized that Trab did not get along well with Vali. All right, said Vali, if this was the case, he would build a house in the back of the compound, and Banu could sit there alone, because he would go to Shiraz no matter what, and his father would no longer have to look at him or his grandson. This was thrashed around a while and eventually gained approval of the main opponents, especially of Tamas, because the plot of land in question was claimed by himself and Trab, and with this solution both their children would benefit from it. Tamas generously presented his nephew with the little corner of land, and Trab said it was not up to Tamas to give it to anybody because it was his, Trab's, but he would give it to his son, and this got Tamas and Trab arguing again.

During all this commotion, Simin looked and listened. Her quick, sharp eyes took it all in: Trab's bullying, Tamas's meekness, Vali's restlessness, Aziz's loud discontent. Avdal had left the scene midway through; she decided he was weak. He did not contradict his older brother, he did not argue with his uncle. He would not trouble her much, she thought, but would not stand up for her in a fight either.

Simin and Avdal stayed in the good room. It was the biggest one in the whole compound, recently painted light blue, and with Simin's long, shiny, veneered cabinet along the farther wall, her large synthetic rug on the floor, and her colorfully embroidered clothes-cover spread over the clothes-stand, it was by far the most present-able and modern one. It furthermore had the advantage of central location, at the main stairway. Whoever was coming up to the west-facing part of the compound had to pass Simin's door, and whoever was walking through the courtyard to get to the south-facing rooms on Trab's side was easily spotted from the same door. A little alertness on Simin's side produced a lot of information on the comings and goings in the whole house. Simin was content. The first round of arguments regarding herself and Avdal had gone well for them without the necessity of actively taking part in the disputes.

Other circumstances worked in Simin's favor too. From the first day after coming back from her father's, Simin had her hands full, helping out here and there. Negin had come home with a cast and in great pains, and Behjad's heart had a bad spell again. With two women off their feet the others had to pitch in, leaving no time for subtle exploration of character, for display of etiquette, for delicate probings into the boundaries of one's place. Rushing here and there all day long, Simin had no leisure to engage earnestly in the who-gets-up-first contests exhibiting and establishing rank priorities; prolonged polite exchanges and assurances of mutual goodwill and modesty between Simin and her husband's people were preempted by the real need of getting work done. Simin did not need any prompting, let alone an open request, to help Behjad knead her bread dough the very next day after she had come back. And Behjad was too weak and too grateful, Simin felt, to lord it over her and see servitude in Simin's generosity. Grandmother helped too with the baking of the bread. Behjad, breathing laboriously, was turning the flatbreads on the griddle over the fire, while Simin and the old woman were rolling out the fist-size balls of dough, each on her own breadboard on a breadcloth on the floor in front of them. Simin's board was new and not yet smooth. The paper-thin dough ripped here and there under her roller. The old woman held a monologue about changing times when young wives no longer could do the simplest tasks, and what was the world coming to anyway, and Behjad pulled a face and apologized to Simin. "Never mind the old woman," she said. Again, Simin felt sorry for her. She had never seen any woman in her own family so sick. The incident taught Simin something, though. When Hakime asked her a few days later to help her with baking bread, she borrowed Behjad's board—she was not going to give her mother-in-law a chance to find fault with her bread baking. And Behjad, ingratiated, lent it gladly.

Despite fumigations and the sacrifice of a kid, Negin's leg did not get better. The doctor came and sawed off the cast with a tiny saw (Simin was there serving tea), shook his head when he saw the badly swollen leg, and told her husband to take her back to the hospital in the city. Negin said she would not go. Her husband said the esteemed doctor should have mercy with his poor wife and himself, his humble servant, and their children, they were good Muslims all, and he should help them here, because a trip to the hospital was impossible at the moment, it would ruin the whole family. They all begged and cajoled, Simin loudly from the door, until the doctor said he would do his best, but it was God's will and he was not to blame for any misfortune. Outside, Simin tried to see how much money Negin's husband pressed on him delicately. It was a bundle, she thought.

Golperi was offered an assistantship at the weaving workshop and took it, against the advice of her mother and the explicit prohibition of her brother Aziz. Her father and Avdal protested only mildly, mostly because the pay was very low; Rahmat was not consulted. So she started walking to the workshop in the next hamlet every day early in the morning, coming home tired and just in time to help with the tail end of dinner preparation. Banu and Behjad complained about her absence, and Perigol, whose classes would start shortly, was even more irritable than usual. Hakime told Tamas and Aziz that it was their fault, that if they had let Golperi put up a loom she would have stayed home. Simin found advantages and disadvantages in both—Golperi at home and Golperi gone—and spoke for her working when she was around and complained about her absence to Banu and Behjad, until Golperi called her a two-faced liar. Now Simin kept quiet.

Within a few days Simin had demonstrated that she could make bread; wash dishes and clothes; watch chickens and milkpots and children; heat the bath; sweep the floors without raising too much dust; shake rugs; brew tea and serve it properly to guests like the doctor and the visitors who came to see Negin; cook the dinner staple, rice and lentils; run errands; mend pants; clean rice; wash wheat; and spin wool. And it took Simin only a few days more to realize that she was working twice as hard as anybody else in the house. The only task she was not expected to do was milking—the cow, not used to Simin, was restless when she milked her the first time and upset the milk pail. With so many other worries occupying everybody's minds nobody made a fuss about it, but Hakime did not let her do the milking again. For Simin it was just as well.

Simin soon found herself employing dodging tricks she had learned at home, where she was bossed around by her mother, two older sisters, two sisters-in-law, and a paternal aunt. One of the tricks, the ill-health claim, had worked well at home, where nobody was seriously sick, but it did not go very far here, where so many women were either old or else a lot sicker than Simin could possibly pretend to be. However, with well-placed groans she turned a sudden headache one morning and cramps at her next period into a few good hours of respite from duty and made the point that Simin too had health to be concerned about. A more usable dodge involved not being where she knew her service might be wanted soon. When Perigol was piling up dirty dishes around the water faucet in the yard, Simin sneaked out to visit her aunt who had a new baby. So what if Perigol growled, "The third time!" after her. A big bundle of fleece on Banu's roof warned Simin in time to accompany Hakime to the doctor, because Banu and Peri would card wool with long switches, which was a dusty and disagreeable job, and Simin's help would only benefit Trab's family anyway. On Fridays, when Golperi was at home, Simin spent half the day in the bath—Golperi might as well work at least one day a week, Simin thought. She pulled off her most daring and successful dodging stunt during wheat cleaning. After helping Hakime and Behjad wash new wheat in the cold water at the pool for two days, and lugging the heavy trays of wet grain up the stairs and a ladder onto the roof to dry, on the third day Simin announced she was going for wild almonds with her sisters and some other girls. This met with heavy resistance from all the women in the house, because as a young wife Simin should be extremely careful with public appearances, but she had judged Avdal right: he only meekly said to the protesting Hakime, "it does not matter," and meeker yet to Simin, "it isn't good if you go out," and so Simin did as she pleased. The backpack of almonds she brought back in the evening demonstrated her industry and made up for her insubordination. Only Perigol kept bitching. She had not been able to go out into the mountains for years and was bitter about it.

Now Simin had wild almonds, while nobody else had. She cracked them with the help of Behjad's little girl, boiled the bitterness out of them, dried them carefully in a flat basket, put them into a bag and locked them into her cabinet, for guests, she said. Anything else she needed she had to ask Hakime for (or rather, go without, because Simin did not like to ask favors) because Avdal was still eating his father's bread, as the saying went, which left his mother in control of the family larder. But when Simin's father sent her a bundle of fresh corn, she roasted the ears herself in the evening, when everybody was at home, and personally distributed them together with the information that they were a gift from her father because he knew she liked corn. She only got to eat half an ear herself but had made everybody say "thank you" to her—everybody but Perigol, who had refused the offer.

Negin had pus in her bone, the doctor said. The doctor's assistant or else Shahzade the midwife (who now called herself Fatmekhanom because a name with "Shah" in it was too embarrassing for her) came twice a day to give her penicillin shots. Negin could not move at all. Even for the smallest tasks she needed help. Strong, belligerent, and sharp tongued, she had been the ruler in Trab's household, but now, having neither a mother, sister, nor daughter nearby to help her out, she had to rely solely on her husband's family for help. Simin soon realized that Banu and especially Perigol used her dependency on them to get even for the many harassments they had suffered from her. Requests for water went unheeded several times before they were honored; choice pieces of food, especially the very rare meat, went to Trab or Vali, not to her or her children. Unless there were visitors in her room, she was alone much. Banu had a good excuse for making herself scarce, because Vali had started to make bricks and to build a tiny house in the back of his father's place, and Banu had to serve him and his helpers. Simin, who had as yet no personal grudge against Negin, could afford to be kind to her. Inquisitive and energetic by nature, she found Negin's visitors interesting, the doctor's manipulations fascinating, and the services Negin requested of her easy to fulfill and very meritorious, handy assets on the Day of Judgment, for sure. Perigol, she both thought and said, did not behave right vis-à-vis the sick Negin; she was a heathen. Simin clearly was taking sides for Negin and against Peri.

With this, Peri's annoyance was heated to the boiling point of action. When Avdal came home that very afternoon and, barely inside the main doorway, shouted for Simin to fetch him his good jacket, Perigol, washing clothes at the pool in the courtyard, spoke her mind. "Ha," she said, "you can shout all you want. Simin isn't home. Look up on the porch at your mother and your brother's wife, and look at me and Banu—working from morning to night, we are, and where is your wife, where is Aunt Hakime's daughter-in-law? Not where she ought to be, oh, no. She is out. She is always out, and God only knows where she is, visiting and showing off her clothes. A scandal, I tell you. Ask Negin to tell you what eyes Simin is making at the doctor's assistant . . . the moment he is here she comes running to look at him . . ."

Avdal kept up a rhythmic "shut up, keep your trap shut, filthy mouth," and even stepped up to her, hands raised as if about to hit her.

Peri knew her mild cousin well enough to take the risk. "Let me tell you, my father's brother's son, my brother, I mean well. Next you will hear the people talk about her in the street, and then where is your honor? And our honor?"

Avdal gave up stopping Peri or getting his good jacket. He turned and left. But this was not the end of it. Simin, upon coming back a little later from a short visit with Mehri (their mothers were distant cousins), who had a bad toothache, met with unexpected hostility from all sides, born of true animosity on the part of Peri and of disapproval about her being the center and cause of discontent by the others. By the time Avdal and the other men returned Simin was sulking in her room, Hakime and Negin were arguing, Peri was squatting on the edge of the verandah in front of her room, shouting that it was all true. Avdal spoke sharply to Simin, who talked back, whereupon Avdal hit her and she screamed that she would go back to her father. Negin's husband, encouraged by Negin, hollered at his sister Peri, and when she talked back he beat her up. Trab did nothing to stop him, whereupon Peri took her books from the niche in the wall and walked out on them, taking refuge with her grandmother. It took the whole house a day to persuade Peri to continue to help out at home and Simin not to go back to her father. Rahmat, luckily, was away for a week in a training camp. At home he was a nuisance, forever after the women for letting their hair show, for not putting on a proper headscarf, for laughing, for not praying right, like the mullahs on television, and he only a boy. And in this case he might have done something rash and indiscreet like denouncing Simin to his fellow guards. Tamas had not been around either. He had been in town to see a doctor. When he came back on the late minibus the storm had not quite blown over yet, and everybody was too ruffled to listen to his woes.

Tamas's prostate complaint could be ignored no longer. The doctor said he needed an operation and so did Tamas himself, more and more adamantly. As Aziz was gone on a building job in Deh Rud, and Rahmat was only a lad, Avdal had to accompany him to town. They were gone for a week. Tamas came back a little more shriveled but vastly relieved, and Avdal came back with several boxes of goods, mostly for the store, but one with gifts and necessities for his people. Simin locked their door from the inside and sat down in front of the box. "Show me," she said, smiling at him. She had not smiled much at him before and Avdal got flustered. He cut the cord and showed her: there were shoes for Rahmat; yards and yards of black, shiny fabric for a new veil-wrap for his mother; a few lengths of cheap purple rayon for a shirt for Grandmother; several pairs of socks; there were toothpaste, soap, a set of stainless steel mugs, plastic sandals for Avdal; a dark blue men's shirt; a green knit cardigan with flower buttons for Hakime; a lacy pink shirt fabric and a plain green one; a bottle of aspirin; and a small flask of perfume. (This was for Grandmother to sprinkle on the graves on Thursday afternoon when the women visited the cemetery. "Crazy new graveyard fashion," Simin thought. "What a waste of good fragrance.") There also were two boxes of cookies and five pounds of tea, in two bags. The smaller one, said Avdal, was expensive; the bigger one was ordinary tea. Simin put the boxes of cookies and the good tea aside. "I'll lock them into our chest," she said, "for our guests. If you give the cookies to your mother, Behjad's children will eat them."

"Well, I don't know," Avdal said somewhat uneasily, "she wanted me to bring her some . . . " Simin put the boxes back with the other things. The shoes, shirt, socks, toothpaste and the things for Grandmother and Hakime she also put back in the box. Of the four bars of soap, she put two aside. "Why?" said Avdal. "You have some in your chest."

"Never mind," said Simin. "I had to give a whole bar to Perigol for the doctor the other day. They did not have any, and Grandmother took the bar I had put in the bath and did I don't know what with it, probably gave it to Uncle Timur. She always takes our stuff to her eldest son. Anyway, it is safer in my chest than in your mother's room." Avdal did not much like this but could not think of anything to say against it. Soap was scarce and expensive. Simin was right. Meanwhile, Simin was eyeing the little rolls of pink and green fabric. "And what did you bring for me?" she asked, and smiled at him again.

Avdal held out the green bundle to her. "The other one is for Golperi," he said.

Simin looked at it doubtfully. "Well," she said at last, "I don't know. Golperi does not like pink, she said so herself." Avdal, who was slightly colorblind, neither knew nor cared about what colors his sister liked or disliked. He only knew that he had meant the more expensive fabric for his sister because she wanted a good shirt to wear to work, while Simin as a new bride had all new fancy clothes. But if Simin said Golperi would not like it. . . . "She would like the green one a lot better," said Simin. "I'll exchange it with mine so she won't be disappointed." And while Avdal put all the other things back in the box, Simin let the stainless steel mugs disappear in her cabinet together with the soap and the good tea.

By sheer coincidence, Avdal was called away right then, leaving the box in their room. Simin, who knew what was meant for whom, got out the things and distributed them—to Grandmother, Hakime, Behjad, the children, and Golperi. She did not make it a big affair, that would not have been proper, but still—everybody had to take their gift from Simin and thank her. It was a good move, she thought, although Golperi was mad about the ugly fabric and bitched and Avdal later scolded Simin badly for it. She was offended at his sharp words and sulked, even pretended she was not interested in him after they had gone to bed, and in the end Avdal had to make up with her. Simin knew quite well by now how much she was worth to him in bed.

Simin had other resources to put to good use. Wisely, her father had given her a kerosene pressure lamp at her wedding. Not a new one, but in good working order. Ridiculed by Negin ("For sure," she had chided, "your father's must be the only house in the village without electricity"), it came in very handy nevertheless during the more and more frequent brownouts and blackouts that struck irregularly and for hours on end. Storm lanterns and old pressure lamps were reclaimed from barns and other places of discard and found broken, bent, and faulty in many ways. Simin lit hers with confidence, guarding it carefully and inviting whoever needed good light to come to her room. At times, everybody was there. Perigol, unable to do her homework in the near darkness of one storm lantern that was carried here and there as need arose, would slide inside her cousin's door with her book. "Sit by the light," Simin would say with honey in her voice, "don't ruin your eyes." And when Peri refused with many polite murmurs through gritted teeth, Simin would move the lamp a little her way and tell all and sundry how hard it was to study if the light wasn't good, and didn't she know it, but of course, her father had always repaired their lamps and kept them in good order.

It was sufferance of an embarrassment and some fast talking that played the key to Hakime's storage cabinet into Simin's hand.

Back from the hospital, Tamas had visitors. His one good rug was taken down from under the storage pile and spread on the felt mat on the floor. Simin's big new thermos bottle, another of the handy things she had brought with her, was put to service to have tea ready—so much more convenient than the fire and the old teapot. (Tamas's bottle had been broken by Aziz's little son only days after Tamas had bought it.) Simin served dozens of glasses of tea from it, sharply watching the children. Hakime kept the sugar and sweets (for the more esteemed visitors) under lock and key. So it happened that when on the third day after Tamas's return Hakime had to walk to the doctor with Banu because of a bad bout of rheumatism, Simin was left behind with a bottle of tea but no sugar and no cookies. That afternoon seven visitors came: neighbors and Tamas's own cousins, a teacher among them, and a few women. Simin borrowed sugar from Behjad. Since it was not cut up and she had to hack and cut the hard cone to pieces first, Simin served the visitors embarrassingly late and after Tamas himself had shouted for it twice. But Behjad had no cookies and no fruits either. Using threats and desperate promises, Simin succeeded in sending Behjad's eldest son to Avdal's store to get some. The boy left reluctantly and did not come back. Simin put her almonds and some raisins on a tray for the guests. Then she went over to Negin and Peri, but Negin said she had no cookies and Peri said she had no key to the storage cabinet. Simin was certain Peri was lying. She was a fool to have asked at all. The visitors were just leaving when Behjad's son came back from the bazaar, empty handed. He had not found Avdal, he said. Simin was good and sore when Hakime finally returned. "What will Uncle Hamdullah's people say about us?" she said with heat. "They always have proper things to serve to guests, not just some measly bitter almonds. We lost honor, we don't do right by Uncle Tamas and not by our visitors either. And just because our stuff is locked up and Uncle Tamas doesn't have a key and I don't have a key and no one has a key. As if Grandmother or I would ever steal anything!" Tamas seconded her. Hakime, shamed for inept hospitality, rummaged for another key but could not find one. Therefore Golperi, who was not at home much anyway, had to give hers to Simin that evening. Golperi was mad and protested, but to no avail. Simin got the key and with it, gradually, control over the provisions of the house. None of the children now could snitch a cookie, Grandmother could no longer take as much as a handful of raisins to her eldest son's house unnoticed, and the lumps of sugar which had disappeared untraceably before were all accounted for now. To Avdal and Tamas, Simin proved a good housekeeper.

To the children, however, Simin was a menace to their customs and ways of subterfuge. They were wild children, all six of them (not counting Banu's baby), ranging in age from ten to three, without fear and respect except for their fathers, who were mostly elsewhere. And they annoyed Simin with their fights, their habit of grabbing whatever they found useful and unguarded (a skill Aziz's eldest commanded perfectly), their begging and whining, their insubordination. Complaints about them were shrugged off. "They are just children," said Avdal.

"Real devils," Grandmother said proudly, "really strong, praise be to God." Their hapless mothers threw things after them, threatened them with needles and with thrashing, with death and perdition, to manage them at all. Simin relied on watchfulness, the key to the cookies and the sugar, and a fast hand for control. But after Avdal unexpectedly drew a lot allowing him to buy a color television set at the cheap government price and put the huge console in their room, Simin had a powerful encouragement for juvenile discipline in hand: admittance was based on good behavior. Negin's oldest, a master devil, was not allowed to watch television at all after he swiped two of her tea glasses in a moment of relaxed vigilance, took them on an outing with other boys to a spring in a high mountain valley, and promptly broke them there. He complained about her meanness to his mother, his aunt, and his grandfather, and when one day soon after Simin, sent by Hakime, came to borrow a meat grinder, Perigol very acidly told her that she should get Avdal to buy her the necessities of a household which her father obviously had neglected to provide her with, instead of wasting his money on a television set. Simin made the suitably impolite reply that Avdal provided his people with meat to grind while Trab's house only had an idle grinder, and she went all the way to her mother the next time she needed a grinder again.

Later in the fall, when the first gray rain clouds were hanging deep over Snow Mountain, Banu and Vali moved into their new house. Immediately an argument broke out about the vacated room: Aziz wanted Avdal and Simin to move there. Behjad and Tamas were against it. If Aziz really wanted a second wife (and Behjad was becoming more afraid of another pregnancy than of a co-wife) he should put her into that room and not next to Behjad, they said. Vali said that their youngest brother, who was in the army, would— God willing—come home in three months and would need this room for his bride. Rahmat said that there was an order out for the revolutionary guards to get married and that he would be obliged to do so soon, and what about a room for him then? And Trab, tired of the negligent care he had gotten lately while Negin was recuperating, and well aware that the service would deteriorate further as soon as Perigol was married, declared that he would get himself a wife—not a really young one, but a well-kept widow who could still see to the household and his needs. At these various announcements everybody was so surprised and stunned that the arguments died, the room stayed empty for the time being, and Avdal and Simin got to keep theirs. But with three men in the house looking for a wife, and one, the soldier, betrothed, space was clearly getting scarce. Negin's husband could figure out the problem as well as anybody else and announced that he was going to build a house down in the fields as soon as Negin would be well again.

Negin's leg was healing. She could hobble around now and pitch in here and there, but Perigol still had to work long hours after school and was very grouchy. Negin sick had not been quiet, but Negin well, or almost well, was a sore trial. No one was safe from her cutting remarks, her biting jokes, her teasing. Simin was not spared. Negin had something witty to say about her clothes, her spinning, her cooking, about the way she walked or sat or worked or did nothing. And Simin answered her. To the relief of Hakime and Behjad, Simin could hold her own in debates with Negin and advanced to being the speaker for all the women on her side of the house. Where Behjad hid, Golperi fled, Hakime meekly said, "but . . . ," and "no, that's a lie . . . ," and "I never said . . . ," and Grand-mother held screechy monologues no one listened to, Simin cursed, accused, argued and denounced with speed, vigor, and accurate aim at Negin's weak spots: her lack of support from her own family while she was sick, her lack of family altogether, her children's mental deficiency (they were failing in school with embarrassing regular-ity), her short temper and evil tongue. "Aren't you ashamed of yourself," she cried at one such occasion, "bawling out Golperi for no reason at all, picking on her, and so what if she spilled water on your skirt, why did you have to push her, because you think you are better than her, so you think, maybe, for no good reason whatso-ever! And where was your sister when you were sick, and who had to wash you and take your dirty imbecile brats to the bathhouse if not me and Golperi? And now you go around like Lady Negin — maybe we should call you Lady Negin from now on because you can hobble on your own legs again? No question why Uncle Trab's wife drank poison, with you in the house — it would make anybody drink poison just having to listen to you, and no wonder that your kids are always over here and your husband is never home . . . " Simin had a long breath and limber legs — Negin's weapon, an aluminum ladle, missed her as she jumped up to the verandah. Neither Simin nor Negin, however, was of the sulking kind, so their angry out-bursts did not weigh heavily on hearts and minds, and no livers burned with quiet rage. For all their bantering, Simin did not dis-like Negin, and she knew Negin did not dislike her. Simin only had to be on guard against being gulled by Negin, that was all. It was Golperi who was fast becoming a problem, not Negin.

The manager of the workshop had not yet paid Golperi any of her salary, little as it was. The agency had not yet sent it, she said, but Golperi was certain this was a lie. Furthermore, instead of letting Golperi instruct pupils as she was hired to do, the manager had her work on a loom with a finely strung warp and a very complicated knotting pattern, which, Golperi was sure, did not even belong to the agency but was the manager's own. Timid as Golperi was, she did not challenge the manager, nor did she tell the agency supervisor when he came on a round of inspection—there was nothing to gain by picking a fight, she said at home. But she was unhappy, tired, and no longer even sure that putting up a loom at home would be of much advantage either: the agency loaned the yarns and the pattern, and the manager allowed herself a sizeable cut off the meager price the agency was paying. To make any money, Golperi would have to furnish her own yarns and pattern, but only her brothers could arrange this for her in the city. Her requests unheeded, Golperi was gloomy, moody, and resentful. Simin, by far the most active of the women in the house, got the brunt of her discontent and was getting tired of it fast. If only, she thought (and said as much to Negin and Banu), if only Golperi would be taken away by a husband soon.

At one of her visits home (to avoid helping Negin and Perigol shake their rugs) she arrived in the middle of a discussion about one of her cousin's chances to be allotted a government-subsidized truck. The chances would be very good if he was married, but about nil without demonstrable duties towards dependents on his part. Simin casually said he should marry Golperi, and how good a cook she was, and that she even had a salary at the workshop, and how good tempered she was, and how quiet and proper. To her own greatest surprise, only a few days later a delegation from her family came to pay a visit to Tamas and broached the subject obliquely. The next day Hakime took Golperi aside and had an earnest talk with her, and Golperi said no, she was not going to marry anybody, but she did not even cry, and only a week and a few visits later the bride price was agreed upon, the marriage certificate was written, a wristwatch and a small golden pendant were sent to Golperi, and Simin's cousin left to claim his truck. And when Simin, the established link between the two families, talked her cousin at his first visit into getting yarn for a rug for Golperi and magnanimously said she would not mind the loom right outside her room between the window and the door, she had nothing to hide from anybody, Golperi forgot the green shirt, forgave her the key to the larder, and quit at the workshop.

Simin made certain she got full credit for arranging this match. "For all the trouble I took for Golperi" became a stock remark to even the slightest hint of criticism by Hakime and usually silenced her instantly. For a while at least she had them eating out of her hand and she felt smug, and smugger yet when she missed her next period.

The first one to know about Simin's pregnancy was Aftab, Bandar's fresh little wife. She had seen Simin in the bathhouse, she said, and it was obvious. Aftab told Maryam, who said Aftab should keep her nose out of other people's business; and Mehri, who told her mother, who was a cousin of Simin's mother; and on her next visit she also told Banu. Banu asked Simin, who denied it in a way that convinced Banu she was lying, and spread the good news to Negin and Behjad. Behjad gave Simin a child-stone to keep on her always as the only potent guard against the fatal attack of another woman's child-stone. Simin's mother brought a bag with seeds of wild rue, a powerful agent against the evil eye, which she had bought on a pilgrimage to the south, where the plant grew. Hakime cooked a big pot of sweetpaste with turmeric and butterfat and fed Simin fried eggs in the morning—"warm" foodstuff to make it more likely that Simin's blood was nourishing a boy in her womb and not a girl. Grandmother insisted that Simin wear two iron bangles on her wrist—ugly things, Simin thought, but she dared not refuse—to ward off possible attacks of the spirits who live around ruined houses, and the washhouse of the dead, and along the water channel, and even in the bathhouse at dusk, those no one spoke of lest uttering their name would summon them. And after Simin's mother had come upon her one day in the middle of winter washing Avdal's shirt in cold water, squatting on the cold mud of the frozen courtyard, she spoke some polite but firm words about it to Hakime, and from then on Simin did no more washing. What if the cold would hit her womb? How would Hakime stand up to the reproaches of Simin's people? From the vantage point at her fire across the courtyard, Negin observed it all gleefully. "Oh, Simin dear, oh, Simin, my life," she mocked them, "oh, precious little devil-dear, don't fall, don't slip, don't make your little fingers wet or else big mother will come running with a stick . . . "

"Shut up," cried Behjad.

But Simin was laughing. "You wish you had something in your belly, that's all," she shouted. "Want some rose water to get your man going tonight?"

"Shut up," shouted Perigol, "dirty mouth."

"Who needs it? Your rose water you can give to Grandmother so she'll smell better in her grave."

"Then cook him something nice for a change, something easy on his teeth, something that smells good and tastes well . . . "

"It's in the pot, thanks be to God, thyme and wild onions and wild garlic, a whole handful—can't you smell it, like food in paradise, no martyr eats better from the hands of the houris . . . but wait, can you smell it?"

"Yes, sure, stinking to heaven!"

"Well, then get over here quick," Negin said and ladled some from the pot out into a bowl.

"You think just smelling it will make me want some?" Simin said. "You have ideas!" But she went over and sat down at Negin's fire and ate a little of Negin's food. Because if Negin didn't give her any or Simin refused it, her child might be born with the evil eye. Negin didn't want this; neither did she.

For the time being, Simin had it all wrapped up. If only it was a boy.

8

Mamalus Is Telling a Story

"The rain," Mamalus said from her kitchen door, "it is dripping through into the store room." Gholam grunted. He shoved a last handful of rice from the tray in front of him into his mouth, wiped his hand on a greasy gray towel, got up slowly, clutching his back, and limped out into the noisy dark. Rain was coming down in heavy sheets, splashing loudly on the flat dirt roofs. Thunder was rolling overhead. Mamalus, short, plump, with quick hands and small eyes in a laugh-wrinkled face, closed the door behind him. "Eat more," she said to the other people seated on the large blue rug around the tray. Her younger sister Mamanir, much like Mamalus in build and manner, shook her head. Her sister's husband Mokhtar, a much older man, bald headed and stubble faced, lifted a jittery hand in a no-thanks gesture. Surprised by the storm on the way to their house in the next hamlet, they had taken shelter in Gholam's house. Amene, a young, small woman with slow, deliberate movements, white skin, long nose, small eyes and pretty clothes, and the foreign lady, a neighbor and frequent visitor of Amene, were sitting on the other side of the fireplace. They, too, were full. Mamalus picked the tray up from the plastic cloth on the floor and carried it out into the kitchen. Effat, in her midteens, round faced like her mother, gathered the plastic cloth with the shreds of leftover bread and onions, and carried it out too. She came back with a teapot, a water pot, and a polished stainless steel tray with tea glasses. She put the pots on the coals in the fireplace and the tea tray in front of Mokhtar. It was Amene's tea, Amene's room, Amene's rug, and Amene's fire. It was also Amene's rice, but Mamalus had cooked it. Gholam and Mamalus owned the house. Amene came from one of the best (and wealthiest) families in the area and was one of the very few local women with a high school diploma. She and her husband, a teacher in a village far up the river who came home only now and then, rented two rooms from Gholam; his only other income came from peddling cooking pots and aluminum wares all over the countryside and whatever he could grow on the two small garden plots his wife's brothers had given her magnanimously, for Gholam was a stranger to the village. He was as thin and quiet as his wife was round and talkative. From somewhere outside he was yelling for the umbrella. Effat yanked it off a nail in the wall and handed it out into the black dampness. Thunder was spluttering like gunfire. Amene got up to pull a plastic bag with needlework from a pile of odds and ends in a wall niche. Mokhtar poured tea with a trembling hand. Amene's two children, a girl of five and a boy of about three, were fighting with grimy hands over the sugar bowl. Amene took it away. The girl threw her head back and howled and the boy beat on Amene's arm. "Hush, hush," said Amene, "be quiet or the foreign lady will cut off your ears." The foreign lady tried to look the part but the children had heard this too often to be impressed.

The little boy climbed onto his mother's back and beat on her head. "I want candy, I want candy!" he cried in an unwavering, piercing screech.

"Stop the racket," Mamalus said from the kitchen door, "or else the bear will get you. Just watch the door and listen." The boy looked at her with disgust. Amene pulled him off her head and sat him in her lap. She gave him a piece of sugar, which he started to lick and munch and poke his dirty finger into, and rolled another over to the girl, who was sulking in a corner. Stomping and scratching sounds came from above through the poplar-beamed ceiling, and hollering echoed down the chimney. Gholam was pulling a heavy oak roller the shape of a huge rolling pin over the dirt roof to press the water out and pack the dirt tight.

"Ah, the bear," Mohktar whispered. "Better be quiet." The boy dropped the sticky sugar, crawled deeper into the rich folds of his mother's many skirts, and started to whimper. The girl came running to her mother. Mamalus laughed. Effat brought in the waterpipe and Mohktar filled the top with live coals from the fireplace. The stomping and scratching from above was very loud now, and a deafening thunder crashed over the house.

"No bear," the boy cried, upsetting the sugar bowl with his kicking legs.

"No, no," Amene cooed, trying to kiss him.

"This reminds me of the bear on Khosrow's rooftop," said Mamalus, squatting next to her sister and gathering the spilled pieces of sugar, "in the story of Gedulak and his mother's brother."

"Tell us," said the foreign lady.

"Lies," said Mokhtar, blowing on the coals of the waterpipe and coughing. "Turn on the television."

"Broken," said Effat. "The little devil pulled two knobs off it." She was leaning against the big console, which filled almost a quarter of the room.

"There are more lies on television than in the tales of old," said Mamanir.

"Tell us," said Amene. She liked tales. She knew many herself and had written down some she had heard others tell, in a school notebook.

Mamalus was rocking herself and clapping her hands. "Ah," she cried, "that bear, wasn't he something. A bear shaving his face, imagine! Bears are sort of like us," she said to the children in Amene's lap. "Their children cry like you do. Because this Khosrow in the story, not our Khosrow in the village, of course, another one, because he had seen him shave his face, the bear gave him the leg of a mountain goat to bribe him to keep quiet about it."

"Ah, game!" Mokhtar said, leaning back against the warm wall next to the fireplace with half-closed eyes. "Good meat, healthy meat, all gone now, nothing left in the mountains, no goats, no birds . . . we all went hunting . . . haven't tasted any in years . . . "

"They ate the meat," Mamalus said, "but Khosrow's wife, may God punish her, wormed it out of him anyway, and the bear was listening at the smoke hole on the roof and yelled down that he would come to visit them tomorrow. Well, they understood what it means when a bear wants to visit. They were frightened. The woman, may God blacken her face, she said, 'Let's cut off the branches so that the tree can grow again before the tree is gone, roots and all.' But their children, a boy and a girl, were listening at the smoke hole, and understood very well that their parents wanted to give them to the bear to save themselves. So they ran away, in the middle of the night."

"Poor kids," said Effat, screwing up her face.

"Yes, they had a reason to run away, not like our neighbor's devil of a boy, stealing his father's donkey and sneaking off with the Haji's son stuffed in the saddlebag, over Snow Mountain pass." Amene and the foreign lady giggled. "And this is nothing to laugh about either. Gouhar was beside herself with worry when the boy didn't come home. The Haji wasn't there, and *she* couldn't go after the boy now, could she?"

"And it was the second time," said Mamanir. "The first time one of Tamas's sons brought him back, half frozen, and this time the boy's uncle found them, sheer good luck it was, on the other side of the mountain, just in time before they could sell the donkey for money for a truck fare. If they had gotten a ride they would have been in town in no time and lost. One can travel fast now."

"I remember," said Amene, "when I was in sixth grade I needed a photograph for the application for the teacher training college, and my father put me on a horse, and we rode over the pass to town for a photograph. We were on the road for three full days each way. That was not so long ago, either. I was so tired, I fell off the horse once."

"This brother and sister now, they fled on foot, because there were no cars then, or anyway, the story says they walked. They came to a house where a rich, stingy old merchant lived, right in his store."

"There must have been as many thieves then as there are now. Mashhadi Yedulla used to sleep in his store most of the time, although he had two wives at home," Amene said. Mokhtar shook his head, chuckling. "You know the story of this mister somebody or the other, who had two wives yet slept in the mosque every night?"

145

"No," said the foreign lady, grinning in anticipation. She was easy to amuse.

"Because when the poor wretch wanted to creep under the quilt to his first wife she shooed him away and said, 'You go to your other wife, don't bother me!' And when he went to his second wife, she said, 'Don't bother me, go to the other one!' So he ended up sleeping in the mosque."

"Serves him right," said Mamanir. "Why did he have to take a second wife?"

"I don't know how many wives the shopkeeper had. He was stingy. He fed the children acorn bread like the very poor people ate in the past."

"Not only the poor. We all ate acorn bread," said Mamanir.

"It is bitter and dark and sits in your stomach like a rock and clogs you up, with all respect, you know what I mean. You eat it if you have diarrhea."

"Hakime made some the other day," said Amene. "I kind of like it once in a while."

"That's what you say now, because you don't have to eat it," said Mamanir.

"And the work it was—getting the acorns from far and wide and grinding them and soaking the flour in the stream and whatnot, for days," said Mamalus.

"But it was fun to be out with all the women—big parties in the woods all day. And then we were not afraid either, not like now with all the strangers around, like poor Turan, you know."

"Anyway," Mamalus recovered the story, raising her voice, "that merchant could have afforded wheat bread and rice, but did not want to. At night he lay down on a mat and instead of a blanket or a rug or a coat he put the pans of his scales over himself for a cover. That's how stingy he was. The brother and sister jumped on the scales on the old man and sat on him heavily until he was choked. And then they threw him in the water and the water carried him away just as it almost carried away Aftab's little son the other day because she doesn't watch him."

"Do you hear?" Amene said to her little son, who was rubbing sugar mush into the rug. "Don't go near the water!"

"The children stayed in the old guy's house. One day a dervish came . . . "

"Ah, a dervish," Mokhtar cried with feeling. "These hoodlums think it is holy not to work but to beg from honest people who work for every bite of bread. This is not what our Prophet . . . "

"Lazy bums who beg their way through the world become streetwise, bad, tricky, even if they wear the green turban of the holy Prophet's descendants. This one was no better. He saw the girl when he was begging food from her and became infatuated with her and wanted her and got her, behind her brother's back. And she became pregnant and was afraid what her brother would do to her."

"Well, what did I tell you," Mokhtar said, nodding his head on a skinny neck. "The brother has to kill her. Remember when our chief once burned this woman and her, well, her acquaintance—he was a stranger from a village down the river—because they had committed adultery. This was years ago . . . " Mokhtar clearly thought those the better times.

"But no one killed Begom's niece a few years back when she was not married but pregnant," said Effat.

"Then the Shah's police did not let anybody kill her," said Mokhtar, "but now she would be killed."

"And her mother fought for her like a tiger until the child's father married her. Even if he divorced her again, so what."

"This girl in the story had no father and no mother and no uncles. She only had her brother. Now she was pregnant, and after only a few days she knew she would give birth presently. She sent the dervish out with her brother, who was herding the sheep. She said, 'Kill my brother. Make him milk a sheep for you at lunch time, and while he is bending over, kill him with a club.' The dervish tried to do this, but the brother was wise and made the dervish himself milk the sheep and killed the dervish with his club."

"Served him right," said Mokhtar.

"Meanwhile, at home, the sister gave birth to a boy, and the boy could walk and speak right away."

"God, have mercy," mumbled Mamanir from behind the water-pipe.

"It is only a story," said Mamalus.

"All lies," said Mokhtar, half asleep again.

"She never had to wash diapers," said Amene.

"Listen to the thunder," said Effat, "I am frightened. What is father doing up there for so long? He'll be drenched."

"The girl cried when she heard that her brother had killed the dervish."

Effat groaned. "Stupid bitch," said Mokhtar.

"Her son scolded her. 'The dervish was bad,' he said. 'Look what he did to you!' The woman stopped crying. She said to her brother, 'Go, bring me some fat from the dead dervish's body.' The brother had a soft heart and did so. Next time when the woman cooked rice and was about to serve it, she poured the melted dervish-fat over the tray of rice in front of the men and put good butterfat on the other tray in front of her. But her son, his name was Gedulak, this Gedulak had sharp eyes and saw what his mother was doing. He snuffed out the lamp and switched the trays in the darkness. He and his uncle ate the good rice, his mother ate the bad rice, and her belly swelled up and she burst and was dead."

"Good riddance," said Mokhtar. Another terrific thunder rolled over the house.

"That's the sound she made when she burst," said Amene.

"Huh, huh," cried Effat. Amene's children were buried in their mother's skirts with terror. The door opened and Gholam stepped inside, dripping wet, a coat over his head. Effat jumped up and hung the coat on a nail in the door. Mokhtar made room for Gholam at the fireplace. Mamanir put a glass of tea in front of him with three large lumps of sugar. Another thunder shook the house.

"Burst again," said Amene, shaking with laughter. The little boy screamed. Mamanir murmured a blessing.

"Listen to the story," Mamalus said to Gholam. "It is the story of Gedulak, the scoundrel." Gholam was not interested. He was cold and wanted another glass of tea.

"Go on," said Effat.

"As if you didn't know the story," said her mother, but she went on over the din of rain and thunder and Gholam's reporting that the barn roof was leaking badly at the farther end.

"Gedulak and his uncle now, they were alone. 'What shall we do?' said the uncle.

" 'I am only a child,' said Gedulak, 'so you go someplace into service and bring your wages back for the two of us to live on.' He gave him some money for the bus fare—it seems they did have cars then after all—and he also gave him a hair and told him he should put it on the coals of his waterpipe whenever he was in trouble, and

Gedulak would come to help him. The uncle, poor dumb klutz, went away.

"He met a beardless man with green eyes. The weirdo was looking for a servant, and the uncle went with him. Early in the morning the master gave the uncle some wheat, a plow, a cow, a donkey, a round flatbread, and said, 'Go and sow the wheat, make some meat, don't eat any of the bread and at night bring home a load of firewood.'"

"That's how they were, the masters of old," said Gholam, slurping tea from the saucer, "some better, some worse."

"Well, the stories I could tell about this," said Mamanir to the foreign lady, "when we had nothing, no land, no cow, no sheep, and bent our backs for the chief . . ."

"He was all right," said Mokhtar. "His two brothers were worse. Remember when his youngest brother came with three riflemen up to the mountains where we were staying with the goats and sheep that one summer after our two oldest children had died from measles? I was not there, and you were sick with fever, and they took our only rug away from under your body? May God punish him in his grave."

"Just as well that I looked so sick and ugly," said Mamanir, "or else . . ."

"And when your grandfather died, may his soul rest in peace," Mokhtar said to Amene, "the chief's cousin came with his retainers and drove off your father's ox and said, 'Why did your father have to die on me? He was a good hunter. Now you pay for it.'" Amene nodded. She had heard the story many times.

"Bless the Shah for doing away with the chiefs," Gholam murmured, and was instantly hushed by everybody in the room.

"This beardless green-eye was worse," said Mamalus. "Our chiefs fed us. The closer you stuck with them, the better you ate, at least the men who were sitting at their tablecloth. We women at home ate acorn bread. But this poor dumb uncle did not know what to do. He was dying of hunger out in the field. He sowed the wheat and cut some firewood and then ate the bread. When he came home at dusk, the master said, 'No meat? Ate the bread? You'll die,' and he laid him flat on the ground to cut off his head."

"This must have been before they had shotguns," said Mokhtar. "The chief's brother shot Tamas's uncle over his wheat payments."

149

"Well, maybe he wanted to shoot him," said Mamalus, "it is not important. The beardless guy wanted to kill the uncle to get his fat."

"What for?" asked Effat. Amene let her stitchery sink into her lap, looking sharply at Mamalus. Mamalus knew a lot about the medicines of old.

"What do I know?" said Mamalus. "Bear grease is good against rheumatism, and the fat of wild boars is good for a hundred things, so human fat should not be good for anything? He wanted his fat, I tell you. But the uncle remembered Gedulak's hair and asked for a waterpipe to smoke before he would die, and sure enough, when he burned the hair, Gedulak appeared, just like that"—and she snapped her fingers.

"All lies," said Gholam, gurgling on his waterpipe.

"Those who are better than us, they can do this," said Effat.

Amene was nodding. She too thought that the *djenn* and fairies could do such things, and this was no joke. "I hear Hakime's brother is really sick," she said, ending with a pregnant pause.

"A cold, they say," Mamanir said, and shrugged her shoulders. "It is not good to talk about it." "It" was the sick man's frightening story of an unexplainable nightly encounter with a strange woman at the washhouse for the dead after a late-evening funeral a week or so earlier. He had told the woman not to hang around there because it was a bad and dangerous place, the washhouse for the dead was, and the woman had gotten up, had laughed (odd enough, this), moved towards the washhouse, and suddenly disappeared. The man, shaking from head to toe when he arrived home, had laid down and stayed down with an unexplainable fever.

"Who knows," said Mokhtar. It was his turn at the waterpipe again.

Another wave of thunder and pelting rain hit the house. The single lightbulb hanging from the plastic-covered ceiling flickered. Gholam mumbled about the barn and the hay and went out again. Amene's children had fallen asleep. Effat pulled one after the other by an arm to a pillow in the corner and spread a blanket over them. Amene poured herself some tea. Mamalus and her sister started to argue about the sick man's illness.

Amene sat back again, sinking into her wide skirts. "Then what happened to Gedulak and his uncle? Aunt Mamalus, go on," she said.

"Gedulak appeared and told the beardless man that he himself would be his servant the next day and do all he wanted if he would spare the uncle. The green-eyed man agreed. Next morning, the man gave Gedulak a cow and a plow and wheat, and a bowl of yogurt, and a donkey for the firewood. 'Go and make the field green,' he said, 'but don't spoon out any yogurt, and make some meat and bring back a load of firewood on the donkey.' Gedulak left for the field. He plowed it criss-cross and upside-down, and threw the wheat seeds every which way. Then he broke the plow and put it on the donkey, and then he killed the cow and put it on the donkey too, and then he carefully made a hole in the bowl of yogurt and sucked the yogurt from below so that the skin on top would not be broken, and then he found some children cutting grass at the edge of the water channel and said, 'Children, don't you know? Your mother has died, your father has died, and the mourners are eating sweetpaste by the shovelful!' The children dropped their bags of grass and ran home. Gedulak took the grass, spread it all over the field so that the field looked nice and green, and walked back."

Amene was laughing into a tip of her headscarf. "It served the beardless master right," said Effat.

Mamalus, spurred by Amene, was laughing too. "It'll get even better," she cried. "The beardless one lost his tongue when he saw what Gedulak had done. 'I beg of you,' he cried in the end, 'go away, and I'll give you a thousand Toman if you leave right away.' And so Gedulak left."

"No, he didn't," said Mamanir.

"Sure he did," said Mamalus. "He left and went to somebody else's door and sniffled. And the master of that house came out . . . "

"It was the same beardless one. Gedulak did not leave him. He wanted not only the money, he wanted the whole house and all the man had."

"Anyway," said Mamalus, "there he was with this master. The master had a house full of daughters . . . "

" . . . like Agha," said Effat. "His wife just had another girl this morning, her seventh."

"Dear me," said Mamanir, "praise be to God."

"In my husband's village is a man who has ten daughters and another with nine sons," said Amene, and she found this funny too.

"God's ways are inscrutable," said Mamalus. "Gedulak now, he is up to something, just listen."

"The people say Agha told his wife not to nurse the girl, you know, like Tamas did when Hakime had four or five of them, one after the other, and they had nothing but their own lives," said Effat.

"How do *you* know?" asked Mamalus. "You were not born then."

"Hakime told me herself," said Effat.

"A lot of children died, back then," said Amene, with a sideways glance at the foreign lady.

"Too many women around, anyway," said Mokhtar.

"Maryam and Begom and I counted the widows in the village the other day and came up with eleven," said Mamalus. "Eleven widows, imagine, young and old, rich and poor."

"I don't believe Agha said this," said Mamanir. "He likes his daughters. I saw him with one of them at the doctor's a few days ago. She had a burned hand and he was very concerned about her."

"What did Gedulak's master do with his daughters, though?" Amene asked.

"Nothing. He liked them too. But Gedulak said to the youngest girl, 'Go tell your father that your oldest sister'—she was married in the city—'that she has died. I don't dare to give him the bad news myself.' The master believed it and got ready to leave for her place. He told Gedulak, 'While I am gone you see to things here. Sweep the yard clean enough to pour butterfat and syrup on it; wash the ox until its legs are red and shiny; and make these six girls sit down with their spindles, and if they don't obey you, kill them.' The master and his wife left. Gedulak sat the girls down to spin. Then he got the bags with syrup and butterfat—that was at the time when we stored such food in skin bags . . ."

"Foodstuff kept a lot better then," said Mamanir.

" . . . he brought the skin bags and poured them out in the yard. Seeing this, the girls jumped up from their spinning. Gedulak killed them and sat them down again, propped up against something, and put raisins in the corners of their mouths to make it look as if they were smiling. Then he also killed the ox and chopped its legs off with an axe, and stuck them in boiling water and roasted them until they were red and shiny. This is what Gedulak did."

"The black death," Effat cursed.

"It served the beardless one right," said Mokhtar, snug against the warm wall.

Gholam came in again. He put his dripping galoshes inside the door on the dirty gypsum floor. "It won't let up," he said.

"We should have the roof tarred," said Mamalus.

"Pirali's wife is on their roof. It's leaking, she says, although it is tarred. I helped her."

"Luckless woman," said Mamanir. "Pirali wrote again saying he can't come. It is more than two years that he left for Kuwait. She has to do everything herself."

"She is thinking of selling her cow because she can't find any-body for the hay cutting and the herding," said Amene.

"He'll bring enough money for her to live like a lady," said Effat.

"Yes, but right now she has nothing but debts and three little children. His brother doesn't help her either." Gholam, sitting at the fire again, shrugged his shoulders. "Has enough to do himself," he said.

"Right," said Mamanir, "stealing Pirali's land while Pirali is gone, right under her nose. When Pirali will come back, there will be a terrific row. And meanwhile, her aunt's old husband with the lame leg, meaning you, has to help her press her roof. Ha, this is justice!"

"Well," Mamalus said into the pause, "when Gedulak's master came back, he saw his daughters sitting there, lazy-like, and grin-ning. Gedulak said, 'Oh, honorable master, look, your daughters are making fun for you.' The master, who was already angry because he had gone to his daughter's town for nothing, cursed them: 'May they drop dead,' he said. Gedulak pushed one a little and she fell on her sister, and one after the other they all fell down dead. And then the master saw what had happened, and that Gedulak had taken all he had said literally and had brought this calamity over his house."

"Dear me," said Amene, holding back laughter with difficulty.

"Yes," said Mamalus, "but remember, the master has one more daughter. So he says to Gedulak, tired-like, 'Go and fetch my oldest daughter, dead or alive, the sooner the better, for the funeral.' Gedulak went there. He said to her, 'I have to drag you home the fastest way possible, which is by a leash.' And he tied a rope around her neck and dragged her home as if she were a cow. By the time they arrived, she was dead."

"Dear me," Amene said again, "the things they did to girls then . . . "

"It makes one glad to be alive now," said Effat.

"Lies, lies," said Mokhtar.

"Gedulak's master was beaten now. He said, 'Gedulak, I will give you a thousand Toman, two thousand Toman'—and at that time this was a fortune—'if only you will leave me.' Gedulak took the money and left. He . . . "

"No, he didn't," said Mamanir. "It was the same beardless one he did everything to."

"No," said Mamalus, "you have it all wrong. He left and came to another master . . . or maybe it was still the green-eyed one. It does not matter—I don't remember. It was old Binas who told us the story, way back then. She was quite a woman, speaking of widows. She had nine husbands and outlived them all."

Gholam grunted, sleepily. Mokhtar said, "This is not true."

"Sure it is," said Mamalus, "and she knew the best stories. She also could read the Koran. We girls visited her often. There was much more visiting going on then."

"True, true," said Gholam. "Nowadays everybody is too stuck-up to go sit in anybody else's house."

"Well, Gedulak is with these people, who have a little son. At night the boy said, 'I have to pee.' The woman said, 'Gedulak, take him out to pee.' Gedulak took him outside and said, 'If you pee, I'll stick a needle in your balls, and if you shit, I'll put a pitchfork in your butt.' The kid was frightened and did not pee. Well, there is nothing to laugh about, Effat!" Amene and Effat were shaking behind their scarves. "I mean, with all respect, I am only telling you the way old Binas told us. Imagine somebody would say this to your boy."

"Three times a night he has to go out," Amene was sputtering, "and I have no Gedulak, I have to go myself!"

"This boy in the story, he of course after a little while started to whine again that he had to pee, and his mother sent Gedulak out with him, and Gedulak threatened him again with the needle and . . . "

" . . . with the pitchfork . . . " gasped Effat.

"Shut up," said Mokhtar, "let your mother talk."

"When a woman laughs she gives way to the devil," Mamanir said, but she could not keep her face straight either.

"The third time the woman got impatient. She said, 'Take him out, Gedulak, and take his legs apart.' Of course, she only meant . . . "

Everybody was laughing now. Amene's little boy sat up, whining and rubbing his eyes. He looked around and, whining louder still, crawled to his mother. Amene made cooing noises in between her suppressed snickering. "I need to pee," whined the boy. Now they all howled, even Mokhtar.

"Effat," cried Amene, "take him out, and if he doesn't pee, stick a pitchfork. . ." They were choking with mirth. The boy threw himself on the floor, kicking and screaming. "No, no," said Amene, wiping tears from her eyes, "No one is hurting you. Just go with Effat."

But the boy screamed, "Lie, lie, lie, lie," and pulled at Amene's headscarf and her braids under it. Effat tried to hold him down by his legs but the screaming turned to bloodcurdling howls. Amene got up and half dragged, half carried him to the door.

"Take the umbrella," said Gholam. They could hear the little boy's whining, quieter now, from somewhere outside through the open door.

"Gedulak, outside with the boy, took his legs and tore him apart. Clearly into two halves he tore him through the middle, and threw the two halves away."

"Wait," Amene cried from outside, "I want to hear it too." She came back with the boy in her arms, sat down, and bedded him in her lap.

"Gedulak tore the kid apart," said Mamalus again.

The boy let out a scream. Amene laughed and patted his back. "Not you," she said, "somebody else, a bad, naughty boy."

"Lie, lie, lie," the little boy cried.

"Hush hush," said Mokhtar. The boy kept whining.

"The boy was gone," said Mamalus, "and the father and mother did not know what to do. They were sad and cried. At night they talked, softly, so that Gedulak might not hear them. The woman said, 'Old man, let us get away quietly.' They got up and put all they had on their donkeys. But Gedulak knew what they were up to and took a bag of grape syrup out of a saddlebag and crawled into it instead. The man and woman left with Gedulak in the saddlebag.

On the way Gedulak had, I mean, with all respect, he had to pee. The old man—now I can't tell the story if you carry on like this—be quiet! The old man saw something dripping from the bag and said, 'Look, the bag has a hole, the grape syrup is dripping.' He caught a drop with his finger and licked . . . " Mamalus herself could no longer speak. Amene was wiping tears with her stitchery. Mokhtar was wheezing. "The old man . . . he said . . . 'this is salty . . . you are . . . you are a slut . . . you didn't even wash the bag before you put syrup in!' "

It took the party a while to recover. Mamalus used the pause to suck and puff at the waterpipe. The bubbling water in the glass flask was getting brownish. "Oh, this Gedulak!" she cried, blowing smoke, "He sure fooled them! They walked and walked and Gedulak rode along comfortably in the saddlebag. They came to an abandoned campsite at a river and the man started to unload the donkeys. 'Hey you,' Gedulak cried, 'be careful, don't hurt me!' "

"Oh pity, pity," cried Effat.

"This the old man and the woman said too: 'Oh, misfortune, oh, punishment, oh, pity!' they cried. The woman took the old man aside and whispered to him, 'Let us put Gedulak between us at night. When he is fast asleep we will get up, you take his hands, I take his legs, and we will throw him in the water to be rid of him.' "

"If the water was anything like the irrigation channel is now, it should do it easily. It is full to overflowing," said Gholam.

"Right, it was full then too, because, listen: Gedulak, the devil, had overheard them again. At night the old woman said with a sweet voice, 'Gedulak, it will be cold tonight, come sleep between us.' But when the man and the woman were asleep, Gedulak moved to the other side of the old man and waited. Soon, the old woman woke up and said, 'How many legs?' and Gedulak said, 'Two feet, two legs,' and jumped up and grabbed the old man's hands, and the woman grabbed his legs, and they threw him in the water—splash— and the water carried him away. The old woman was very glad and said, 'He is gone, he is gone!' "

" 'Sure,' said Gedulak, 'he won't come back, just as you say.' And now the old woman realized that Gedulak was alive and the old man was gone. 'Ashes on my head,' she cried, 'God have mercy, Gedulak, you are here? Now I don't know which way to turn, what to do. I will have to take you as my son so as not to be all alone.'

" 'Fine with me,' said Gedulak. But then he did something to the old woman and she died too."

"Gedulak did not kill her," said Mamanir. "She died of grief right away."

"Like Huri's father," said Effat. "He died ten days after his wife died, yet he had never been sick before."

"Or like old Qeta," said Mokhtar. "She almost died when her husband and her one son were killed, and then the other son died a few days later. She went crazy. This was the summer our first son was born, when so much fighting and killing was going on."

"She was here this morning, begging tobacco," said Amene. "When she left, she danced on the verandah and sang as if she were at a wedding."

Mamanir nodded. "She is an embarrassment to her brother. His wife says, no matter what they do, she won't stay in the house. At night she wanders off and sleeps in the mosque."

"The old woman in the story died, crazy or not. Maybe she was crazy. Binas did not say. She died, and Gedulak tied her on a donkey with a rope around her feet and shoulders. Then he took the donkey into a green wheat field, and the donkey of course grazed the sweet young wheat as fast as he could. The owner of the field was quite away on the other side of a hedge. He saw the donkey and hollered across the field, 'Hey, you woman on the donkey, take the beast out of the field.' The woman, of course, did not answer. Only her head nodded, like this." Mamalus let her head bounce up and down on her ample bosom. Effat, her hand pressed against her mouth, was rolling on the rug behind Amene. Amene, too, was shaking with laughter, and so was the foreign lady. "The man got angry. He shouted, louder yet, 'Old woman, by the black death, take your donkey out of the field!' The donkey just grazed faster. The man was furious now. He picked up a rock and yelled, 'Get out of the field, you son of a bitch'—I mean, *he* said this, and I beg your pardon for the language. And he threw the rock, a big heavy one, and it hit the woman's head, and she fell down from the donkey. Gedulak all the while was hiding behind a big stone. Now he jumped up and shouted, 'You son of a . . .' —I mean, he cursed him, and said, 'You killed my mother over a mouthful of grass. I will kill your mother, I will kill you, I'll take you to the Shah, to the gendarmerie.' There were no revolutionary guards then, or he would have threatened him with them too. 'What do you want me to do so you won't hurt me?' the man asked. He was shaking in his shoes with fright. Gedulak said, 'I want my hat full of gold coins.' The man left. Gedulak made a hole in his felt hat and he made a hole in the ground and put the hat over the hole in the ground. The man brought a bag full of gold coins and poured them into the hat, but of course they fell through. 'It is not full,' said Gedulak. The man went back to his people and brought more gold coins. Still the hat was not full. So he left again, sweating with fear, and got all the gold coins his relatives had—he cut them off the caps of the women, and off their necklaces, and off wherever he could find any; no bride had a single coin left, but the hat still was not quite full and Gedulak wanted more. In the end the man got his family together and they fled, and Gedulak took over their house and their wealth and their fields, and then he brought his uncle, and they sat down in the house, and that is it."

"Ah," Effat sighed.

"My tale is nice and beautiful, throw a handful of rose petals over it," said Mamalus. "That's how Binas always ended her tales."

"Very well," said Amene. "Then what?"

"The uncle needs a wife and Gedulak needs a wife," said Effat. "Or else who is going to bake bread for them and wash their clothes?"

"They'll live like the Afghanis," said Gholam.

Mokhtar cackled. "If there are as many widows there as are here, they each can get themselves two wives or three—Gedulak is rich and widows are cheap . . . the older the cheaper."

"Let's hope Gedulak did a better job guarding his gold than the Haji," said Mamalus.

"It is better to be poor—if you have nothing, you can't lose anything," said Mamanir.

There was a loud thump at the door. Effat went to open the bolt. A shriveled old woman with brightly hennaed hair sticking out from under her wet, dark scarf stepped over the high sill. She held her bony arms in thin sleeves outstretched in front of her, shaking. "Look," she said in a low voice, "cold." Stepping closer into the light and bending down she stretched her lips with her fingers to reveal an almost toothless mouth. "Look, look," she murmured again, "empty." Then she let go of her mouth and grabbed her sagging breasts under the threadbare shirt and jacket. "Empty," she said, "all empty."

"Yes, Qeta," Mamalus said, soothingly, "we all are getting old. Why don't you go home?"

"The mosque roof is leaking," Qeta said. Mamalus sighed and shook her head.

"This is the old mosque," said Mokhtar. "The new one has a tin roof. You should go there."

"No," said Qeta, "they won't let me cook my rice there." Mamalus sighed again. Qeta sat down behind Amene.

Mokhtar poured tea into a glass and Amene passed it to Qeta on a small saucer with a lump of sugar. "Are you hungry?" she asked. Qeta shook her head, slurping the hot tea from the saucer.

"Weren't you afraid of the thunder?" Effat asked her.

Qeta shook her head again, slowly. "The fire is a little voice, the thunder is a big voice," she said. "It is in the hands of God. The foreign lady gave me matches."

"Mamalus was telling the story of Gedulak," said Amene. "Do you know it? He tricked everybody."

Qeta cocked her head, listening. "The drums and the oboe are voices too," she said, and started to hum.

"There is no more music now," said Mokhtar, "and no more landlords. We talked about how things were back then, when people ate acorn bread and there were no cars and no radios and everybody had guns and went hunting . . . "

Qeta fished a cigarette from an inner pocket of her ancient, frayed velvet jacket, and matches. She lit the cigarette and put it into her toothless mouth. Drawing herself up straight she looked around with filmy, red-lined eyes. "Tata, ta ta," she hummed, snapping the fingers of her left hand over her head and rocking to her own beat. "Ta, tata, ta . . . no chiefs, no Gedulak, no acorn bread, no blood, no rain, all lies. Just lies." She leaned over to the foreign lady, squinting through the smoke. "Life and death," she mumbled, "tales . . . all sounds, all lies."

The storm had passed, the rain stopped. A cold breeze gently pushed the door open. The night was filled with the gurgling of runoff water. For a little while they just sat, listening.

9

Watching the World from Sarah's Loom

Looms, like other successful survivors in Deh Koh, are plain, sturdy, and indifferent to abuse. Dismantled and thus reduced to their essence—a bundle of lumber—they also are hardy travelers, if need be. Cheap and homegrown, a loom is nothing more elaborate than a couple of five-foot-long beams, each resting on rocks behind two short, hard stakes driven into the ground a little farther apart than the planned length of the fabric; three thumb-thick, straight sticks (two for the heddles and one forked at one end, to keep the weave from being pulled together); and a couple of flat, slightly bent, short pieces of wood moving back and forth over the crossbeam of a tripod (otherwise used for buttering) to lift up the heddles alternately. All parts are stretched taut and held together by twice-spun strong yarn—wool or cotton, or a coarse string of wool and black goat hair, so tough and scratchy that even the leatherlike skin on a weaver's hand will blister. There is no nail, no hewn, planed, or polished part on this tool. Knocked down, it is just so much old lumber dropped casually along a wall. Set up, it covers a patch of ground— a corner of a courtyard, maybe, leveled roughly and swept clean—

with the weaver working her way from one end to the other, squatting on the already woven part. During pauses (all weavers have duties other than the loom as well) a large bath-cloth or an old veil might be thrown over warp and weave to protect it from the ever-swirling dust, the chickens, and the small children, who will pull at the yarns that are left, along with scissors and the heavy, comblike weaver's reed, right where they will be wanted shortly again. If it is necessary to move a loom (in the past looms were taken along to the summer camps) the tripod is disconnected from the heddles, lifted, and folded up; the stakes are pulled; and the beams are rolled towards each other from both ends, warp and weave with them, and tied on a donkey. It is something of an art, though, and an exercise in patience, to readjust the tension of the warp later at the new place, and sometimes the cloth will get a little crooked because of sags here and there, but no more harm will come. For Sarah, a weaver since she was a little girl, this nomadic tool is unimprovable in simplicity and functional ingenuity. Sometimes she wonders about the first woman to have sat on a loom. She must have been somebody clever, somebody who had sheep, she thinks, living near trees, and with a father or husband willing to spare two good pieces of lumber.

Yet its very simplicity makes this loom an old-fashioned device in the eyes of the villagers, and the rug dealers in the city consider its products—knotted rugs as well as more humble flat-weave floor coverings, breadcloths, and bags of many sizes and functions—as unmarketable relics of a bygone era. (If the rug dealers had their way, all young women in Iran would be sitting at commercial, vertical looms, swiftly knotting away for the export market using patterns and colors that sell well in Europe and creating products they themselves cannot afford to use. The manager of the government workshop in Deh Koh knows this very well; so does Golperi and most everybody else. But working at a city loom is modern, and who wants to be called backward?)

There are a handful of traditional weavers in the village. They have more business than they can handle and make four times as much money as the girls working on government looms. Many more women than these few know how to set up a loom and to weave at least the simple fabrics used for storage and saddlebags. On her porch, Maryam is sitting on one of many rag carpets she and her

161

nephew's wife have woven over the years; just before the nephew moved, the two women together finished a big saddlebag for hauling manure. Mamalus is weaving for relatives in return for quiet economic favors. (Sometimes, if no one is looking, Effat will help her. Aloud, she will declare not to know how to handle a weft beater.) Tamas's mother once had a loom and taught Hakime to use it. But these women only wove for themselves then, and now they would do even this only under dire necessity; Begom can't even remember where she put her beaters now that Ali brings home a steady salary. Her daughter Mehri's trousseau was woven by Sarah.

Sarah's transport bags are firmer, the patterns on her breadcloths more regular, the colors in her backpacks more pleasing than anybody else's in the village. Everybody agrees about this, even patrons of other weavers. Her customers come from far and wide and often will wait patiently for several seasons for her to get around to filling their order. In winter, when most of the other weavers quit altogether, she installs her loom under the protective roof of her porch. She does not like this workplace, though, because despite a fireplace at her back her fingers are stiff with cold, and the light that gets to her from over the low wall is dim and gray. Also, only a few people keep her company in winter. Come spring, the loom is moved out as soon as the rains are over. In the old courtyard, a shade of poplar twigs and rags was fashioned along the morning-sun wall (it would crash down on loom and weaver several times a season, to be redone with fresh boughs) to keep the sun off her head and out of her eyes. But after her son built a row of new rooms behind the old house a year before the revolution, Sarah set up the loom next to it under a huge walnut tree in the neighbor's (her cousin's) vacant lot. This was by far the best place she had ever had: light, airy, and shady most of the hot day, pleasant not only for herself but also for whomever came to sit with her. The walnut tree, Sarah's niece Mahin once said, was a generous and tireless host.

From her vantage point under the walnut tree, Sarah had a panoramic view of a long stretch of path along a minor water channel. The path emerged from bramble thickets beneath poplar trees into the sun-bleached openness of the vacant lot, ran past Sarah's loom at a comfortable distance, and disappeared behind her son's house to join a bigger alley a few houses further on. Beyond the path Sarah looked into a neglected orchard with hedges in such ill repair that nothing behind them was hidden: the neighborhood chickens had the run of the packed, dry ground; young children quite regularly used it as an outhouse; boys went sparrow hunting with their slings; dogs, chased and stoned elsewhere, found shade there and respite from persecution; and after school, girls often sat under the withering apricot trees, veil-wraps drawn around them, a circle of black backs against the world, talking about God knows what. To the left, Sarah's view was bounded by the wall of her cousin's son's house beyond an untidy heap of poplar lumber dumped there carelessly by a neighbor wanting for space, and a stretch of the kind of rubble that seemed to grow everywhere: paper, cans, shreds of plastic, old batteries, old shoes, more plastic blown about in the dry, dusty wind. To the right, without any effort she could observe what was going on in front of her son's house. He had not yet built a wall around his yard, and his apple trees were too young still to obstruct the view. To her back a broad mud stairway led up to her old house— two rooms where she and her husband lived, except that more and more often she stayed overnight in her son's house now. Craning her neck a bit she could, if she cared to, see who was on the verandah of Leila's husband's house, rising on the slope above and behind her son's place. Of the next house she could not see much, but when Nargez, the young, sloppy, quick-tempered lady of the house was scolding her children (loudly and often), she heard it; in fact, she could easily witness arguments in seven houses around the walnut tree, not counting her own. And although Sarah traveled the world less than many other women in Deh Koh, moored to her loom most of her waking hours, some of the world, she often said, traveled to her along the rocky path.

As a rule, very few strangers were among those who traveled her way. It was just as well, she thought, given what she heard about them. "Decent folks among them, I am sure, but odd," she said, when Mahrokh, her pregnant daughter-in-law, and Nargez, her pregnant neighbor with the piercing voice, tried to count the strangers in the village and found no end. Sarah was crouched behind the head beam, placing the warp which her youngest granddaughter, passing back and forth between the two beams, was rolling off a big ball of thin, white wool yarn. The girl was sliding the ball alternately under Sarah's beam and the other one, which was manned by her mother. Warping a loom ideally takes three people: stretching the warp and keeping it tight, at precise intervals, is an exacting task which can't be done well alone or with only one helper. Sarah was testing the warped yarn. "Tighter, Mahrokh," she said, "it is strong yarn, it won't break." Mistakes at this stage spell troubles later, requiring patient and cumbersome readjustments of tension.

"Odd people, strange people," she murmured again, shaking her head. Just about an old woman now, with her hair more and more taking on the bright red of henna on white under her dark blue scarf, she could size up people from afar, even if her broad, weatherbeaten face and hard-worked, blue-hued hands (modern dyes are not very fast, she will explain) were never far from the loom beneath her. There were eyewitness stories aplenty. Earlier that same afternoon her two older granddaughters, high school students both, took some books to their history teacher, a young woman from Tehran who wore chic black shoes with high heels and an expensive-looking veil-wrap drawn deeply into her face during school. (In fact, they said she had several veil-wraps.) At her home, if one can call a rented room "home," they found her bareheaded, without even so much as a small scarf, and a tight skirt covering only half of her bare legs. And all this in front of her host and their two sons, and even outdoors in the courtyard. In her presence, in a strange house, the girls felt hot and embarrassed—whether about their teacher or about themselves, sweating under all their clothes and the heavy black wrap, they could not say. She invited them to tea, but they left in a hurry. "If a revolutionary guard ever sees her, . . . ugh, ugh," said Nargez, sitting on a log with a spindle in her lap, idly plucking at a long tear in her pink tunic-shirt. A discussion ensued about whether anyone would eventually start talking about her loose habits (the consensus was probably yes), followed by an admonition to Sarah's granddaughters to keep their mouths shut, and what would happen if someone did talk about it (nothing good). Mahin, who had had to deliver a message from her mother, Sarah's sister, and had stayed to be helpful if needed, tried the argument that at home a woman could go bareheaded as far as the religion went, but she had to admit that Miss Salimi was not at home but among strangers and should be more circumspect and careful. And then Nargez, Mahin, and Sarah wanted to know what Miss Salimi's skirt and blouse looked like, and whether she wore a bra and slip under it (the girls did not know and their little sister, the yarn passer, just about forgot her business and had to be told to be careful and to hurry up), and they speculated where she got her clothes from and whether she knew how to sew, or did her mother? Tehranis, it was decided, had a lot more resources than poor villagers, and their ways were different, if not evil. The little girl was getting tired of bending down. She dropped the ball twice into the dirt and tried to talk her older sister into taking her place. Sarah was measuring the width of the warp with her hands: a breadcloth took five spans and four fingers. Only one more span to go.

"Odd, in any case, very odd, these strangers," she said again. "Just as well that school is over soon. She'll go home for the summer, certainly."

By the next afternoon Sarah had tied alternate warp strings onto the two heddles and had fastened them onto the two short, slightly convex pieces of wood, dark and polished from long use, resting on the cross-piece of the buttering tripod. Sliding the wooden pieces back and forth over the cross-piece opened the sheds alternately. But the tension on the warp was not right; the left half had slackened. Mahrokh and Sarah's sister (here to borrow some henna to relieve an aching head by packing it in henna paste) and Banu (returning with her baby from a visit to the doctor) were pulling hard at the beam at the loose side so Sarah could insert a piece of flattish rock between the beam and the post. "Oh, Ali!" Mahrokh cried. But now a few strings on the other side were not tight enough, and a granddaughter, just back from school, had to tear a piece of paper from a notebook, which Sarah folded and slid between the strings and the beam.

She was running her fingers over the warp, muttering to herself, not quite satisfied yet, when Leila stopped by on her way home from school. Two young women had arrived in the village from Isfahan or Tehran or maybe even the holy city of Qum, she reported, to teach Koran and religious studies to girls and women over the summer, without a salary, for the love of God . . . "There are good people in this world, by Holy Abbas," she said. They were to live in one of the smaller classrooms in the girls' school, alone by themselves, and had brought with them all necessities for setting up house, a kerosene stove for cooking and a teapot and such, but so far no one had been able to take a good look at them. They were totally enveloped in black and nothing at all showed but one eye:

Leila demonstrated this, to everybody's amusement. Even she, a practiced veil-wrap user of the new, strict way, failed to keep the wrap in place while moving her head. One of the two women, she said, had glasses, and both wore blue jeans and dusty sneakers—that much one could observe with some luck. They spoke very softly with voices like little girls, like the announcer on the children's program on television, but when a man approached, the janitor or a teacher or even only a boy, a sort of little boy, Leila said, who still thinks his birdie is only there to pee, the women would turn around completely and stop talking altogether. The granddaughters said that this was all true; they had seen them move through the bazaar, two figures of solid black. They wore gloves, a girl in school whose father was a shopkeeper had told them, so that not even their hands would be visible to men. Sarah was so astounded she forgot the warp.

Mahrokh grinned until her eyes were mere slits above her high, puffy cheeks. "If they looked at me," she said, "they would call me a heathen. White scarf," she enumerated, plucking at it, "hair showing in front, hair showing at the sides" (she wore the twisted sidelocks of married women), "and if one wants to one can even see the braids—here, and here."

"And the neck, if you throw your head back like this," said her older daughter. "Don't do this." She was annoyed with her mother for making fun of the new dress code. Even Miss Salimi told her students they had to be true soldiers of Islam and make sure their mothers and grandmothers at home complied with God's orders. But her mother was unteachable. And Grandmother—well, at least she wore the dark clothes of an old woman.

"One wonders who is right," said Leila, "the two religion teachers or Miss Salimi, who goes around in the village and visits her students—she came to my brother's house the other day, just like that, and last weekend she went on an outing to the White Spring with two other teachers from the school and their husbands!"

"We will find out in the other world," said Sarah's sister, pressing her aching temples. "Until then all kinds of men will try to make fools of us."

"Well," said Leila, "at least I will recognize Miss Salimi if I meet her in the next world—the two religion teachers I won't know unless they keep their veils." There was nodding and grinning all around.

Sarah's sister got up. "Ow, ow, ow," she moaned. Rolling her eyes and clutching her throbbing head, she climbed the staircase and disappeared.

Sarah was squatting behind the head beam, rummaging in a gunny sack with balls of white cotton and colored wool yarn. "Orange!" she said, "Look at this, a breadcloth does not have orange, as if Abi didn't know better." She wound several loops of white cotton yarn over her palm and elbow, wrapped some around the skein at one end, tested the warp again and the heddles, groped for the beater (she was sitting on it), murmured "In the name of God the Merciful" by way of a blessing, and pushed the first weft through the sheds, separating them with her free hand, about two spans at a time. A new breadcloth was under way.

Her visitors had seen her do this many times without getting tired of it. It was something to watch endlessly, Banu said with some regret as she picked up her crying baby and headed for home. Leila too rose to walk with her. Just when they had disappeared behind Sarah's son's house, two black figures emerged from the shade of the thicket beneath the poplar trees, moving slowly along the path. Sarah had no difficulty recognizing them. As Leila and her granddaughters had said, one could see nothing but black. For a moment they seemed to hesitate, and Sarah thought they might move over to her as many a passerby had done, but they turned suddenly and picked up speed again. Sarah's brother was descending the staircase behind her. "Poor girls," Sarah said, "running from an old man." Their veils were trailing the ground. Every step stirred up a little cloud of dust behind them. Alone for once, Sarah felt exposed and not quite proper, sitting in broad view, naked, so to speak, without her veil-wrap.

"They should be home with a husband and children," said her brother. Sarah thought he was right. So many young men killed in the war—what was this country coming to if young women like these two and Miss Salimi were made to walk among strangers, alone, in the name of religion? She looked over to the tired orchard where her granddaughters had taken their stitchery. "Who knows?" she thought, "Maybe they too will be like them one day." For Sarah, a lot was amiss in the world.

Later, towards evening, after Sarah had decided to quit for the day, Mahrokh tied a blue bead onto the tripod against the evil eye.

One had better beware of strangers who were unsparing with dangerous praise and admiration.

It is no hardship to weave a breadcloth without help, because it is only hands wide and except for the two ends the weave is simple, in white, interrupted only by a few rows of colored lattice- and diamond-shaped patterns (called "cow's stomach" and "flower"). By midafternoon the next day, having spent the morning in the bath, Sarah had finished the linenweave stripes of red and green and the damaskweave in blue and white, which mark the beginning. She was working on the first row of latticed rectangles (blue, purple, green, and pink) by the time Nargez had hung washed fleece on the hedge to dry and had joined her for a short visit. Keeping somebody company who was working on a lonely job had religious merits. "I talked to the two Koran teachers yesterday as they were walking by," she told Sarah. "They were out for a walk, they said." Sarah and Nargez looked at each other. Sarah shrugged her shoulders and Nargez raised a thin eyebrow quizzically.

The granddaughters came back from school and headed straight for the teapot in their utility-kitchen-living room. A little later, Sarah had no difficulty recognizing Miss Salimi as she moved along the path in a graciously flowing, shiny black wrap, nor did she guess wrong when she asked whether the lady had come to visit her granddaughters. Miss Salimi insisted on sitting outside though, with Sarah, to watch her weave ("Never have I seen this, I swear," she said. "Please let me watch, I beg of you, and forgive the trouble I am causing you"), and therefore a rug for her to sit on was dragged over from the house hurriedly. Mahrokh got the fancy tea glasses and a stainless steel tray out and dispatched the younger daughter to the store for cookies and the older one to brew fresh tea. In no time, a dozen or so children and four more women had congregated, and Miss Salimi was being grilled, politely but firmly. She spoke in the hard-to-understand, melodious drawl of the northerners, but was so polite and friendly and refined, and made so many nice remarks about the girls and about Sarah's work (which slowed down considerably during all this), that everybody was charmed.

"Aren't you lonely?" she asked Mahrokh when she learned that her husband was working in Kuwait. When Sarah's sister answered with a proverb ("A happy life: No wife to choose your food. A happy life: No man to answer to"), she laughed in a pearly giggle that Sarah's little granddaughter tried to imitate for days. There were noises of pity and sorrow when she said she had only one brother and one sister, and general commotion and consternation when she announced—in answer to a blunt question from Leila's mother-in-law—that she did not yet have a fiancé. City people were truly strange.

The two older granddaughters—the alleged objects of the visit—stayed in the back, not uttering a word. Their little sister, however, squeezed herself between her grandmother and the sack with yarn and stared at the lady unabashedly. In the evening she gave a much appreciated performance of the funny way in which Miss Salimi moved her mouth every which way while talking and pursed her lips when she was listening, and of her bouncy, high-heeled hop-walk with tiny steps.

After the party was over and Miss Salimi had left under many blessings and assurances of mutual respect, Sarah voiced a reasonable opinion: "The lady goes around the village to find a husband," she said.

Before Sarah was halfway through her breadcloth the school year was over, Koran school had started, and the fasting month was upon them. The two Koran teachers were fasting, of course, despite the special hardships of a summer fast: no food or drink, not so much as a drop of water on your tongue, from before sunrise to after sundown. Sarah's granddaughters fasted, even the youngest one, who was barely ten. When they tried to get their fourteen-year-old brother to fast, he shrugged his shoulders. He had to work, he said. Fasting was for idle women who had nothing to do all day. This, of course, was a wrong, heathen notion: a fasting true believer, the religion teacher had said, will be given the strength to work at any task, under any circumstances, by God. The girls, however, slept after their heavy early-morning meal until well into the day and then hung around, listless, weak, with parched lips, stinking from the mouth. Mahrokh and Sarah teased and scolded them. The oldest girl said she did not dare to break the fast, because if somebody would tell on her she might get into troubles in school; she wanted to try out for the teacher training college, and not fasting would be seen as moral weakness. But after the second one fainted, Mahrokh refused to wake her daughters any more. She said she would rather be guilty of that sin than of hurting the health of her children. The youngest, who was in summer school with the bespectacled religion teacher, was glad and embarrassed at the same time. Sarah said that if the teacher asked her, she should say that her parents did not wake her up and it was their fault, not hers. But she preferred to lie and to pretend she was still fasting. By then, Miss Salimi had gone home for vacation, and no one knew whether she fasted or not. "Probably not, though," Mahrokh said.

Nargez, sitting at the foot of the loom with fleece to be plucked and fluffed, agreed. "People in the cities fast less," she said. "They pretend to, but they don't. I was the only one last year in the house we were living in, and the others made fun of me. I was almost glad when I got the ulcer and the doctor told me I should not fast." For half a year Nargez had lived in Shiraz while her husband was working on a construction job there. Now she was a local authority on life in the city.

"The two new doctors from Mashhad don't fast either," said Mahin, who had a kidney problem and was down at the clinic often. "They told Abi she had the miscarriage because she was fasting."

"Tsk, tsk, tsk," clucked Sarah. The breadcloth she was working on was for Abi's oldest daughter.

"They also told me not to fast, but I have obeyed the rules of the Prophet since I was a little girl, and I still do, no matter what the doctor says," Mahin said defiantly. She was in a belligerent mood because after seeing a pair of men's shoes outside Banu's door she had not dared to follow through with her intended visit and had turned back. (Later it turned out that they belonged to Qeta, who had fallen asleep in Banu's kitchen.) Stopping at Aunt Sarah's had been a second choice.

"If it is bad for your health," Nargez defended her position, "you should not fast—it is a sin to fast. That's what the mullahs say in Shiraz."

"Right, right," cried Mahrokh. She was a picture of health, but during the month of fasting the aches and pains in her arms and legs got so bad that fasting was out of the question. "Somebody has to work around here," she said, looking meaningfully at her daughters.

The girls were quiet. Somehow, the arguments they learned in religion class (by rote, out of a book) did not quite fit what people at home were talking about. "If not fasting is such a sin," said Nargez, "then many more men will go to hell than women. In town, the men even went on smoking—they kept cigarette boxes in their socks under the pants so that nobody would see them. One man in our house was searched in the street by a revolutionary guard and taken to their station. His wife went after him and pleaded with them and got him out again."

"Served him right," cried Mahin.

"And what about her?" said Mahrokh, "and what about his children?"

"Indeed," said Sarah, pounding a weft down firmly with the heavy, iron-toothed and iron-plated beater. She had no desire to travel to a city, except Mashhad. It was a dear wish of hers to make the pilgrimage and see the glories of Imam Reza's shrine. With her son in Kuwait and an indifferent husband, however, her chances of being taken there were slim . . . unless she would go alone. "I am glad to live in the village," she said.

"Well spoken," Nargez said with feeling. "I told my husband I would return to my father if he would not take us back home. Here, at least, I have my own house, and not just a tiny filthy room in a filthy house full of filthy strangers, and I have chickens, and I can keep a goat, if he ever gets around to finishing the barn, and my children can be out in the streets without me getting nervous. In Shiraz, just to get bread every morning took me an hour waiting in line, and then the baker would only give me four pieces and I had to go back in the afternoon again. My neighbor had two big boys, and they pretended not to belong together, so they each got three or four and had enough for the day. And the bread was so bad—salty, doughy inside, and burnt outside. I think it was the bread that gave me the ulcers."

"Like the bread of the Isfahani baker in Hassanabad?" Mehri suggested. She had been at her brother's new house and had taken the longer but less crowded path past the walnut tree. She felt she still had some time to spare to sit with Aunt Sarah, a relative on her father's side. Sarah had never eaten the baker's bread, but the girls said it was not bad; he put sesame seeds on it. The other day, though, a health inspector came and closed his bakery again because there were so many flies.

"Then he better close up the whole village!" cried Mahrokh, "If it is for the flies."

"Yeah, Aunt Sarah, watch out, if the health inspector sees the flies around here he will close your loom," said Nargez, fanning herself with her fleece.

Sarah kept pounding on the weave. "No one has to eat what I make," she said. "The health inspector, with all respect . . . "

"The health inspector should go to Shiraz and see what is going on there!" Nargez said. "Half the time we had no water, and the other half the lights were out and the refrigerator. Here I don't have one and I don't need one; we have cool water here. In Shiraz we had one, but what is the use if it is down all day long? There was so little water we had to get up at midnight to fill a few bottles, because come morning there would be only a trickle, and at noon it was all gone. Speaking of flies! The children had diarrhea all the time, and the doctor said it was because of the flies and the dirt, and we should wash their hands more often. 'With what?' I asked him. 'Bottled lemonade?' But what could he do?"

"The war," said Mahin, but no one wanted to talk about this.

"Setara is making eyes at the Isfahani baker," said Mehri. "I saw her myself. She is down there all the time, as if she couldn't bake her own bread."

"And what did *you* have to do at the baker's?" said Mahrokh sharply.

"Ali sent me, because Golgol had no time to bake bread." Mehri's blank face belied a smirk.

"Young widows," Sarah murmured.

"Lies," said Mahin.

"The baker has a wife and children in Isfahan," said Sarah's grand-daughter. "Bibi told us in school. He is rooming with them. His wife does not want to live in a village, but he is making more money here than in Isfahan. He is hiring Bibi's brother."

"Maybe he is looking for a second wife here?" Mehri suggested. "It is easy now for a man to take another wife." This was met with pointed silence. Sarah's husband was looking for a second wife, and they all knew it. Mehri had been tactless.

The story was a short and familiar one. Sarah's first husband was killed in a battle shortly after her second child, Mahrokh's husband, was born. As was good and reasonable custom then, his brother Jomhur, as yet unmarried and much younger than Sarah, took her as his wife and brought up his own and his brother's children. They had five together, but his two sons died. Lately he had gotten restless. Sarah had always neglected him, he complained, although he had taken good care of her, and now she was treating him even worse. (It was generally understood that this meant she refused to sleep with him.) Sarah said she had had to support him with her income from the loom because he was lazy and only would hang around the house most of the time, and anyway, she was an old woman now. He had locked his radio and his clothes and his bedding into the bigger of their two rooms and announced he did not want her, he would find a better wife. Sarah was upset, and so were all her daughters and her son. They talked to both of their parents, pressing for a reconciliation, but to no avail. By now the family was split between those who were for him taking another wife and those who were against it, with the pro faction becoming more numerous. His youngest daughter, after seeing him cook his own dinner rice one day (his own choice, said Sarah; he refused to eat with her), was criticizing her mother and scouting for a wife for her father quite openly. However, since no one in the village was willing to give him a wife—out of respect for Sarah, said her supporters—he left to find a bride elsewhere. Rumor had it that Amene's brother, his son-in-law, was trying to find one in the village where he was teaching. Amene, who had been a frequent visitor at Sarah's loom, did not dare go there now.

Mehri, either oblivious to the dampening effect of her blunder or in an unfortunate attempt to cover her mistake with an anecdote, made matters worse. "At least you are well off," she said to Sarah, who kept a stony face behind the tripod. "You have your son and Mahrokh and you earn your own money. Yesterday at the doctor's Setara told us about this relative of the gendarme's wife who is renting a room in her house—she is from somewhere east of Shiraz, and her cousin's husband wanted a second wife but she did not agree, and then he wanted to divorce her but did not want to pay the divorce money. So he beat her up and at night stuck needles into her and burnt her with a poker, until in the end she agreed to a divorce without severance pay. Now she has absolutely nothing and goes begging." The pause after this story was even heavier. Mehri pulled her veil-wrap across a flushed face.

Nargez, never short of words nor themes to talk about, saved the situation. "The gypsy blacksmiths are here, Aunt Sarah," she cried, gesticulating with her wool-covered hands in the direction towards Hassanabad. "I saw their tents and heard their 'bang bang' when I was at the doctor's yesterday with Maryam; here, look how bad the eczema on her cheeks is, but there is no medicine, the doctor said. I'll have to take her to Mortesa—his spit really helps. You should get yourself a new beater at the blacksmiths'; the one you are using is all crooked."

"I need some more chamomile herbs," said Mahrokh hastily, getting up. "I am glad they are here—surely their women will come around the village again selling their stuff."

"They are Afghani blacksmiths," said a granddaughter darkly.

"No, no, no," Nargez cried, horrified, "that would be bad. I am sure, not. If there are Afghanis among them, I won't let my children out of the house. There was this neighbor of mine in Shiraz, and she swore it was a true story; she said she was going on the bus somewhere, and there was a woman wrapped round and round in a veil sitting next to her with a baby clutched against her. Now this neighbor of mine started wondering why the child did not make a sound, and did not move, and in the end she said something to that woman, but she just shrugged her shoulders and shook her head, like she did not understand her. My neighbor got suspicious and told the bus driver, and in the end—now I tell you, by the life of my son Hassan, I swear this is what she said, it is true— in the end it turned out that it was a dead child which they had stolen, and killed, and all the innards taken out, like a chicken, and then they stuffed it with heroin to take someplace to sell. Afghanis are awful; they are filthy heathens. They also go around and break into houses . . . " But this was an anti-climax which drowned in the noise of wailing and clucking and shouting. The episode with Heidar Khan Afghani and Aftab was remembered in a new and sinister light. Mehri, who had been a neighbor of the Afghani workers, furnished the party with so many odd details of their life that the women wondered how in the world Mehri could know. As they often had before, they decided Mehri was a liar.

Sarah had kept working at full speed during all this, then paused and muttered a curse. She had made a mistake: on the left side she had missed the start of one of the diamond patterns a few rows earlier. It looked like a glaring blank space to her. "Never mind," said

Mahrokh, looking down on her. "Start one now, a small one—nobody will see the difference."

"Sure," said Mahin, gathering her veil to leave, "big or small, red or green, the whole thing will be caked with flour before they notice it. It is all the same to the dough."

Sarah was not convinced by these arguments but had no other choice. She felt discouraged and tired. "Enough for now," she said, and got up, supporting herself on the sack of wool.

A terrific screaming had started from the direction of Nargez's house. Nargez jumped up, ripping her skirt. "By God," she cried, "The devils are killing each other!" Shouting threats and curses, she rushed off, dragging little Maryam with her.

Sarah was stretching her bent back and locked knees. "Dear me, ow, ow," she groaned, but no one was left to pity her.

The next day Sarah did not get much done. When early in the morning word came that her second daughter was in labor, she went there straight from her bed. Even so, the baby was born already—her daughter's seventh, a little girl. Sarah reproached her daughter's in-laws severely for not sending for her earlier, but they said that her daughter herself had told them not to wake Sarah too early. Not that Sarah could have done much for her, anyway, they pointed out; her daughter was well taken care of by the midwife and the women in the house. Sarah hung around until noon, refused lunch because it was fasting month, and left for home when she felt hungry, thereby missing a drama that shook the village thoroughly.

A few weeks back a fight had started when a certain Khorshid had started to build a new house, only to find that Ata, a neighbor between himself and the road, would not yield him the right of way. Arguments were forwarded, documents of purchase of land produced, witnesses called. The case for and against both parties was thrown back and forth among the public agencies—from the newly established local citizen's court to the gendarmerie, to the county office, to the judge, to the governor's office—and each contradicted the other. That afternoon some members of Ata's faction fell upon Khorshid and knocked him bloody. After he was taken away to the doctor, the fight continued among the bystanders who had congregated in the road.

After a lunch of bread, green onions, and tea, Sarah resumed her position at the loom. She had heard distant noises of a commotion, but not knowing what was happening she stayed put, especially as she had found the whole neighborhood deserted. Not even a child was left to ask. The first one to emerge from the scene of upheaval was Bandar carrying his son and driving a sobbing Aftab in front of him: "Keep you mouth shut, be quiet, stop the racket," he hissed. "Maybe you have nothing to do at home, to walk around other people's houses? You should be ashamed . . . no honor . . . "

The two were almost instantly followed, at a brisker pace, by an elderly woman, a neighbor of Leila's, urging her limping husband along with the same words: "Old man has nothing better to do . . . ashes on my head for having to put up with a good-for-nothing husband . . . serves you right getting killed . . . "

This made Sarah very curious. She ran into the house for her veil-wrap to go see for herself what was going on when her grandson came hobbling in the door, holding his side and groaning, accompanied by Nargez's six-year-old son. An errant rock had hit him, an innocent bystander, in the ribs, he sputtered. He asked for water, and tea, and a cold compress, and lay down, assisted by his grandmother, who kept asking what and how and why. He managed to tell her what had been going on while she put a large adhesive bandage (from Kuwait) on his ribs; the battle was just about over, now that the fighters finally had been separated by level-headed, neutral onlookers. Nargez's son furnished details: "Ata," he said with satisfaction because he had a grudge against Khorshid's son, "Ata broke Khorshid's head, and then broke his arms and legs, and then ripped open his stomach, and blood was flowing from head to toe, and so they dragged him off to the doctor's."

Sarah was aghast. She did not dare leave her grandson, but she was on the lookout for more news, and when Nargez, Effat, and Banu were coming her way Sarah hailed them. Effat, related to Ata through her mother Mamalus the Storyteller, told her that the previous day Khorshid himself and, even more outrageous, his wife, seven months pregnant—heathens both—had taken shovel and pickaxe to the disputed wall Ata had put up to guard his property, but they found no one there to hinder them. Unchallenged, Khorshid went home disappointed, to return this afternoon, certain to find someone to fight with now. Meanwhile Ata had summoned two of his sons and his brother to help him restore the wall, and when Khorshid started foulmouthing them, assisted shamelessly by his wife, who had the dirtiest mouth in the county, they pushed him back, in the process of which he fell off his own wall and broke his skull. Nargez said, "Lie, all lies, not true" all through the narrative and was fairly shouting now. Loosely related to Khorshid's mother, she had heard quite a different story: Last night, she said, Ata and his sons had made the rounds of their relatives to ask for assistance in a final showdown with Khorshid which would end the matter once and for all, since the authorities had proven totally ineffective. Today, when Khorshid was heading for the minibus, to pursue his complaints in town like any good Muslim, Ata told him he wanted to make peace and he should come to the new house with him. There, however, Ata's relatives were waiting and beat Khorshid up. Surely, Ata would go to prison for this. Effat in turn accompanied this story with noises of disapproval, and now she and Nargez started a fight about who was right, and Banu and Sarah had to beg and reason and scold and talk honey to make them let go of each other. Nargez finally left in a huff when a familiar screaming from her house told her she better see to her own peace at home.

There were no winners to this fight, only losers. Some were pitied and some had ridicule added to their injury: Effat's eldest sister, who had spoken her mind at the top of her lungs at the scene of the fight, not only was pushed and pummeled by Khorshid's wife and had her hair pulled and scarf ripped by Tala, Khorshid's cousin, but at home, instead of finding commiseration, was scolded by her mother-in-law and slapped by her husband's brother for having mixed in an affair that was not hers. The whole neighborhood found this funny.

Sarah, who often said that the loom was a place of rest for her, of peace, where her thoughts cleared of worries, now found no solace in her work. Automatically she wrapped the selvage in a red and blue braidweave but then fidgeted. She repositioned the stretching stick that ran under the weave, fastened by a smooth-worn chicken bone on one side and a long iron needle at the other, and pushed back the tripod. "Fighting over a speck of land!" she murmured. "Never ever has there been such an indignity!"

"The citizen's court should have taken care of it before it could become a fight," said Banu. Sarah clicked her tongue disapprovingly.

Her oldest granddaughter was appointed to serve on this court. No wonder it was no good, if mere children were made judges, she said. Sad and worried, she fingered the bright pink yarn irresolutely, found fault with her scissors and the way the heddle sticks moved, tested the tension again, and promptly broke two warps. She gave up and left to look after her daughter and the new baby.

The next day, Thursday, the loom remained deserted because Sarah joined a group of other women for the weekly wailing session in the cemetery. The three "martyrs" of the village were mourned loudly with singing and crying, and the women not only remembered their own dead relatives but pitied themselves and each other and grieved for the hardships of this life. It was a time-consuming and exhausting outing which drained Sarah of any energy for work.

But on Friday Sarah was back at the loom in full swing when Setara, the young and spirited widow of an esteemed man from Tehran who had settled locally and had died not long ago (and now the ex-wife of Abbas the rapist as well), came along in the afternoon, recognizable from afar by her size and brisk gait. "May God grant you strength," she cried by way of a greeting, slightly breathless after the climb from her house way down beyond the road. When she sat at the foot of the loom with her many skirts spread around her, moving her body and her head and her hands as she talked, everything around her seemed to shrink. From under her well-worn and slightly faded veil-wrap she produced an old rice sack with yarns in different colors: orange, red, green, and blue, dyed by Begom's brother, who supplemented the meager income from his fields and his goats by this craft. The yarn was for a new backpack, Setara said, because her daughter—black death—had burnt a big hole into the old one, careless, oh, so careless the children nowadays; and Aunt Sarah could work on it whenever she cared to, the sooner the better, but there was no hurry. Next from under her veil appeared a small plastic bag with sugar, cut up and ready for use, and a smaller one yet with tea. (Cash for the work would be paid upon delivery.) Sarah, seemingly ignoring this, murmured that Setara should not have troubled herself for Sarah's worthless work. Setara also brought news about Khorshid: he was released from the hospital in town and was home again. His injuries were not serious, his mother had told her, but his wife swore she would not rest until the whole Ata family was in jail. She was fairly raging, Setara reported. It was very unhealthy for her. The child surely would be born with some defect—bad parents, worse children.

"The whole family is bad," said Leila. She had seen Setara walk purposefully in the direction of Sarah's rhythmic, ringing pounding, had collected her veil and her little one and followed her. Sarah's loom was neutral ground, and she had not seen Setara in a long while. "My mother-in-law says that at the fight yesterday Ata's brother dropped his pants and shouted he would do such and such to Khorshid's wife if she did not shut up." Setara gave a suppressed hoot.

Sarah put down her reed, mirth and alarm fighting in her mild face. Chuckling slightly, she cried, "Unheard of! Rude! Shameful!"

But Leila said she was sorry she had missed it, and Setara said she was too, and knowing what she did about the men in Ata's family, she believed it. "They are vulgar, like Abbas," said Leila.

This reminded Setara that she also had news about Abbas and Turan. She had it fresh from her roomer, the gendarme's wife, that Abbas had been caught while visiting (or hiding) with a relative who was living in a village on the road to Isfahan. It seemed that somebody had seen him there and denounced him, and Abbas then was tricked into leaving his hideout by the clever lie that his mother was very ill and promptly was arrested by the gendarmes. Now he was in jail awaiting his trial. "I hope they won't make Turan marry him," she said, "he is bad all over. And I hope I'll get my divorce-payment now . . . "

"Most young men are bad," Leila sighed.

"Some are worse, though," said Setara, eyes sparkling under her famous, high-arching brows. "This Miss Salimi, now, I tell you— Khalil's eldest son, you know, the one who works down at the clinic . . . "

"Oh, yes," cried Leila, "he is the handsomest of Khalil's children . . . "

"He is after Miss Salimi. Really, Aunt Sarah, I swear, you can believe me, I have seen him with my own eyes; listen: he is hanging around outside her window all the time to see a glimpse of her . . . "

Leila was laughing. "The window is too small and too high," she giggled. "He won't see anything, but just the clinking of her tea glasses will make him die of craziness." Sarah moved back on the loom, tying in green yarn for the last row of diamonds. She was not surprised—she herself had said that Miss Salimi was looking for a husband.

"Huh, huh," whispered Setara, bending over so that she almost came to lie on the loom, "and he got on the same minibus with her when she left. Now I say. . ."

"Pssst," said Sarah, who had seen her youngest granddaughter walk over from the house with a tray of rice. (She had to fill in for her mother, who was out harvesting lentils.)

Setara could shift gears in midsentence. She straightened up and faced the girl. "Now, this will be a good bride," she cried, slapping her on the knee such that the rice jumped on the tray. The girl blushed, hid her face in the folds of her wide, dark scarf, and muttered indignantly. "Never mind," Setara cried, chuckling and slapping her again. "Your time will come soon enough!" The girl abandoned the tray and ran back to the house.

"She is touchy," Sarah explained, "because she is fasting again. Her black Koran-teacher-lady promised her a new black veil-wrap because she is such a good student . . . well . . . "

"Making widows of young girls," said Setara. She picked up the tray and started to clean the rice, over Sarah's protest. Leila's little daughter was playing with her mother's braids, with pebbles, with the rice, and with the yarn in Setara's bag; she was shooed from one after the other and finally toddled away towards the path where Nargez's two sons and three more kids were fighting loudly over a young sparrow tied by its legs to a string. "Mashhadi Fatima," Setara cried after her, "Hello, Mashhadi, I will be your servant, don't run away . . . "

" 'Mashhadi' indeed," said Leila. She herself had made the pilgrimage a year ago with her husband, all their children and her mother-in-law, at the pesky old woman's insistence. It had cost a fortune—a year's worth of her salary, she had figured out resentfully. "Avdal and Tamas left for Mashhad this morning with Hakime and Golperi and Simin," she said. "Simin talked Avdal—he is gaga over her—into going. Now we will have to call loudmouth Simin 'Mashhadi.' "

"Their fate is kind," said Setara. "I wish I had somebody to take me. What about you, though, Aunt Sarah? When will you go? Your daughter told me they want to do the pilgrimage—her husband likes you well enough, he'll take you."

Sarah swung her beater with confidence. "I'll go as soon as I have the old man off my back," she said. "You'll see." And she dismissed the old man with an upward flick of her hand.

The old man was off her back sooner than she had figured. She had just put in the last row of colored lattices on the breadcloth and was working on the final repeat of stripes at the end when Amene's husband received word from his brother, Sarah's son-in-law (through a man peddling rugs from that village), that they had found a wife for Jomhur and would bring her shortly. The girl, the stranger volunteered, was a very good girl—a little older, and not at all flighty (this translated as ugly or impaired in some way)—and her people would not ask much bride price for her, they were good people (that meant poor and in no position to be choosy), and she would take good care of him, for sure. Amene passed the word to Mamalus and Effat, who in turn told Banu and Mahin. By the time Mahrokh and Sarah's daughters tactfully broke the news to Sarah she had picked up enough rumors to take it more calmly than other members of the family, who were divided still and arguing hotly.

Amidst a hubbub of coming and going, of discussions, accusations and discontent, the granddaughters helped Sarah carry her belongings past the loom to their house: a bundle of clothes, a few bags, pots and pans—old, well worn (the new bride would bring her own, bought by her father with the money Jomhur had given as a bride price, although Sarah wondered where he had gotten it), her bedding and her new henhouse with the three chickens. She left the gas burner for the new wife because she pitied her, a poor girl from the back of beyond, and did not need it in her son's house. She would eat at his tray and sleep with her granddaughters now, not as a guest but as a permanent member of her son's household.

Sarah was not left alone a minute. People came to pity her, to cheer her up, to curse her husband, to remind her that she was well liked and respected by a large family; she had nothing to be afraid of. Her eldest daughter urged her to come to Mashhad with them— they would leave as soon as the alfalfa hay was in. One granddaughter tried her religion teacher's sermon on the subject: "If a man desires a second wife, and if he can take care of two wives adequately, and if he provides for both equally, and if he treats them equally, and if he divides his time and attention equally between them, and if he does not prefer one above the other, then his first wife commits a sin if she resents it." But the reactions to this were not what her religion teacher had made her expect. Mahin snorted irreverently; Sarah's sister said no man had ever done this; and Nargez said that it amounted to an awfully heavy bag of "ifs." Sarah's sister then recited a proverb about the unpredictable ways of a bride: "A bride's fate is written on her forehead by God. Just wait and see," she said.

Into the final rows of the breadcloth was woven the much-voiced opinion that it was a cruel fate for an elderly woman to be saddled with a young co-wife, and for a young woman to be brought to a strange village as the second wife of an elderly husband. "It is not her fault," everybody said, "only bad luck."

Finally finished after the many delays, Sarah cut the breadcloth off the loom with her blunt scissors. She shook it thoroughly, folded it up, threw it onto a pile of wheat bags in the corner of her son's porch, and sent word to Abi that it was ready to be picked up. She dismantled the loom and stored the beams along the porch wall of her son's house with the help of Nargez and Mahrokh. Now the place under the walnut tree looked strangely deserted and clean, with tufts of colored wool floating in the wind amidst the surrounding rocks and garbage, but only for a day or two. When an old, battered pickup truck arrived with Jomhur and his bride and her meager belongings, welcomed in a subdued way by some of his daughters and sisters (who had even cooked a good dinner for them), the shady patch under the walnut tree lost all traces of a special place. Sarah, so as not to be in the path of her new co-wife, planned to set up the loom in her son's garden under the small apple trees. She would have fewer visitors there but more privacy. But before that she would make the journey to Mashhad with her son-in-law and her daughter, paying her own way with the loom money she had hidden in her clothes bundle.

She would be a pilgrim first and worry about everything else later.

10

Setara, Six Proposals, Four Engagements, and Three Husbands the Wiser

What a weak and skinny little girl I was once—hard to believe now, but I well remember how I suffered when I carried the heavy waterbag down from the well, two, three times a day. Although I did not fill it to the top, it sat so heavily on my hip that I was bent double by the time I got home.

I was tough, even then. A whole summer long I kept house for my father and my uncle and my cousins, baking bread and washing clothes at the water channel, and lugging water, and cooking rice and sweeping the floor, everything, while my mother and my uncle's wife with the younger children were tending the sheep and goats in the mountains. I must have been no more than eight or nine then—so lightweight that the wind once almost blew me off our roof. I was not much to look at either, I am sure—thin, tired, braids matted like felt, lice on my head, rags on my skinny bones. But my father's eldest sister watched me work—watched, not helped—and saw how industrious I was and how capable, and decided she wanted me as a bride for one of her sons. One day my mother gave me a new red shirt and a new skirt and a new scarf, and I was very glad about it the way dumb children are. The clothes were from my fiancé, but Mother only said they were a gift from my father's sister. I did not like the aunt much, but I liked to show off in my new clothes. When Huri, who was a neighbor, teased me about my fiancé, I beat her up.

Years later, my mother told me that my aunt had wanted to take me to their house right away, but Mother could not spare me, so my parents stalled. They said, "after the harvest," and "after the grape syrup is cooked" (for days we were stirring the huge pots), and "after the mourning period for this old man or that old woman is over," and such. My aunt got more and more impatient, but meanwhile one of their sons had gone away to study to become a teacher, and one of their daughters married into the landlord's family—this was before the land reform, when the chiefs were still big and powerful. Actually, they were related to the landlords in some remote way (which had not kept them from being poor like us), but now all of a sudden they remembered their position and started to make themselves "big." For example, whenever my aunt or her husband entered a room, especially my aunt, their children rose in greeting. It showed great respect. And when *they* got up, whoever else happened to be there had to stand too, whether they wanted to or not, out of politeness. And they started to call her "Lady," even amongst themselves, and to hang around the chief's house and to call him "Khan." I was too little to notice, but people have told me. My aunt has others call her "Lady" to this day; "Lady Mahvash," indeed, the toothless ogress.

The cousin I was supposed to marry went to high school in the city. This was very expensive and unusual then. The boys had to go away and live in some hovel, for an outrageous rent, fending for themselves. Being suddenly much better than us, and hoping for more wealth and honor yet, my aunt decided I was no longer good enough for my fiancé. She had her eyes set on one of the chief's sons' daughter, and my former fiancé indeed married her at last. They dropped me. My mother was furious but I was glad. My mother says they even tried to get back the gifts they had given me . . . stingy, stingy, even if it is my father's sister.

All this happened before I had any brains, before I knew anything of this world, anything but how to cook rice and fetch water and such things. Whenever we could get away from our mothers and their endless chores we would play, five, six of us girls. Leila was one of them, and Mahin's sister, and Huri and her sisters. We would go from house to house around the neighborhood and chant, "A dry house is full of mouseshit," over and over, until the people in the house gave us a handful of flour. When we had enough we hid in a garden and made a dough with a pebble in it and baked a thick, soft pancake over a fire. The hardest part was getting matches for the fire. Usually we had to steal a few live coals from somebody's fireplace. The bread we divided into pieces, one for each of us. And whoever bit on the pebble was in trouble: we would grab her by her arms and legs and bang her butt against a tree or a wall. That's why this game is called "Butt on Butt." Leila always cried when she was "it." Once she even swallowed the pebble, she was so afraid.

We lived in our old courtyard then: seven, eight rooms on top, barns below. Dirt wherever one looked, with all the animals milling around in the yard. On the far end of the half-circle lived a cousin of my father. He had a wife who kept running away for seven years. She would leave, and then they would bring her back and after a few days she would run away again, for no apparent reason. She just did not want him. In the end she killed herself—hanged herself in the barn by a calf rope. My mother found her. It gave her such a fright that even now she won't go into a barn alone. Since then we keep a good medicine against fright at home. Mashhadi Janjan gave us the recipe: saffron, turmeric, caraway seeds, galangal, dried balls of a wild ram, mixed together and well ground in a mortar with soot from an iron kettle. One drinks it with water, heated with a hot iron. Leila took the rest we had when her mother-in-law's heart stopped because Leila's little daughter fell off the porch. Maybe the blacksmith women have wild rams' balls for sale—around here there are no more wild goats.

A few weeks after his wife had killed herself, my father's cousin sent for me. My father said no and my mother said no. But he was insistent and came again and again. He helped my father cut wood, and lent him a donkey to get our hay in faster, and offered to help him thrash the wheat . . . in the end he made it impossible for my parents to say no to him. I was about ten or eleven then, before I even had my first period, but I had grown quite a bit and no longer was so weak and skinny. I cried and screamed and kicked and scratched and bit like a cornered cat, but they just beat me up, my mother and my father did. My sister cried with me. My father's brother, when it came to sign the marriage contract, even clobbered me with his rifle butt until I said yes. Mashhadi Yedulla lived in the next courtyard, the most pious and knowledgeable man in religious matters. He heard me cry and he told my father that it was a sin to give me into marriage if I did not agree. But my folks and everybody else said that it had nothing to do with the girl. What does a girl know? Can an ignorant child judge a man? Indeed, they are right, I say now. Leila was not forced into marriage, and yet she and her husband fight a lot. And Amene's sister, the one who is a teacher, she married late, and no one forced her, but they were fighting so badly—mostly over her salary—that he divorced her.

As to myself, I just had this aversion . . . I mean, I did not even know what it meant to be husband and wife. I thought it meant to get new clothes and to get bangs cut, and musicians drumming for a dance, and to be taken to a different house on a mule and somehow to get children. I had no idea about anything, only how to work in the house and how to play. I could also spin, but not very well. I never learned to do this as well as my mother.

The man was much older than I. I had called him "Uncle," like his own nephews and nieces who lived there. And I did not like his mother either. She and my mother did not get along very well. The day they came for me there was a feast, and the women sat around, singing, and the little girls were dancing. We were too poor to hire musicians. I was taken to the bath and a lot of fuss was made over a new set of clothes. The barber's wife packed the palms of my hands in henna paste to color them red, and lined my eyes with mascara— soot and grease, which you smeared all over yourself if you touched it. I was sitting at home not daring to move, with my hands clasped to keep the henna from cracking and flaking until it was washed off eventually. The barber's wife, who cut my bangs and side-locks and bathed and dressed me, hung a necklace of glass beads around my neck and one made of cloves and wild cherry pits dyed red and green and blue. It kept its nice smell for years. She also put a red velvet cap with tiny glass beads and a few small gold coins on my head. The cap is gone now—no one wears these things anymore— and the gold coins are gone too. One I have kept for my daughter or a bride, if I can hang on to it long enough.

The women were singing and ululating. Oh, how many weddings I have been to since—the best dancer in the village I was! And I know more songs and I can ululate longer and louder than any other woman. No use for such skills now. Quiet as the graveyard the weddings are, except that this is not true either: now there is more going on in the graveyard than in the village. The world is topsy turvy.

They had to lock the bridal chamber after me, or else I would have run away, new clothes and all. I screamed and yelled and tore up the bedding. It was not necessary though, because it turned out that he could not do anything.

I was too young and too ignorant then to know what happened, or better what did not happen. All I know is that next morning I went home. They dragged me back the following evening, and in the morning I went home again. This went on for a while. And then his family and my family started to fight, and everybody left me alone. His people accused my mother of having tied his penis by black magic. It is a great sin to do such a thing, and nobody in Deh Koh does black magic now, but there are plenty of evil people in Deh Rud . . . once in a while if a girl is married off while she is still very young and her mother feels sorry for her, the mother will ask somebody to do this. My people said that it was not us who had tied him, but that instead his dead wife's mother had tied *me* because she wanted him to marry another of her daughters, she liked him. Now the fight spread to his dead wife's people. It went on for two years. And we were right, because finally he let me be, we returned all the gifts (my wedding outfit my mother wisely had put away so that I would not ruin it), and he married his dead wife's sister and had six children with her, right away. His mother-in-law clearly had untied me when he let go of me, and everything was all right. Only the person who does such an evil thing as tying somebody can remove the tie.

He divorced me, but this was no big deal; we had no children, I was still a virgin, my parents did not insist on the payment of the divorce money. I don't even know how much had been written into the marriage contract, if any at all. At that time there was not much divorce, and especially poor people like us did not pay much attention to the divorce money. In any case, now as then, not long after a woman is married her husband will say, "Pardon the divorce money."

If she does not, and he dies, in the other world it will hang around his neck like a rope. It is bad. It shows that his wife distrusted him or that maybe he did not treat her well. So he will ask her to pardon it. She will say, "What will you give me for pardoning it?" And then she can bargain for something: a gold coin, a cow, whatever. That is, if she is clever. If she is a humble, pious, quiet woman, she will say, "A holy Koran," or she won't ask for anything at all. Some women pardon it at the deathbed of the husband. This is a little better than not forgiving it at all, but still not so good for the dead husband. Not to pardon it at all is a sin for a woman, the people say. I don't know. I'll find out soon enough, because I pardoned mine only at the deathbed of my husband. Nowadays some women who want to appear especially pious will not write any divorce payment at all into the contract. Mehri told me that Golgol's payment is one kilogram of fly legs. This means her people want to play up to his family; they give them a lot of honor. I don't know if this is true, though. Leila says it is not, and Mehri often is telling lies. But in the city they now write divorce money of hundreds of thousands of Toman into the contracts. Of course, men then find all kinds of ways to keep their wives from collecting if they want to divorce them. Nargez knows quite a few such stories. Because if it is the woman who asks for a divorce, and she is lucky enough to find a sympathetic judge who will see her point and grant it, then she forfeits the divorce settlement. Amene's sister never got a single penny of the divorce money in her contract—all only on paper, because he made life such a hell for her that she actually asked for the divorce. And she had to go to court three times, all on her own money. What if she had not had a salary, I ask?

Although I had been spoken for twice and married once by the time I was about twelve, my younger sisters were really married before I was. People in the village were afraid to come for me after what had happened to my first husband. In the end it was a stranger who asked for me, some three or four years later. By then I was almost as tall as I am now, and no longer skinny. A man from Hassanabad made a song about my eyebrows—he did not put my name in, but I knew it was about me. My mother was worried because I was not married. I had to be very careful about everything so that people would not gossip about me. My father did not even let me go to the evening school for illiterate women which was started under the old regime; Leila taught it for a while and Amene's sister, and Aunt Sarah's youngest daughter, all women we are either related to or know very well. There were no strangers in these classes, but my father still did not let me go. He was also worried because I had no brothers—my father had only one son, and he died—so I really had no one to look after me except my father, and fathers get old and die eventually. I was fifteen or sixteen, and people whispered that I was "old." Nowadays there are many older unmarried girls in the village, and no one says anything, but then ... then it was seen as odd, as a flaw, as bad. Leila was not married yet, but she was in the teacher training college and had a fiancé. Only I was left, and Mahin, but no, she is younger than I am. At that time, the young men in the village took local girls as wives. Nowadays they travel all over and get married to outsiders. Take Khalil's son—he followed Miss Salimi all the way to Tehran, and this morning his father and his mother left to go there. This means he is going to marry her. And meanwhile Mahin and Effat and Mehri and most of the girls in high school and a dozen others are without a fiancé. No wonder that our daughters sit at home, doing nothing but stitchery. Iran surely is self-sufficient in needlework now!

There was this man from the north working at the hospital in town. His name was Tehrani, but he was not really from Tehran; he was from a small city in Azerbaidjan, and he spoke Turkish better than Farsi. In Turkish, he said, my name was Yildiz, which means *star*—how pretty. He was educated, and strong, not a young lad but wise and knowledgeable, and well traveled. He had seen something of the world in his jeep. Of all places he liked the mountains best, he said, especially around Deh Koh. I don't know how he came to try to buy land for a garden from my father's brother. It was fate. But my youngest cousin said the money should go to him because he was taking care of his father, and my uncle, who was old and decrepit by then, said he himself wanted it. Tehrani, who was a careful and wise man, did not want to get stuck in a family fight or to cause one—he was a real Muslim, a good man—and so he asked my father instead who owned the land next to the one he wanted. My father was getting old too and was tired of the work because he had no sons to help him, and so he sold that piece of land. At these occasions, when Tehrani was in our courtyard bargaining for the garden, he saw me. Then he asked around, and people told him that

I had had bad luck, that I was still a virgin, that I was a good and honorable girl and a good worker. Well, and that I was strong and good-looking with a white skin—then it was white; now I am dark from the sun because I have to work outdoors so much—that much he saw himself. A few times he also watched me dance at weddings, round and round with the other women—they all danced then except the old ones and women like Mashhadi Yedulla's wives and the mullah's wife, of course, no matter what they say now that it is forbidden—he watched me stepping like the best of them and waving my kerchiefs high, and he wanted me. All this he told me himself. He sent Mashhadi Yedulla, whose youngest son was working in the hospital office, to ask for me. It was done very properly, and I had nothing against him; I had none of the aversion I had felt in my heart against the other two. I say it was because I was older and wiser, but my mother says age has nothing to do with it—whether a girl gets along with her husband or not is entirely her fate. I just don't know. Our Prophet said a girl can be married when she is nine; the doctors and Tehrani and all the teachers and midwives under the old regime said a girl should not get married before she is fifteen. I only know I won't let my daughter go until she is fifteen, if I can help it at all.

Although my father did not really bargain hard for me—I think he was plainly glad to see me get married—Tehrani gave him a good bride price, and he and my father together (which is unusual, and people talked) did the shopping for my bride wealth. I had the first gas burner in the village, and the first pressure cooker—no, Amene's sister had the first one. This very rug I am sitting on . . . thick blankets . . . all good, expensive stuff from the city. The little blue rug on the wall over there is a silk rug from Nain. It is one of a pair; the lighter space is where the other one was hanging—I had to sell it last year. And this picture of Saint Mary with baby Jesus—it is so old, it is covered with flyspecks—this he brought for me from Tehran, and he brought one for my mother. She gave hers to my sister, though. But the picture of the battle of Kerbela with the white horse and the martyrs—the blood is painted as a tulip, so sad—this I bought myself from a poster peddler last spring. Next to the Imam Khomeini up there is a photograph of Tehrani himself; oh, how heavy my heart is when I look at it.

For saying "yes" to the marriage contract he gave me a golden bracelet of the kind only the teachers here wear, and earrings with red stones. I had to sell them; they are gone, no matter what people say about my gold. I danced at my own wedding—musicians played for two days—and my clothes were so pretty that many women copied them. The divorce money was eight thousand Toman, which was a lot of money then, about what a teacher could make in three years. Tehrani would never have divorced me, though. We got along very well, and I never heard a harsh word from him . . . well, almost never.

Ali's father—he wanted me to call him by his first name, but I never could bring myself to do this; I called him Tehrani or "Ali's father" after our first child was born—he was a widower. His first wife had died in childbirth, a sad story. It did not happen often here, thanks be to God. Leila's sister almost died when she had her first child. They took her to the city, in the middle of the night, an eight-hour drive, and she stayed for a long time. The doctor scolded her in-laws for allowing her to get pregnant so young. She was not more than thirteen then, and a real runt.

We lived in town for a while, in a row of townhouses the government had built for government employees. It was summer, and very hot and dusty, not cool and breezy like here. The houses had tin roofs which the hot wind was clanging and banging on. During the rains in winter the din was deafening. And there were so many flies that I could have easily provided divorce money for three Golgols! There was a row of trees in front of the houses, and one in the back, but they were only knee-high then. My neighbors were strangers from all over the country. They were nice, most of them, but I did not feel at home there at all. My next-door neighbor I could hardly understand, and she could not understand me. Most were also dressed differently, and I felt embarrassed. When Ali was born and Ali's father saw that I had no help and was unhappy, he let me go back home. He was kind and reasonable. He built this house with his own hands, of sun-dried bricks like the old houses here but with a hall and an indoor shower like the most modern houses have now, and with nice plaster inside and outside—only that outside it has cracked and inside it is sooty and dirty, what can I do? He was very clever with his hands. His job in the hospital was to see to the equipment. He could build and repair everything; there are dozens of radios and clocks still in the village which he fixed.

The following summer he added the two back rooms with a separate entrance and their own toilet. Everybody wanted to rent from us because our place was so nice and clean. Tehrani even planted flowers. They didn't do too well, though, because of the chickens.

Our house was one of the first outside the village, in the fields. This, too, had been his idea. Everybody was afraid for us—there would be thieves, people said; it was dangerous. But in fact it was cooler, and we had fewer flies and less dust here. He was gone all day, and my sisters visited me and my mother, and slowly more and more people realized how much better life is out here and started to build their houses around us. Now it is almost as crowded here as the old village.

My father liked Tehrani—he planted the garden around the house for us and put in the irrigation ditches. Tehrani also was kind to him. He brought watermelons from town and good medicines for my father's weak heart and my mother's rheumatism, and he bought meat with his money and we ate it together. Now people say—and don't I know it!—that we fought a lot, that I did not honor him properly, that I was lazy and cheeky and whatnot, but this is not true. People were jealous of me because I had a nice, clean house and an understanding, educated husband—he even tried to teach me how to read and write, but I did not have enough leisure to practice, so it never amounted to much. Now I have more time, but in the illiteracy classes for women they teach only holy scriptures. I mean, I have nothing against the religion or studying the holy book, but it won't teach me how to read a doctor's prescription or to write an application for assistance to have the roof tarred.

People were also jealous, especially the women, because in town I had learned to cook all kinds of food, not only the good old rice and lentils and such. I know how to fix macaroni and meat balls and many kinds of soup and "Istanbuli rice," which now is served in every house, but at that time no one but me knew even what it was. Tehrani appreciated the food I cooked very much. And then the people were jealous because he bought me new clothes and I never had to beg for whatever I needed. And when our third child was a big, healthy boy again—Glory be to God—and not sickly and weak, people got even more jealous. And there is nothing more deadly than the wagging of tongues.

The winter before he died, when we had so much snow that Tehrani could walk down from the roof after he had swept it, I and the two older boys fell sick with a cough which almost killed us. Tehrani was very worried. I asked him to allow me to make a promise to visit the Imam Reza's shrine in Mashhad, and I pledged a pilgrimage to Bibi Masume. All three of us recovered overnight—a miracle—oh, the saints are so good to us. My pledge to Bibi Masume I fulfilled last year; I went there with my mother and all four children. But I still owe Imam Reza his visit because Tehrani could not take us there after all.

In early spring he started to feel sick for no reason whatever, and weak. His skin was pale; he lost weight. The doctor said he had cancer of the blood. We gave him so much blood . . . I gave him my own blood, and my sister's son gave blood, and my cousin, good Muslims all, but it was not God's will for him to live. He died in the hospital. My father held his head. When the people brought him back here and washed him, I pardoned the divorce money—my mother reminded me, bless her, or else I would be burdened with a grave sin. At the funeral I fainted, and the people thought I would die too, right there on the spot, next to his open grave where he lay swathed in the white shroud. Since then I start trembling with fright whenever I see something white, like a white shirt on somebody's back or sheets drying in the sun.

A few days later, when I still was feeling weak and very sad, and the mourning guests were coming and going, the wife of one of my cousins took me aside and asked me if I was pregnant. I said I did not know. She said we should go to town to the women's doctor because if I was, people should know right away so that no one could start gossiping later. She was right. She got her son to take us to the doctor because I was so weak, she said. The lady doctor did not even look at me but only wanted some of my urine. But neither my cousin's wife nor I could read the report of the examination. We asked her son, and then her husband, who is also literate. Both said it only was a prescription for drugs. They were too embarrassed to tell us. It did not matter, though, because they knew, and that was important. In the end, Shahzadeh, the midwife, read it and told us that I was pregnant. Now I was even more sad and angry. I did not want another child, fatherless. I had three already and no brother and no relatives on their father's side to guide them, to help them. How was I to bring them up? To care for them? I did what I could to lose the child: I jumped up and down and kneaded my abdomen, but God wanted me to have it, and now of course I am glad. I had always wanted a daughter. With only three sons, a mother is alone at home—daughters-in-law are good for nothing.

But long before my daughter was born I had a curious visit. Tehrani had never talked about his family. I did not even know whether he had any brothers and sisters, or whether his father and his mother were alive. But one day the noon minibus brought a strange, rather old woman and a little boy, who asked the way to my house. The woman was Tehrani's mother, she said, and the boy her daughter's son. It turned out that she had been a widow, and when she remarried Tehrani was angry. He fought with her and did not get along with her second husband, and when Tehrani's wife died he left because of his discontent. She said that a friend of Tehrani at the hospital had written her about his death, and she had come to cry and pray at his grave, which she did. But she also looked around very carefully and asked whose garden it was and whose house we were living in, and how much rent the back rooms brought in. She had her hands and eyes in everything when I was not looking. A few weeks after she had left, this friend from the hospital came and told me Tehrani's family had phoned to ask whether I would marry the old woman's second husband! Me, a second wife of my own mother-in-law's husband! I guess they must have figured that I would do as a servant. Or else she wanted the children, but because her second husband was no relation to Tehrani's own father, and therefore had no right to the children, she would have to persuade me to come with them. Tehrani had no brothers—only they would have been able to claim the children. Or else they thought Tehrani had money, and by taking me they would get it too. Whatever their reason, I said no, of course. This was my fourth suitor.

Shortly after my daughter was born my father died of a heart attack in his garden. Since then I have had to fight about his land with my cousins, that is, my father's brothers' sons, who all want it, and also with my sisters' sons. They all either claim it as theirs outright or else they pretend to want to take care of it until my boys are old enough to take over, which is a lie. In either case, there won't be any of my father's land for them unless I am on my toes. I even do the garden around the house myself. As well as I can I tend to the apple trees and the vines, and the boys help me a little—children nowadays don't know what work is, heads full of book stuff—because otherwise one or the other of these heathens would even steal this patch of land right from under my nose. Only one of them is a good man: he takes care of the first garden Tehrani bought from my father, and he brings me apricots and grapes—not as much as I should get, but I won't complain—and wheat. I have raisins and dried apricots for the winter, and bread to eat. It won't be long before the boys can work the land themselves, if they want to, and if they can manage to get back any.

Here I was, a widow with four small children, no brothers, father dead, an orphan myself, and surrounded by greedy relatives. My father, they claimed, had gotten more land from our grandfather than their fathers had; this was not true at all. The difference was that my father only had three daughters, while they all had their houses full of sons and therefore their fathers' land seemed so little after they had divided it amongst them. And then they argued I did not need any land because Tehrani had left me well off anyway—a small widow's pension they called "well off." We barely survived on this and the child support from the insurance company. If I had not had the two rooms to rent, and the jewelry to sell, we would have starved. People talk about my gold and my bank account and whatnot—all lies. With the profit from the jeep I bought a new refrigerator and a television set and clothes for the children at New Year, and I paid for the expense of the funeral and the mourning guests. I had to buy sugar and tea on the expensive open market, not to speak of the dinners we cooked day after day. I wanted so much to have the grave surrounded by the wonderful ironwork "bridal chambers" that are put up everywhere for the young martyrs. They have a roof and a little glass box in the middle with a photograph in it and a bottle of perfume, and plastic flowers; there are quite a few now even here in the village, but they are very expensive. Tehrani only has a small gravestone, it grieves me every week when I go there to mourn. When it rains, I am on the roof with the oak roller because I don't even have the money to tar the roof. Ours must be the last house in Deh Koh with an unprotected dirt roof. Yet, people say I am rich. Such is the justice of this world.

A young widow without brothers has a hard life. If I went to town to complain about something or to go to the doctor alone because I have no brother to accompany me, people talked. If I was out haggling with the shopkeepers because I have no brother to do it for me, people talked. If I passed the time of day in the alley with my aunt or a neighbor, people talked. If I rented my back rooms, people talked. Even now that a gendarme with his wife and three children is living there, people talk, and all because I am on my own, I am not afraid of anybody—I can answer, I can argue, be it with the governor himself—and because I don't let any crooked shopkeeper cheat me, and because I don't blush like a dumb little girl when a man looks at me. The other day a revolutionary guard—a stranger, I had never seen him, and a young boy to boot—stopped me in the street almost outside my house and told me to pull my veil-wrap over my forehead, my hair was showing. I planted myself squarely in front of him and looked him in his face and said he should be ashamed to look at a strange woman, and he should get himself a wife instead of walking the streets ogling honorable widows, and ours is a country so free that a criminal like Abbas can freely molest women and little boys dressed in fatigues can freely behave immodestly. My neighbors cheered me after he had beaten it with a red face, of course, but behind my back they say I am brash and brazen. Double-tongued lot.

Because of all the talk and to-do, I did not say a word to anybody about how one of the two revolutionary guards who roomed with me, two lads from some godforsaken village I have never even heard of, was after me. He kept asking me to marry him. He told me it was a sin for me, young as I was, not to be married, and that he would do a good work by marrying me—ha! I told him I would complain about him if he did not leave me alone, and he and his roommate (who was much better, but a little slow in the head) should leave. He did not, though. I locked the house and my room at night and had my mother stay with me day and night, I was so afraid. Yet, even in this I can see my ill fortune. Because if I had married him I would be rich now: he volunteered for the front (because I would not marry him, he said) and was martyred within a month. As his widow I would have gotten a lot of money and my roof repaired, and a much better pension than the one I got after Tehrani. My luck. Worse luck, however, that Abbas ever saw me—the same Abbas who is in jail now because of Turan.

Abbas saw me in the bank in town when I tried to get a loan for tarring the roof. He worked there as a clerk. I noticed him staring at me, but of course I ignored him. He saw me again a few times and went crazy about me. People told him who I was. Many people in town know that I am Tehrani's widow. He is younger than myself, quite a bit; a mere lad he was then. Several times he sent somebody to ask me to marry him. The first time the messenger went to my father's brother, what a joke. His wife told him to ask me personally, that I was the master of my house because I wanted it that way. This is one sensible woman.

It was wrong of me to say yes, of course, but hindsight is cheap. However, I did not accept his proposal because of what the people say. They say a young widow is lusty, and that is why I married Abbas. People say that a man marrying a young virgin will stay young himself because she is not interested in this husband–wife game, she does not like it. But marry a widow, they say, and you will be old soon—a widow has the sleeping roll ready the moment she sees her husband, and he will spend himself . . . that's why I married Abbas, people say behind my back. Such nonsense! Heathens with their foul tongues! They also say I was glad that he preferred me over Turan, his fiancée, that I wanted to rub it in. In fact, I did not even know he had a fiancée. What do I care about the affairs of people in Mahmudabad? I have not even been there more than once or twice in my life. If I had known about Turan, well, maybe I would have married him anyway, who knows? I made demands, though: he would have to take charge and responsibility of the children, I said, and he agreed; I would stay right here in this house and not go to Mahmudabad, and he agreed to this also; I would continue to rent the two rooms and keep the money for the education of the children. This, too, he agreed to. And I wanted thirty thousand Toman of divorce money written into the marriage contract. This he did, too, and I checked it personally: I had my cousin read me the document to make sure no one was cheating me.

Nothing but grief and problems I had from then on. For one, he did not really live here. He did not bring any of his things, he did not work in the garden, he never even was around to talk to; he would come in the evening, eat my good food, and leave early in the morning to go to work. On Friday he would go to Mahmudabad and not come here at all. This happened three weekends. In the middle of the fourth week the gendarmes came here, to this house, and asked if he was here, and when I had seen him last, and where his things were. It turned out he had stolen money at the bank, and now the gendarmes tried to find it. He had smuggled it out in his sleeves—the long-armed Islamic shirts are good for this, indeed—and in his pants. The gendarmes believed me when I told them I knew nothing of his business. Indeed, they found some of the loot later in his father's house in Mahmudabad, and no one blamed me for anything, thanks be to God. I shudder to think what might have happened if the gendarmes had found the money here, or anything else. I remembered that he had said he would bring some television sets to store in our good room—he had bought them cheaply from somebody returning from Kuwait, he said. These, too, were stolen. He and his brothers had a smuggling and thievery business going, it turned out. Bad people, the whole lot of them. I had not gotten a penny from him, not even for the food he ate, let alone for my expenses. But I lost the small widow's pension because I remarried. So there I was, four little children, no widow's pension, no one to turn to, and a criminal hoodlum for a husband who was in jail. I went to court and asked for a divorce. The judge, a mullah, after hearing my case, granted me a divorce, and even said that Abbas would have to pay the divorce money—this was one good judge, God bless him. It did not help me much, though, because to this day Abbas has not paid anything, and now, of course, after what happened to Turan, he will be in jail for a long time, and where is my divorce settlement? I'll have to go on fighting for it as soon as he is out again. I know he has money stashed away someplace, and thirty thousand of this is mine.

Now I am in town all the time going from office to office with a petition to have my widow's pension restored. The other day the district secretary, one of those young guys with a black shirt and a black beard, had the nerve to tell me it was my duty to get married again, I was still young enough to bear many children! I am powerless, I need help. Maybe the governor will help me or the Friday Prayer leader in town. And why not? "In the city of the blind put your hands over your eyes." This is another true saying. And surely, even now at the time of the turban and the black shirts, somebody will have pity on a brotherless widow and four fatherless children?

Yet, I won't complain. What if Tehrani had had a brother who had taken the children away because they belonged to his family? This happened to Nargez's sister: she has not seen her two children at all since her husband died four years ago and his people sent her back to her father. One of her husband's brothers should have married her, of course; then there would not have been any problem. But they are heathens. And she was too meek and honorable to go to court. I think she would have gone, but her father said no, he did not want a fight. Compared to her, I am lucky. Or Huri's cousin: nice mother-in-law, a good family, they are kind to each other and devoted, never a harsh word among them. Her husband got a job in town and took her there into one of the houses where I had lived with Tehrani. The trees are taller now, but of course, strangers all around still, and dirt, and filth, and many odd people. Cities are ugly places now. She wanted to go back to her mother-in-law so badly, she was crying day and night. After the second child her sadness got worse. Now she is back here, but crazy. She lies in a corner all day long, crying and laughing without reason, not speaking at all. And her mother-in-law is so worried that she too will get sick. What are my pains and aches and troubles compared to theirs?

Eventually my children will grow up and take care of me, maybe—though there is this proverb: "A daughter will be taken away by a man, and a son by his passion for a woman." This is one true proverb, indeed. They'll have to go away to find a livelihood, and where will this leave me? But the future is up to God. Meanwhile I'll look for help where I can find it. Like the Friday Prayer leader in town. This new young mullah who is here sometimes for sermons— a brand new mullah who just has learned how to wrap his turban— maybe he can write me a letter of introduction . . . he is always watching me out of the corner of his eyes. I'll ask him . . . I'll tell him . . . "Honorable, exalted servant of God," I'll say . . .

11

About Crazy People and Butterfly's Silence

In Deh Koh there are many ways to be odd without necessarily causing much concern. Simin's sister won't drink tea, ever. She puts hot water in a tea glass and drinks it with a lump of sugar in her mouth as if it was tea. It took her mother-in-law a while to get used to it. "Crazy," she would call her. Mahin, who refused three suitors in one year and speaks her mind whether asked to or not, is sort of crazy, she says so herself, but so what? "What would people have to talk about if it were not for me and Setara, who is just as crazy?" she says. What indeed? Mahmud the Cripple can neither walk nor talk right, he is weak in mind and body, but he has a wife and three children he is feeding and clothing with his alms. Qeta, whose craziness in the village is agreed upon unanimously, had a fright which dried up her brain and her soul; she is neither shunned nor feared, and ridiculed only by the ignorant children. Yusuf's cousin gets inflamed easily by the sight or probably just the thought of a woman. He forever and embarrassingly is trying to bargain for another wife, meanwhile beating up on the one he has—a sore craziness this, like drunkenness, bringing sorrow and discontent to everybody. But although people remonstrate with him when he is mistreating his poor wife, he is a well-respected carpenter otherwise. One of Maryam's nieces sometimes falls down suddenly, moaning and muttering incoherently. People say that a *djenn* hit her years ago when she was washing clothes all alone at dusk at an infamous well below the village. But the doctor sent her to Tehran with her husband to a hospital for the mentally ill. Her craziness, it turned out, was a disease—not that knowing this made much difference in her behavior.

Parvane, which means *Butterfly*, is crazy like Maryam's niece, some people say; others think that she is crazy like Qeta, only less so, from shock and grief; still others, including most of her relatives, say that she is only plain and quiet and in need of a little help and consideration, which she does not get from her husband.

The summer Parvane was born in a branch hut high above the fields, gardens, and scrub oak, up above the cold springs, her mother Atri remembers in many ways. It was the summer when Reza, Parvane's father, was chased up an oak tree by a pack of wolves while looking for a stray cow in the wilderness. He was hanging on to the branches of the lonely oak for dear life, from midmorning to late afternoon, when some men on their way home from outlying fields chased away the wolves. With blood curdled from fright and nerves dried up from shock and exhaustion, he never was the same afterwards and often was gruff or silent. It was also the summer when the locusts fell over the village one hazy afternoon, darkening the sky and eating most of what should have filled storage bins in the walls and skin bags and wool sacks stacked for the winter. Earlier that summer Reza's mother had died, leaving Atri to cope by herself with the products of one of the largest herds in the village. It was the same summer measles and whooping cough took away some thirty children in the village, including Parvane's two brothers and Maryam's only child. It was a hot summer with a parching sun that dried the springs and brooks to mere trickles. During the long and tired afternoons, between milk boiling and evening milking, Atri, aching in every bone with her fifth pregnancy, would squat in the shady doorway of the small branch hut, looking down the dust-colored, sun-baked slopes towards the village, spinning. Pulling a fine and even thread with the steady movements of long practice, she wondered how fast the grass was turning the color of sand under the blue sky and watched twisters moving hither and yon

201

over the Deh Koh plain, twirling slender columns of dust up high into the shimmering air.

Although the animals gave little milk that summer, Atri had to be up long before dawn to get the buttering done while the air was still cool enough to make the butter fall out in firm little lumps in the churning sack on the tripod. For Atri, the rhythmic sloshing and thumping of yogurt and water in the goathide sack was the most endearing sound of the night, rising up into the still sky from each and every one of the six branch huts and mingling with the soft scratching and tinkling and coughing of the sheep and goats in the corral.

On such a morning Parvane was born, right after the second butter sack was emptied. The day before, a tiny fly of the sort that hides in the animals' hair had gotten into Atri's mouth while her cheek was resting against the flank of a goat she was milking—a dreaded occurrence, because these flies cling to the inside of the throat and make swallowing, talking, and drawing each breath itchy and painful, so irritating that water wells up in the eyes and the tongue swells until it hangs heavily in the mouth. There is nothing one can do but suffer in silence until the affliction subsides after a few long, intensely unpleasant days. When the labor pains told Atri that the child was about to come, she could or would not utter a sound because of the fly in her throat. Instead, she walked over to the next hut (Reza's cousin's) and got Zari to understand that she was about to give birth. Zari shouted the news to the other women, and they left their butter sacks to help Parvane into the world. Reza and his cousin, the only two men in the camp that night, got up and left to claim their share of irrigation water in the village. The two shepherd lads slept through everything.

Parvane was a tiny little thing, says Atri, red faced, and only a girl—praise be—better than a puppy, certainly, but after the loss of two sons, a hope disappointed.

Zari finished the buttering for Atri and the women did her milking at noon and boiled her milk and set it to yogurt, but at night Atri was back in her place, still not able to say anything.

This is what Atri remembers of Parvane's birth. Nobody seems to know why the baby was called Butterfly. "Parvane" sounded pretty, and as no other woman in the village had this name nobody could be annoyed by a duplication.

Zari remembers how very quiet a baby Parvane was from the beginning. The little thing hardly ever cried. This was not good, Zari told Atri. It was probably a sign that she might be a changeling—that the *djenn* had stolen her that first night in the mountains and replaced her with one of their own children, which would turn into nothing but bother. But unlike a changeling, Parvane was growing as well as a healthy baby should and was hardly ever sick with even as much as diarrhea or a cold.

For Atri, the first sign that Parvane was different appeared after Parvane got badly burnt when she was not quite two, up in the mountains again, in early spring in another camp. One night while Atri was kneading dough for bread, Parvane's side of the blanket caught fire from some embers; space was dear in the small oak beam-and-stone huts there. By the time Atri noticed what was happening Parvane's left leg was badly burnt. Parvane did not scream; she only whimpered, with her little fists pressed on her mouth, and from then on she was quieter than ever, for a long time not even using the few words she had learned so far: "Mother" and "no" and "Dada" for sister and for most everything else. Without hardly moving at all, she would sit and watch, or stand and watch, friendly-like, but as if she was not really interested in what she was seeing. Atri got a little concerned then. She hung amulets on her and punctually week after week burned seeds of wild rue to ward off the evil eye. She got iron bracelets from the itinerant blacksmiths and put them on Parvane's arms and around her ankles against the *djenn*. When Parvane walked, slowly and with small, measured steps, there was a constant tinkling around her. No little girl had more beads around her neck than Parvane. No little girl was better protected from any imaginable danger than Parvane.

Setara, Negin, and Parvane's eldest sister Kokab say that what they remember about Parvane as a child was that she hardly ever played, or fought, or ran, and that when the other girls teased her, she did not answer back but slinked away at the first occasion to hide. For the most part, the other children left her alone. Kokab took to looking after her smiling, dimple-faced sister, dragging her along to the vineyards and the walnut trees and to gather vegetables in the high valleys above the village in the spring and acorns in the woods in the fall. The girls remember how once they unwittingly roused a wild boar during such an outing and fled every which way in sheer panic, except Parvane: she stood fearlessly and watched the boar, and the boar turned away and sped down the hill. It was an amazing story the girls told about Parvane standing on a boulder in the sun, skirts aflutter in the wind, looking at the ranting monster (the girls said) without blinking an eyelid.

Kokab remembers another odd quality about her: she would not get dirty. Parvane walked carefully, sat primly, ate tidily, avoided puddles and dirt, and kept her hands to herself. Not even her hair got mussed or matted. It hardly seemed necessary to take Parvane to the bathhouse. One time, Kokab remembers, Parvane somehow got left outside the bathhouse. Patiently she waited at the door, and when Atri herself came there a while later, she thought Parvane had already finished her bath, so clean was she, and sent her home.

Atri says that Parvane was good at gathering plants, cracking walnuts, and carrying loads of grass and heavy bags of water. One cold winter day at the well (this happened long before the village got its water piped to every courtyard) she did not tie the bag properly, and it leaked. By the time Parvane came home her skirts from the waist down were frozen stiff on her right side, but she did not even feel it.

In time, Parvane learned to card wool, to spin, to sew. She was easy to teach, Atri says, because unlike other children she was patient and did not hop up and down while being shown something. Soon Parvane's yarn was spun flawlessly; every one of her stitches was placed exactly next to the others. Setara, a neighbor then, clumsy with her hands and lazy (so she says), often bribed Parvane with a handful of raisins or a lump of sugar she had pilfered at home to spin a little for her or to help her do chores. Parvane liked sweets more than any other child did, Setara says.

Parvane learned to make a fire to cook rice and to knead dough and to bake bread, to churn butter, and to weave. She worked without protest, but only if told to in a soft and friendly voice by her mother, her father, or Kokab. If anybody else ordered her or shouted at her (she struck people as being a little hard of hearing), she only smiled and did not respond at all. Left to herself, she would sit and watch; take a nap, maybe; and sit and watch some more—hands in her lap, rain or shine upon her, flies or no flies, smiling to herself, and speaking a few words only when caring to answer a question.

"A good girl," people said about her, "a humble girl, a girl without guile in her heart, poor thing, and without poison on her tongue. A pretty girl, may God protect her." So the people still say today, talking about her as she was back then when they all were young.

One can still see Parvane's prettiness, her tanned face notwithstanding (she never tries to keep the sun out of her face). Her skin is so smooth that it seems stretched tautly over the frame of her high cheekbones, her large eyes are half-covered by heavy lids, and her small, friendly mouth sets below a straight nose. Every part of her round face, every one of her spare gestures and spare words, exudes a kind of deep, faraway calm. On her slight body, held straight and still, even an old shirt looks proper, clean, and better than it really is.

Huri, from her observation spot in the courtyard behind Reza's, and Negin's mother, recalling the time when she was Atri's next-door neighbor, agree on how Farid wooed Parvane. Farid was one of Huri's relatives in the same courtyard. At that time he was a young man, some ten years older than Parvane, living with his father and mother and three younger brothers. "The boys were always looking at us girls," Huri says, "and we were looking at the boys and talking about them, pretending not to notice them. This probably is a sin, but that's what we did and what the young people do now, and that's how Farid noticed Parvane." He took to using Reza's stairways to get to his courtyard whenever he was coming down from the fields — it was not really the shorter way, says Negin's mother, but it gave him a chance to take long, good looks at Parvane squatting by the fire, Parvane leaning against the verandah post, Parvane cleaning rice, Parvane spinning, Parvane doing nothing. He liked what he saw and liked what others had to say about her, especially his mother: Parvane was "short of speech," they told him, "not a troublemaker, never talking back, not one to fight anybody or about anything. A docile girl, an obedient girl."

He asked for her and got her. There was no reason on earth to refuse him, says Atri. Parvane said "yes" clearly when told to (unlike most other girls, who mumble tearfully and barely audibly) and left for the other courtyard without a word of protest. She was about thirteen. Her older sisters were married already, and Atri did not like to see Parvane go. Although not much of a companion as far as conversation went, Parvane had been her most willing and reliable helper. Now she had only one daughter left at home (as jumpy and quick and full of mischief as Parvane was slow and quiet), and a son who would not bring home a bride for many years to come. He was in third grade by the time three goats and a sheep were slaughtered for Parvane's wedding and the women came together in an open space above the Haji's house (long since built over and gone forever) to listen to the drum and the oboe, to dance a round and to watch others dance.

Life in her husband's house was not at all bad for Parvane at first. Farid, a peasant with only little land, was literate and enterprising; he bought useful stuff in the city like aluminum pots and shirts and shoes to peddle in the isolated villages and camps. He lent money and got interest, and lent more money. Young and full of energy, he minded neither hard work at home nor travel, although at that time traveling was still dangerous because of robbers and soldiers and the feuds between villages.

Parvane stayed at home with her mother-in-law and did what she always had done: work as told to, and sit and smile to herself otherwise. She got pregnant and bore a son, to everybody's satisfaction. But she had little milk and seemed to nurse the baby only hesitantly, and the baby died. Atri blames this misfortune on Farid's thoughtlessness: he once brought home pomegranates, which, tasty as they are, nevertheless have to be eaten with caution and in moderation because of the tendency of their intrinsic "cold" quality to upset the natural balance in the body, and put them—no doubt with the best of intentions—next to the pregnant Parvane. "Parvane," says Atri, "ate the whole box. No wonder she had no milk and the baby was weak and she felt chilly all the time and came down with a cold fever. It dried up the nerves to her head."

A year later she had another child, a girl. Again Parvane did not show much interest in the baby. Her mother-in-law and Atri fed the child cow's milk, and bathed her and swaddled her, and told Parvane to rock the cradle and to wash the soiled rag diapers, which she did without a word. And when she was told to unstrap the baby off the cradle and to hug it, she did this too, and after a while seemed to like it. "She will learn how to take care of children, for sure," said Farid's mother when Atri showed signs of alarm at Parvane's indifference. And she made sure that her other daughter-in-law did not

206

scold Parvane or yell at her. One smiled at Parvane and spoke to her endearingly as to a favorite child.

Her third child—another year later—also died, of measles, when he was only a few months old. Parvane cried when the tiny body was taken away. She cried silently, her head bent back, heavy tears rolling down her cheek. No wailing, no singing came from her lips. This sight more than the loss of the baby made Atri cry too, and Reza, who had never seen his daughter so miserable, was moved to tears himself and became very grouchy.

It was obvious that Parvane was a woman who got pregnant easily and that this was not good for her. Her cheeks turned hollow, her fingers bony. Often she would sit with her eyes closed, dozing even in the bright sun of midmorning amidst the noises of a thousand goings-on around her, and then would get up with the careful and tired motions of a much older woman. She smiled less and sighed more. Nothing could be done about it. Some women just were like this, pregnant all the time, God only knew why or what for.

Between the middle of spring and the first of the summer, just before Parvane's fourth child was born, Farid's mother shriveled up and died. She was gone so fast that the whole house was left bewildered. "Like a bird took off," her stunned daughter-in-law, Aferin, said over and over again; she struggled to fill the sudden vacancy of manager and caretaker for so many people: her father-in-law, her husband, her three children, her husband's two teenage brothers—and Parvane.

Aferin had never quite been able to figure Parvane out. Her pretty sister-in-law appeared lazy, sitting idly amidst pressing work, but it was not that she refused to work or else did whatever she pleased, as a truly lazy woman would. Rather, it seemed to Aferin that Parvane's body was one place but her mind was elsewhere. Parvane simply did not feel the flies on her face; she did not hear the bells of the cows in the evening. Yet, again, no one baked thinner bread, no one churned finer butter than Parvane, and both required mastery of tricky skills. Whenever the clack-clack of a rolling pin on a breadboard cut the clear darkness of a deep night, it was likely Parvane's. She liked to work at night. And her slosh-thumpy butter-sack rhythm was the first one in the neighborhood on many a crisp early morning. There was no laziness in any of this, nor in Parvane's smiling responses to her mother-in-law's requests. But now that the old woman's strong and kind voice was quiet forever, Parvane had nobody to listen to. No matter what Aferin tried—coaxing, pleading, demanding, yelling—nothing made Parvane respond even faintly adequately. Aferin, overworked and tired, felt put upon and exasperated. Once she left a pan of bread dough (her largest pan, bread for nine hungry people) to rest in a corner of the kitchen. She and Parvane together had kneaded the water-flour dough and would bake the bread later. Aferin covered it with a cloth, closed the door behind her, and left on an errand. She did not think of locking the door because Parvane was sitting right outside it, spinning, and Aferin knew she was not likely to move. But the children started to run in and out of the kitchen, past Parvane, who did not say, "Don't do this," or at least "Close the door again." After the children, the chickens found their way into the room through the open door, just about hopping over Parvane, who did not mind them either. When Aferin came back the dough was all theirs. They had scratched away the cloth over the pan and were pecking and jostling with great determination, all under Parvane's eyes. "I hit her then," Aferin says years later, "and I will be sorry for it to the end of my life. Now it is a funny story that makes me laugh, but then—there I was, ready to bake bread, but where was the dough? Dirty and half gone it was, covered with chickenshit, and Parvane was sitting next to it, not shooing the chickens, not throwing a pebble, nothing. I was so angry, I hit her and yelled at her, although I knew it was not her fault; she just is like this, simple-like. I always tried to be kind to her, not to get angry, not to frighten her. But that time I hit her."

Parvane's mother fell into the habit of trying to be in two places at the same time. She was forever coming and going between her home and Farid's, working from morning to night. Atri was afraid for Parvane and afraid of what Aferin's people might say about Aferin's workload. Nobody likes to see one's daughter having to take on more responsibilities than are reasonable. Caring for a husband's married brother and his wife and his children was not reasonable. But Reza warned Atri. "You are meddling in Farid's house," he said. "They will resent it. It is none of your business." They had arguments about it, Atri and Reza. "Parvane needs help," Atri would say, and Reza would counter that she was no longer their responsibility but Farid's. "If you go on pampering her, she will never learn how to work," he said.

"She is sick," said Atri.

"Just because she likes to sit with her hands in her lap doesn't mean she is sick," said Reza. There was no end to this argument.

Thanks to Atri and Aferin, and a little help here and there from other women such as Setara's mother and Negin ("Parvane, your baby is crying; pick him up, feed him" they would shout across the courtyard, Negin recalls), and because it was the will of God, her fourth baby, a boy, survived. Unlike his sister he was a weak and sickly child, although Parvane cared for him much better than she had for her daughter. She smiled at him and made little noises when she held him, and nursed him often and quite willingly.

Farid, when he was at home, played with his daughter and the baby. He was pleased with his family. He did not talk much to Parvane—she answered only monosyllabically, but he did not mind that; he had not married her for her talking but because he knew she was the quiet sort of woman. He heard enough from Aferin to appreciate Parvane's silence all the more. "He thought I was a troublemaker," Aferin says. "He thought we were like so many other brothers' wives living together, fighting about everything. Parvane's older sister thought so too. But Atri herself knows it is a lie. I told Farid that Parvane could not work like other women, but he did not believe me. 'Good for her,' he said, 'if she is not your servant. Leave her alone.' He did not realize how much I worked for her and for him. When my husband told him, he argued with him too. Atri spoke for me—his own wife's mother!—but he did not listen. I told Farid he should bring a servant from one of the little villages, a girl who knows how to do chores, to help Parvane. He thought I was joking. 'You think I am a khan?' he said, 'and Parvane is a lady? Then treat her like one.' He was unjust. If only he had listened to me."

Advice came from another quarter too. Setara had married Tehrani, who, on his visits to his father-in-law, often saw Parvane across the courtyard. Setara and the others in the house talked about her. Tehrani, with the relaxed social constraints enjoyed by trusted outsiders and the grace of an extroverted and esteemed half-stranger, struck up conversations with Atri and Aferin about Parvane, who seemed to intrigue him. Once he made a point of walking across to

Atri to tell her that he had talked to a doctor friend in the hospital about Parvane, and the doctor had offered to come to Deh Koh to look at her; he thought she could be helped in the hospital in the city, and Atri should talk it over with Farid. Atri brought it up with Farid, supported by Aferin, but Farid became furious. Nothing was wrong with his wife, he shouted; they should get off her back and his back; he was tired of Parvane this and Parvane that. "No!" he shouted, "I don't want to hear any more about your nonsense. And anyway, what is my wife to this stranger?" They were lucky he did not pick a fight with Tehrani.

At home Atri had to listen to Reza's opinion too. "What have I told you?" he said. "A hundred times I said you should shut up and stay home." Atri cried, and this made Reza gruffer yet.

Farid's younger brother got married. The courtyard was crowded now. The new bride was a saucy and quick little thing with a fast tongue and a mind set on her own advantage. Working for Parvane ("lazy and dirty" she called her) was not to her advantage. The many children irritated her, especially Parvane's daughter, who (fair game to everybody's bossy demands because her mother did not stand up for her) was disobedient and disrespectful, she claimed. Whenever something went wrong in the house she was quick to blame Parvane or her daughter for it. "Maybe it was Parvane," she would say, shrugging her shoulder, when a pile of pots and pans toppled and crashed. "Surely it was Parvane's bratty kid," she said, when a line of wash broke and the laundry ended in the mud. "Parvane did not watch the fire," she said, when the rice burnt; "I saw the girl eat it," she said, when the sugar bowl was unexpectedly empty once again.

Although the others doubted these claims more often than not, Parvane slowly grew into the role of a convenient scapegoat. She started to look neglected then, says Setara. She was no longer smiling, scrubbed clean, and spotless. Her scarf often would sit crookedly on her head, her feet were dirty, tears in her skirts were not mended. Once she burnt a big hole into her shirt (the new fabrics just melt away when one gets too close to a flame) in an indelicately conspicuous spot. It was ignored until Setara mentioned it to Atri and Atri made Parvane change the shirt and repair the hole. The children started to make fun of her. "Crazy Parvane," they would shout from safe distances, and make obscene noises. Setara shushed them many times. "She is a poor woman, it is sinful to mock her," she told them, but who can get children to listen to reason and the voice of kindness? And some of Parvane's habits indeed were embarrassing. At the mourning party for Farid's father (he died shortly after the new bride joined the house; prematurely, people say, probably of grief over the loss of his wife) Parvane, sitting among the women guests who had come from far and wide to grieve for their dead relative, lifted her skirts all the way up to her thighs to scratch herself loudly and forcefully. A little while later she broke wind, unperturbed, into an awkward silence, and did not mind at all when a child accidentally pulled down her scarf from behind so that she sat among the visitors with a bare head. When her legs stiffened from squatting too long in one position, instead of getting up and walking around outside, she just stretched them out in front of her like a child too young to care about not being rude. The younger women giggled. Farid's sister hissed at her to pull her scarf back up and to sit properly. But not even she could make Parvane cry and wail along with the others. While the others sobbed, Parvane kept looking around her, with an expression of astonishment and a little smile out of place for the occasion. "What is the matter with Parvane?" the women whispered to Aferin as they were leaving.

Aferin pretended ignorance. "She does not feel well today," she said. She was glad when Atri took her to their house the next day.

But towards noon Farid missed her and called her back. Aferin sat her at the fireplace to brew tea for the guests. That afternoon, Parvane drank "ten, twenty glasses" of tea, says Aferin, which was not good for her cold disposition, and they went through two cones of sugar because Parvane let the children steal all the sugar cubes they liked.

Most people who care enough about Farid's affairs to have an opinion about them say Farid built his new house because he was at odds with his brothers and their wives (a very common situation, unfortunately), and also because his business had expanded and he could afford a house. Farid's sister says that he needed a bigger house to entertain his clients. The house is surrounded by a walled-in courtyard next to that of Farid's sister. Atri was a stranger there. Her visits became less frequent. Parvane was alone with her two children most of the day. Atri thinks that Farid did not let her visit her father's house and that his many guests made life hard for her. But Farid's sister says that Farid was good to Parvane. "He often cooked rice when he came home in the evening, tired, and found she had not prepared any dinner. He took his daughter to the doctor when she knocked her head bloody. He even washed his children's faces when he saw they were dirty. It is a lie to say he neglected her or beat her, a great big lie." That Parvane occasionally cooked an extra pot of rice or brewed a pot of tea for guests was amply balanced, in her opinion, by an otherwise easy life: Parvane had no goats to milk, no butter to churn at night; she had water right in the courtyard and all the food she wanted. Besides, she had a helper in her daughter. All the women agree that Atri and Aferin had trained the little girl well. She was barely five years old when she was seen carrying the baby around competently, washing rag-diapers, taking yogurt home from her grandmother, sweeping the house. When she was six her father enrolled her in school, and Parvane lost her helper for most of the day. Parvane got worse.

Parvane's sister Kokab, who lived only a few houses away, and Farid's sister next door slipped in to see Parvane now and then. What they found in Farid's house often filled them with sorrow. One day Kokab came upon Parvane trying to soak sugar, obviously thinking it was rice. And Farid's sister once rescued Parvane's baby from being washed in ice-cold water under the faucet in the courtyard in the middle of winter. The most harrowing incident for Kokab, however, happened one afternoon in late spring, when she found the dripping wet body of a premature baby on a rag in a corner of the yard ("tiny, tiny fists it had," she remembers) and Parvane washing her bloody skirts at the pool. She had had a miscarriage, silently, alone by herself in the big, empty house. That night, Farid's own sister was the one to tell Farid that something was amiss with Parvane. "Take her to Mashhad," she said. "Chain her to the Imam's shrine and ask him to have mercy on her and to allow the chain to fall open. Or at least take her to a doctor for some medicine to make her stronger." Farid, embarrassed and distressed, grumbled assent. "He hired the taxi to take her down to the clinic," his sister says. "He was considerate with her."

The doctor, however, failed her. Parvane, he said, was weak because she had too many children in too short a time. "She does not have enough blood," he said. There was nothing else wrong with her. Pregnant too often, he said, but don't give her pills, they are

212

bad for her health. Have her tubes tied in the hospital. He wrote a letter for Parvane for a hospital in the city.

Farid did not like the idea of having no more children. He only had one son. But he was a reasonable man, and he agreed with the women and the doctor. Parvane, he decided, should have her tubes tied—it was the only reliable way to prevent pregnancies, everybody said. But first he would see to it that she was well fed and a little stronger for the long journey. Towards the end of summer he packed his family into the crowded minibus and headed for the city. After three days of waiting for their turn, a doctor examined Parvane and said she was pregnant again. He could not do anything for her now. They should come back right after the baby was born. Angry and disappointed, Farid took his tired and dirty family back home and never again asked a doctor to help Parvane. Doctors did not want to do anything for her, he decided; it was useless to try.

Why Parvane's only brother, fourteen then, volunteered for the front the first time is another matter entirely and has nothing to do with Parvane, the women say. He left with two other boys in a truck of the revolutionary guards who had come to Deh Koh to recruit fighters. Atri walked around with red eyes; Reza's heart was broken, she said. For days he sat in his room, head in hands, hardly uttering a word. It was just as well that by then he had sold most of his animals because he was unable to work. His brother irrigated his fields for him at his next turn at the water. However, a few days later the boy was back; the officer in charge of the camp for volunteers was a man from a neighboring village up the river who knew Reza. He had taken the boy aside and told him that it was a sin to leave his old father and mother alone, and that it was of greater merit to stay with them than to fight at the front. He had given the boy money for the bus home and sent him away discreetly. The joy at home did not last long, however. The boy, used to looking after Parvane's firewood and the kerosene in her heater once in a while, upon his first visit after his return found Parvane "half naked" (meaning, in this case, without a scarf on her head and with only one shabby skirt under a thin shirt) sitting "on a rag," he said, in a chilly room, rocking the cradle. She was shivering with cold. Unhappy already for reasons of his own, and now brimming with frustration about his sister, he went looking for his brother-in-law. A loud and ugly argument ensued in Farid's store which ended by Farid throwing the boy out. He went home, packed a few things into a knapsack his mother had woven years ago, and left again, this time for good. Two months later he was killed at the front.

Parvane bore another child, a girl "weak and tiny like a little sparrow that had fallen out of the nest," Atri says. After this she got even worse. Her days of withdrawal were broken now with spasms of insult in such foul language that people wondered where she might have heard it. Several times she refused to be taken to the bathhouse, even by her mother. If her daughter bugged her about something, she threw things at her. More and more frequently Farid's sister, Kokab, or Atri collected the toddler in the street and fed him, or else Farid would take him with him to the store. Even the older girl spent much more time with her aunts and grandmother than at home. Parvane looked disheveled and forlorn, thin and tired. There was not the ghost of a smile left in her face.

Farid's relatives talked about a second wife for him, a good worker. Couldn't he find some nice, sturdy woman—a widow even, if need be—in one of the villages? In Deh Koh, they knew, nobody would be likely to give him a wife. Deh Koh girls could do better than serving as a servant-wife; and besides, Reza was a highly respected man whose feelings would be hurt if his daughter was slighted by a second wife. Farid was not interested in another wife, however. Reza and Atri were dead set against it. No second wife would take care of a sick and meek elder wife like Parvane, they were convinced. Parvane would be just as neglected as she was now, and her children just as ill fed. No woman likes to care for other people's children. It was also a matter of honor: if he took another wife, people would talk, and neither Farid's nor Reza's family was the kind others talked about. Surely there must be a better way to handle the problem.

One evening, Farid paid his father-in-law a rare visit. After politenesses were exchanged, tea drunk, and sweets refused, he offered a suggestion. Their son was a martyr in heaven, he said. They had nobody to watch over their interests, work their land, take care of Reza's animals, repair the house, do chores. He, Farid, had his big, modern house. He gladly would make room for them there and be like a son to them, and they could live together and eat the same bread. Of course, it would be good for Parvane too. They should think it over and be assured of his devotion.

There was no way to budge Reza. He said no and stuck to it. It was against all good custom for a father-in-law to live with his daughter's husband. No. Farid's people, his sister, his brother's wife Aferin, his brothers, did their best to be persuasive. "Nobody will think less of you if you move in to care for your sick daughter," they assured him. "Farid and all of us hold you in high esteem. Farid is your servant, not you his." Although Atri had her doubts about this, she did not care whether anybody would think she was lowering herself to the role of her son-in-law's servant. All she could see was a miserable Parvane, sliding into a lonely darkness under their very eyes and suffering from a lack of the kind of attention this strangely weak daughter of hers needed. But Reza said no. It was God's will for him not to give in.

Not long after this debate, one gray afternoon when the last snow of the winter had turned the main road into a slippery, half-frozen mudslope, a young man on a motorcycle, miscalculating the bend in the icy road in front of Farid's store, skidded sideways and bumped into Farid, who was standing outside his store. Both fell. The young man got up unharmed, but Farid had to be dragged from under the motorcycle with a smashed foot and a useless left leg. He could not get up. In great pain, he was shoved into his cousin's pickup truck and driven to the doctor, and from there to the hospital. The cousin came back the next day and reported that he had had to try three hospitals before he got somebody to care for Farid, and that Farid needed an operation on his foot and thigh and would have to stay in the city for several weeks.

The older women, including Farid's sister and Atri, were crying and wringing their hands, asking all and sundry what sins they were being punished for by God. The younger ones, such as Aferin and Kokab, looked at each other with grim faces, sighing. Parvane seemed not to understand Farid's misfortune or else not to care about it. When Atri and her husband's sister told her, she kept spinning without saying anything. The next day, Farid's sister left with her son and Farid's daughter to visit Farid.

Atri fell ill with a fever that chilled her bones to the marrow. Her younger daughter, who lived in Mahmudabad since her marriage, was sent for to stay for a night, and Kokab milked the cow and cooked dinner for her father. After a few days, when Atri felt strong enough to walk, she summoned Kokab to accompany her to Parvane. She was not sure whether she would be strong enough to climb the steep hill alone, she said. Kokab was a little put out about this request, because she had a pile of wash and a cranky old mother-in-law at home, but later was glad she had not refused. "Mother still was sick herself," she says now. "She would have fainted or maybe died of a stroke if I had not been with her, such a fright we had." When the two women entered Farid's courtyard, they heard pitiful mewing sounds from the house. The three-year-old was tottering towards them through the cold mud, pantless, barefoot, munching on a dirty roll of bread. "Mother is crying," he said. They found Parvane sitting in the house in the center of the room, head bent back, beating on the rug beneath her with a dough roller, swaying to and fro in and out of swirls of rug dust illuminated by shafts of light streaming in from the open window. In her lap she held the skinny, limp body of her baby, its head, still covered with the cap Atri had made for it, dangling over her arm, lifeless.

Parvane, with tangled strands of hair in her dirt-caked face and her eyes closed, and engulfed in the catlike whining that welled out of a depth of misery, did not see her mother and sister, did not hear their shouts and sobs. The little boy threw himself against her, yelling "Mother!" "Hey Mother, listen!" But Parvane had slipped into a world filled with death and coldness and was listening only to her own voice of sorrow.

No one was to blame. No one had acted out of turn, maliciously, disrespectfully. On hindsight, of course, one could see that if only Farid had not married her, or else had looked for a servant, taken a second wife, stayed close to Atri and Aferin, been kinder to Parvane, spoken to her more softly, helped her more, brought fewer guests, taken her to the doctor . . . and if only Reza had not given her away in marriage so early, had taken her to the doctor when it was first obvious something was wrong with the quiet, smiling girl, had swallowed his pride and moved in with Farid. . . . But what difference did it make now? They were all good men and good women and had done what they could and what was proper at the time. Aferin had done a good deal more, and so had Farid's sister and Atri. God had not watched over Parvane. It was His right to watch or not to watch; only He knows why things happen to people.

Atri and Kokab had to wrestle the dead child away from Parvane. She pressed its little face against her breast as if trying to suckle it, all the while moaning in small high-pitched noises broken by cries like choked sounds from a reed flute. "Dear . . . dear . . . my baby girl . . . my life, my baby dear . . . "

Atri brought Parvane home without asking Reza. Although tempered by Farid's inability to care for Parvane because of his accident, taking Parvane up to her father's house through the village amounted to a public statement of criticism of Farid's and his family's treatment of her. Atri knew that people would talk, but she was not going to face this problem now. When Reza came home at dusk, Atri caught him outside on the verandah. "Parvane is here to stay," she said, looking him in the eye. "The child is dead, she is numb with shock. Nobody is taking care of her and the children. She stays." Reza looked over his wife's head into his shadowy room. He could see Farid's two little children lying under a quilt on a pillow. They were not his to decide over, and neither was his daughter. Farid's brothers should . . . but then again. . . . "We will see what will happen," he murmured. Slipping out of his shoes at the door, he stepped over the sill into his warm house, bent from work and worry and hungry after a long day. Inside, Parvane, fed, washed, in clean clothes, hair combed under a white scarf, was sitting on his thick, soft rug next to the fire, her empty arms in her lap, rocking herself slowly. Reza sat down on his side of the fireplace, facing his daughter, and his heart felt as heavy as his tired body. With unseeing eyes Parvane was staring past him into the dusty blue evening, a deep silence around her like a blanket of snow.

12

Huri on Beads, Stringing a Necklace of Embers

The necklace was much longer once: pretty beads and powerful beads and dangerous ones too, strung left and right of the amulet—powerful words on a slip of paper, sewn in red velvet. All but these red glass balls and the two silver pearls are good for something or other. The shell comes from the sea. It prevents infants from foaming at the mouth. The tiger's tooth is against *djenn*. It hung on the cradle for all of my five children and will hang on the cradle of my sixth, God willing. Unlike myself, who is wrinkling more every year, the beads get smooth and shiny with age. Amber beads are good in a general way, as are red corals. The bead with the soft red and pale green stripes prevents attacks of screaming in babies. The salt crystal and the blue bead are against the evil eye. A few scrapings off the yellow bead given to a baby in water will prevent the child from getting jaundice. The iron bolt keeps the *djenn* away. This black, shiny bead will shatter when the evil eye is deflected onto it from a child. I had several, but they all burst eventually. This long, dark one is good for something, I forget. Here is the dried eye of a sacrificed sheep: it keeps a person healthy. And this mud-colored, round one will counter a powerful word: when we are angry at children, we often curse them—"May a *djenn* get you," we say, but of course we don't really mean it, and the bead will prevent it from happening. The date pit is against exhaustion in babies. The white one is a milk bead which strengthens mother's milk. The donkey bead comes from a hard growth under the skin on the neck of some donkeys. One can use it secretly to make a man or woman want you. Similarly, this light bead makes a husband want his wife so much that he won't take another one. And this black-and-white one is put into the clean powdered clay onto which babies are delivered, so that the child will be beautiful and protected against the *djenn* and the evil eye. The midwife and the doctor won't let us use them anymore, but the other day Hakime sent for it when she had to help Simin deliver her son because the midwife was taking a religion course in town. My father found a whole handful of these old blue and white glassy beads in the field—the people of old must have known about beads too. I am sure they are good for something, but there are only two left. This big, heavy, dark one is a livestock bead, good for sheep and goats, as is this brown one: scrapings of it sprinkled on water help against diarrhea in sheep and goats. It was used so much, it is all but gone.

I had more beads—my daughter took some with her, although she is a Party-of-God Muslim and married to a revolutionary guard. When it comes to pregnancy and infants, it seems that they want all the protection they can get, even if their religion does not quite approve of it. I also had a child-stone. Begom borrowed it for Golgol and when I needed it back after she was through with it, I sent my son to fetch it. I told him to put it into his shoe; it would be less dangerous there, near the dirt of the road. But he went to play on the way home and lost it. It does not matter, though: it is lying somewhere on the ground among other rocks and pebbles and won't harm anybody.

Beads are powerful. Like talk, like words, they have to be used with care. Treated with respect, they help a woman do what she is supposed to do: protect herself and her children. But the mullahs say the beads are bad, superstition, magic, and one should only trust in God. Still, I say: God made those beads and God gave them their power—where else would they have gotten their efficacy from? So what is wrong in using what God gave us? It is a matter of knowledge: some women know, and therefore can keep their children healthy and themselves strong. And some women don't, or they are too lazy to do what is necessary, and then their children die, and they themselves are weak and can't work.

Of course, beads have to be handled with care. Just as you don't wear your heart on the tip of your tongue if you want to be polite, so we don't wear beads around our necks anymore. We stopped protecting ourselves to be kind to others. We are quiet now and have taken to wearing golden chains with golden inscriptions of *Allah*. But I keep my beads. Hardly a week goes by without somebody asking to use one: to put it in water, to scrape off a little, to hang it on a cradle. We used to be our own doctors, our own counselors. Now we need men from the city to tell us what to do. Is it better so? Well, I'll keep my beads, although my son-in-law, the revolutionary guard, warns me that like gossip from my tongue they'll be hot coals around my neck in the other world.

Behind the branch hut I was listening . . .
What my wife and her mother were saying about me
Made my heart heavy with sorrow.

When men talk it is like rose petals falling to the ground, gently falling in the summer's breeze. When women talk, people say, it is like poisoned darts and red-hot swords cutting the air. This is true. Yet: who would console me when I am sad but my mother and my sisters and my neighbor, who is my cousin? And why do I get so angry when my husband is calling me names and scolding me like a child? Is it bad of me to sit with my sisters to lighten the burden of my heart? And then again, it is said that the talk of the people can be helpful.

There once was a young widow with a son. The son grew up and got married. The widow, who was young still, let a man near her and became pregnant and bore a son at the same time her daughter-in-law had one too. The bride was full of honor and modesty and did not want her mother-in-law and her husband to be talked about by the people. She pretended her mother-in-law's child was her own, that she had borne twins. Then she herself brought up the child. The widow died eventually. But when the people wanted to lift the bier it was so heavy it would not budge. They sent for the

Prophet. He ordered the daughter-in-law to come before him and asked her about what evil her mother-in-law had done that the bier could not be moved. She told him. The Prophet himself told the people, and the people started to talk: "Have you heard about the old woman? Who would have thought it of her . . . she fooled us all . . . may God have mercy on her," so they talked, and the more they talked, the lighter the bier got, until at last it could be moved and the old woman could be buried.

For better or for worse, the wagging of tongues is inescapable. The Prophet himself once was going somewhere with a caravan. They stopped to eat at a caravanserai, and his wife went outside to relieve herself. There she lost her necklace. Afraid to tell her husband, she looked around everywhere. Meanwhile the caravan moved on without her. After a while the Prophet missed her and the people told him she had stayed behind to have an affair with the owner of the caravanserai, that they had seen her talk to him and move about outside the gate. But the Prophet, who could see everything if he wanted to, said that no, she only had lost her beads and was looking for them. But the people would not stop talking, and everybody had still more to tell about her and the owner of the caravanserai. In the end the Prophet said that not even he, a prophet, could contain the tongues of the people, and he divorced her.

Such is fate. One does not need to be guilty to be punished. When I was pregnant the first time, I felt very strange. I felt like crying and then like laughing—one minute I would be content and quiet and the next I would fight with everybody. I did not like my husband at all, and whenever I saw him I felt rage rise up in me, and my liver burning. I could not help it. Pregnant women, it is said, often are like this: their reason is impaired, they become like stubborn children. Once I kicked over a pot of milk because I was furious about something my sister-in-law said to me. My husband chased me through the village and then beat me up so badly that two of my ribs cracked. I was six months pregnant then, and my father took me back home. They scolded me at home for behaving so badly and eventually I went back to my husband. From then on, however, I was calmer and more even tempered. It helped that he beat me up, although it was not my fault.

> You know it and God knows that my eyes are on you.
> But you won't look at me—
> It is all your mother's fault.

Once a man fought with his wife. He threw a rock at her and hit her on her forehead. The skin peeled off and beneath, on the skull, he could plainly read, "This woman will live in a brothel for forty days." A few days later his mother was baking bread and did not have enough water. She sent her daughter-in-law for water. At the well was a man who took her arm and led her away, straight into a whorehouse. She stayed there for forty days. When she came back, the people talked: "Beat her up," they told her husband, "divorce her."

His mother was the worst: "Kill her," she said.

But he said, "No, I myself have read what was written on her forehead. It is not her fault, it was her fate, ordered by God." And he took her back as his wife.

We are naturally bad because we are descendants of Adam and Eve. The saints are descendants of the Prophet and therefore without sin. Once a blind man came to the door of the Prophet's house. Saint Fatima pulled the veil over her face and left. "Why did you do this?" the Prophet asked her later. "He was blind, he could not look at you anyway."

"But I am not blind," Fatima said, "I could have looked at him." This is a saint. If it happened to one of us, we would take an extra good look at the man. This is so because Saint Fatima came from the family of the Prophet, and we are children and children's children of sinners.

We are what we are through the will of God, whether we like it or not. A menstruating woman can't pray and can't go to the mosque. Her blood is dirty and can make others sick. It is said that in the beginning, after God had made Adam and Eve, men had to put up with this nuisance. They complained about it to God: "We don't

want this bother," they said. "It makes us dirty and weak, it is defil-
ing. Take it away from us." They kept imploring God and in the end
He took it away from them and gave it to the women. That's why
women menstruate and men don't.

> The woman's beads were strung on leather, not brittle thread.
> But the necklace broke,
> And corals and amber fell into her lap.

All that wailing for Behjad—people say she died because of her bad
heart, because she was pregnant again; that she should have had
her tubes tied, and she should have taken the pill, and whatnot. It
was the will of God. It was her fault too. If she had not made a fuss
about Aziz wanting a second wife, maybe he would have left her
alone. A wife is committing a sin if she refuses her husband. It was
better she got pregnant and died than to commit a sin, surely. And
it was her fate. What does the doctor know? Is he maybe God? Or a
prophet? When my sister got married she was very young and tiny
and weak, a mere child. She got pregnant and the doctor said her
husband had to take her to town; she would not be able to deliver
the child because her bones were too narrow. But when the time
came, he did not take her to the hospital. She had a hard time with
the delivery, for sure, but she survived and the child survived too,
no matter what the doctor had said. As to Behjad, ei, poor woman. I
dreamed of her the night after the funeral: she was sitting in a green
meadow full of flowers, like the gardens in the south in spring, with
the scent of a thousand blossoms in the air. This is heaven. Behjad
is in heaven, but who knows where I will be in the end?

Like most of us, I too had doubts about what was said about heaven
and hell. "Who knows?" I would say. "Has anybody come back yet to
tell us?" But then I had a dream. I saw my grandmother, who had
died a few months before. She was sitting in my brother's courtyard
watching a pot of rice. "Grandmother," I said, "You are dead! What
are you doing here?"

"Dear, I have come to help your brother," she said, "they have
guests and so much work to do. I thought I would lend a hand."
Now, I say: how could I have seen this in my sleep if Grandmother
was truly dead and gone, being eaten by the worms in her grave?

No, indeed—she is somewhere. In heaven, it seems, because she did not look unhappy at all. She looked quite like herself. I was glad about this, because I don't think many women make it into heaven.

> Looking down from the hill I saw her swing her hips.
> The beads in the valley between her breasts
> Made me faint.

Like a wolf circling a herd of sheep and carrying off the one that strays, so men are always on the lookout to find a stray woman who is not with the others or safely at home. It is their nature. God must have wanted it that way, although I cannot think why. Maybe to make women stay in their place. Maybe to show each and every one that it is indeed better to be at home and devoted to her husband and her children instead of showing herself off in public. There was a man from a village further up the valley who had no sons to do the herding for him and was too stingy to hire anybody. He sent his daughter, who was a child yet, but still, men were starting to look at her. She was out with the animals one day when a ghoul came in the form of a mountain goat, a ram. He took her up with his horns and carried her away to a cave and made her his wife. She could not do a thing against it. Her father searched for her, the whole village searched for her, but they could not find a trace of her. She stayed with the ghoul and had two children by him.

One day a shepherd came to the cave. It had a dark and narrow entrance, and he rested just outside. From inside the cave the woman whispered to him: "Ali," she said, for she had recognized him as one of the village boys. "Go home and tell my people that Mahvash is lonely in the cave." He did so and they came after her and took her away. The ghoul did not know what to do when his children cried, and he killed them; and the woman's people did not know what to do with her, who had been sleeping with a stranger, a ghoul to boot, and they killed her too. What else could they have done?

With a woman who is truly immoral, it is like this: There was once a man who had an affair with his neighbor's daughter. Her brother swore he would revenge her. Hearing this, the man fled in fear. But his wife knew that the brother would take his revenge by sleeping with her. She locked the door and dragged a sack of wheat behind it to make sure he could not come in. But at night the young man came through the chimney. She saw that it was her fate. She said, "It is my fate, so be it. But don't put your semen in my womb, put it into this rag." He did so. When she looked at the rag later it was full of worms. This means, the semen of a man who is doing such a thing turns to worms inside the woman, and once in a while they move and stir inside her and make her do it again. From then on she will be a bad woman.

> Rose-blossom girl,
> Keep your eyes off the dirty-eyed scoundrel
> On the wrong path.

Once a woman puts one foot on the wrong path she will have no choice but to go on. And once she has been on the wrong path of sin, her womb will be poisoned by the sin for all her children: they will be bad too. It is the same for a man who fathers a child while in a state of sin. His semen will carry the poison of sin for his children. Our former chief was the worst philanderer in the area. Wherever he saw somebody's pretty daughter or wife or sister—it made no difference to him—he wanted her. And if her father or husband was not willing, he would burn his wheat and steal his sheep until the poor man had no choice but to give in. His friends would sing and clap outside while he was doing his business in his house. And now? His son is in jail, his daughter is doing worse than her father. She does not even dare show her face in the village. She moved to the city, where there are more men at her disposal. I shudder to think what will happen to her children. It will go on and on, and the poison will spread. Thus the world gets more and more evil.

Maybe Soheila got to be the way she is because of her parents. People say they fought a lot, and her father was a rifleman for a landlord and has arguments with all his neighbors. They live in a village way up the river. Soheila made friends with the forest ranger in Deh Koh, a man from the deep south. She would talk to him in public and in private, and would ride to town with him on his motorbike. Her husband had no power over her. He would throw her out one day and then take her back the next because he had nobody to take care of his children. His mother was dead. Once a neighbor found him slinking around the ranger's house with a rifle at night. It was a big to-do with screaming and a gun going off, and the neighbors thought the war was upon them, or a band of robbers. But Soheila tricked them again. In the turmoil she slipped out a window and ran home, and when the people came to her house she was sleeping peacefully next to her children, and her husband was a fool twice over. But we knew it would take a bad end eventually, although the ranger left. Her daughter married a man from town and moved there, and she too had a lover, or maybe more than one, but with this one man she conspired to kill her husband, an old man who had married her out of pity for her bad reputation. The two together killed him and now she is in jail, and her lover is too. The rot is in her blood.

While this forest ranger was carrying on so shamelessly with Soheila, his wife once came to visit. She saw what was going on (wives see it; men whose wives are cuckolding them don't) and was very sad about it. He beat her up and made her all kinds of troubles when she reprimanded him.

One day a theater group was in Deh Koh and we all went to see it. There were snakes and huge pictures of the scenes at Kerbela—blood and such, it made one's skin creep. The ranger's wife was there too, standing next to me. When the performance was over, the two men collected money. The ranger's wife gave me ten Toman and asked me from beneath her veil to take it up front for her, because if anybody would see her do it, people would talk. I did, and then she said she had offered the money for Saint Sarah, with the request to punish her husband. I was worried, and justly so: three days later the ranger's truck turned over on the way to Shiraz and the man was badly hurt.

> God gave me a flower, a blossom,
> But I was not good to her. I looked into her eyes
> And became a sinner.

Not long ago in Deh Rud there was a man who had a wife but not much else. He went to the city to work and earn some money. There he missed his wife and found himself another one. He brought her back with him. His first wife resented it. She and the other women—

Deh Rud women are clever—cast a spell on her co-wife and used their beads, so that the husband would no longer want his second wife. It worked. He came to dislike her so much that he killed her and buried her under a huge pile of stones in the fields. But the children found her and now he is in jail.

In Deh Koh a man went crazy over a girl who had been talked about a lot. Some even said she had borne a stillborn child secretly out in a pasture camp, although for sure such gossip is sinful. He married her, against the advice of his people. He wanted her badly. For three days and nights he did not leave the bridal chamber, and then he always was at her service, bringing her the best food and the finest clothes and beads, and necklaces of gold, but she always wanted more. People laughed about him behind his back. He would press pieces of fabric his wife fancied onto anyone who happened to leave for the city, asking him to bring it back. Or he would give money to someone to bring back such and such shoes, and such and such perfume, and whatnot. He was not rich, though, and had to work harder and harder to keep up with her wishes. If he had nothing to give her she would pout and not cook dinner for him and not let him near her. In the end he split his guts over the hard work and died. He will go to heaven and she will go to hell.

Binas now, she was a wise old woman. She could read the Koran and she knew everything. Once she told us she had been to hell in her dreams. There was a woman hanging from her breast on an iron hook because she had nursed another woman's baby without her husband's permission. And there was a woman with a red-hot iron plug through her tongue who had talked badly about others; and there was one with red-hot iron shackles because she had gone places without her husband's permission; and there was a woman immersed in boiling water because she had refused herself to her husband; and there was an emaciated woman who was swallowing rocks, because she had not fed her husband and children properly but had given her food to her lover. And there was a woman impaled because she had given alms without her husband's permission and had not given alms when her husband had ordered her to. A woman who had laughed a lot had fire coming out of her mouth; one who had not pardoned her divorce money settlement was weighed down by a bag of rocks. There were women with needles stuck in them, and with their eyes poked out; with cut-off noses; standing in fire, standing in snow. Hell, Binas said, was full of women who had committed sins that hung around their husband's necks like necklaces of glowing embers.

> My baby boy is playing with the beads on his cradle.
> The beads around a girl-blossom's neck
> Will take him from me.

There once was a widow who had only one son. Because she had no more children she kept him like a little child. She let him drink milk whenever he wanted to. He could walk but still drank her milk, and then he could talk, and run, and work, but still he would drink his fill from his mother's breasts each morning before he left the house. He did not want to marry, he said. "What for?" he said, "I have my mother." The old woman got worried that she would not get a bride to work for her. She was old now and getting tired. So she told her son she would let him drink milk only if he agreed to take a wife. "All right," he said, "give me a wife." The mother looked around for a good wife, a pretty one for her beloved son, and chose carefully.

After the wedding, he did not want to go to his wife in the bridal chamber, and his mother had to push him in and lock the door behind him. She expected he would do his job quickly and come out to her again. She waited and waited, but he did not come. The stars were fading, dawn was breaking, but he still did not come outside. The sun was rising and he still was inside. The mother got restless. "My soul, my dear," she cried, "come drink your milk."

"With all respect," the son shouted from inside, "take your breasts to the graveyard, old woman, I have better things to do."

Many years ago when the locusts had eaten the crops, the widow of a Seyed—a descendant of the Prophet—came to my grandfather with her young daughter. They had nothing, and my grandfather was well off. They stayed with him as his guests. The little girl was very beautiful: her skin was white like opaque glass, and she had eyebrows like a ram's horn and little breasts like budding almond blossoms. One of the chiefs saw her and wanted her as his wife. When he slept with her the first time there was so much blood that the bedding was soaked. Because of this she became his favorite wife — it showed how much of a virgin she was.

When I was little my father used to play with me — I was the oldest of his children, and he liked me. He would lie on his back and put me on the soles of his feet and move his legs up and down so that I felt like I was flying. And sometimes he would throw me in the air a little. But my mother told him not to do this, it might break my hymen. She was right. The sports for girls in school, all this jumping and running, is bad for them. Nargez told us of her neighbor in Shiraz whose daughter got a letter from the school director before she got married saying that she had been very active in sports, because her mother was afraid she might have a broken hymen. And indeed, she had. What an embarrassment for the groom and the girl's father and brothers! If she had not had that letter from the school, who knows what might have happened to her?

> Lady bride blossom is shedding tears
> Like precious beads
> Into a green meadow of flowers.

Girls have to look out for themselves. Red lips and black eyes and a white skin under the skirts are enough to make a man crazy, but not enough to make a good life for a woman. A good woman has to know when to talk, when to be silent, when to work and when to jingle her beads, when to use her eyebrows and when to use her voice.

One of the sons in the family next to Ali and Golgol's new house — the one they just sold, I mean — got himself a wife from a village on the other side of Snow Mountain, where he was a teacher. She came to the village a total stranger; her people had let her go only reluctantly, and only after having looked the young man's family over very carefully. His are good people, though, and in the end they gave the young teacher their daughter. She was a very good

229

woman from the beginning, polite and pleasant, hard working, never gossiping and never speaking out of turn. But somehow her husband's people made life hard for her and she was crying a lot, Golgol said. Even in her unhappiness, though, she was quiet and proper and did not complain to her neighbors. She had honor—still has, of course. Well, one day something especially upsetting happened to her. Unlike one of us, however, who would have started to scream and scold and swear—Golgol once, our sweet and pious Golgol, ripped Mehri's necklace off during a fight—well, this young woman did nothing of the sort. Instead, all of a sudden, out of complete silence, she started to wail, loudly and piercingly, as if somebody had died. The people came running from everywhere, and although she stopped almost as soon as she had started, talk was in the air, gossip was loose. Somebody took the news to her people, and two days later her father and two of her brothers and some more people came in a car to take her back, no matter how sweetly her husband and his mother talked. It took her husband two trips with all his relatives, a whole caravan it was, until he got her back, and only after he signed a paper in front of a whole council of elders and notables promising never to make her trouble again and never to permit anyone in his family to mistreat her again. Without losing any words at all, she had managed to make an agreeable life for herself—what a clever and strong woman she was already as a mere bride.

Over the years I have come to understand many things. I know when to talk sweetly and when to scold. I know which beads work and which are just good to look at. Through trial and error I found out what food suits my temperament and my children's. I found out who can write good amulets for what and how to determine lucky and unlucky days. I know that if my husband is the first one to open the door on New Year's day, he and I will be fighting all year. But if I am the one to open it first, there will be peace in the house. On the last evening of the old year we had an argument. A little after midnight my husband woke me: "Go, open the door," he said. But I was mad at him still. "I was not the one to close it last night," I said, "you were. Go open it yourself." But then I thought about how much I would suffer under the fights to come, and so I got up and opened the door. Wisdom and knowledge are the crutches for this world.

> Heia, heia, I am rocking a new cradle.
> Let me count the beads on the cradle's beam
> Into the hands of my baby, one by one.

Epilogue

Huri, who thinks and talks in stories, is a widow now with five children, two half-grown sons among them. Supported by a small pension, her strength and her considerable wits, she hustles to keep her family fed and clothed; her cows and two goats in fodder (now and then, when all other arrangements fail, she carries grass home on her own back like a very young girl); and her fields ploughed, sowed, and harvested. Her sons, with her blessing, don't work their father's few plots of land, not even during their long summer vacation—most high school students with aspirations disdain peasants' chores. All these worries give her a big ache in her heart, she says, an ache that feels as if her heart was weighed down with a heavy rock; but there is little pain in her eyes. Her husband's relatives did not claim her, her children, or his land; her old father is protective, her mother is helpful, and her brothers, all younger than herself, are devoted. And she knows she can manage easier now than before, when a sickly and querulous husband was providing only marginally and with a heavy hand. Her "beads of wisdom" were formed at that time. Better than any life narrative they show the parameters within which she constructs her life with a measure of success, despite a frustration so great that years ago, at the death of one of her infant daughters (a death she could have prevented had she earnestly tried to), she said she was more glad than sad about this death because it spared the baby girl the miserable life of a woman.

Parvane's condition is much better by some accounts, a little better by others. Nobody, not even her husband's people, claims she is any worse off in her father's house than she was in her husband's. Her husband's circumstances have changed drastically, which has made things different for everybody around Parvane but not for her. For all practical purposes of role performance, routine, and decision making, she has been taken out of the arena of social interplay. Life flowing and ebbing around her, she is sitting on an island sheltered by her mother and a still reluctant father, a worry to everybody but herself. Her mother hopes to live long enough to see Parvane pass into the loving care of her grown son—a thin hope, requiring more faith in the kindness of a future daughter-in-law than is reasonable, but the only one she has. So far, the safety net around Parvane is holding up. It has empowered her to perform, marginally at least, throughout the progression of her condition all the way to a point of catatonic withdrawal—a triumph of cohesion and solidarity of family and of women, and of the stubborn and compelling expectation of a woman's routine in the division of labor.

Rumors are flying around Setara as usual, and she dismisses them with grand gestures. These rumors and what is behind them enlarge on her story but don't amount to a new chapter, at least not yet. She got her roof tarred, but now the water pipe to her house has dried up, and this necessitates more trips to town and more petitions. For Setara, life essentially has become a challenge to recreate or at least approximate the good old days when Tehrani took care of what she deemed proper and necessary. Trying to relive her own myth, she creates a drama that satisfies and frustrates her simultaneously and keeps her going, going, going.

Sarah the Weaver is "Mashhadi Sarah" now, a successful pilgrim to the shrine of the Imam Reza. She has seen something of the world, yet, she says, it has made less of a difference to her than she had expected. Out there, she says, people are worried, and the pace of life is frenzied. At home, the focus of her world has shifted to under her son's apple trees behind a new, massive stone wall. Clients and neighbors still find their way to the makeshift sun shelter, made of an old veil-wrap tied to three trees (inferior to the shade of the lost walnut tree by all counts), and her two remaining granddaughters (the oldest was married after graduation from high school and has left) still bring home stories of school and strangers. Sarah wants for nothing in her son's house; if anything has changed for her, it has changed toward the side of ease. But she looks and acts older and talks less, and with a softer voice, as she bends over her loom. The story plot in her family has shifted to the young ones in the house and to her husband's new bride.

Around Mamalus the Storyteller things have been happening so fast that even she, one of the most restless and resolute women in the village, has found it hard to keep up with it all. Her favorite son died from a mysterious disease; another son built a house away from the crowd, moved the whole family there, and then married the daughter of a cousin of Mamalus who reappeared out of nowhere after twenty years of total silence—a factory worker in a big city, with a fast-talking wife with a huge nose and shrewd eyes and two dumpy, marriageable daughters with short, frizzled hair and blood-red varnished fingernails. It is one of these two who stayed on as Mamalus's son's wife . . . and quite a story that has turned out to be. Mamalus's daughter Effat had a suitor who was accepted, but then Mamalus spotted a better one and extricated Effat from her engagement—a maneuver that was complex, nerve-wracking, and wholly successful. Mamalus's store of grotesque and absurd tales is disappearing from her memory, but she is not sorry about it. Life for her provides all the excitement she can handle, she says.

Of the others around the story of Gedulak, Qeta died without fuss in her brother's house one hot evening the following summer and was missed by many, strangely enough, considering she was only a crazy, ugly, and poor old woman. Amene's story (or, more appropriately, stories, for she is linked to many) is untold. She and her sister the teacher, the first woman to fight for and get a divorce in the village, along with their mother, one of the most formidable women I have ever known, are in a class wholly by themselves. In their lives the women's world is connected with the history of the whole village, with the interplay of power, nobility, and politics, and the beginning and end of several eras are mirrored in them.

Soon after Simin moved to her husband's house, Behjad died in childbirth. Aziz, urged by his mother and the other women who soon tired of taking care of his children, married again after only a few weeks. His wife is a bland and pleasant young woman, a distant relative of Sarah's who was, Simin said, glad to have found a husband at all. Peri negotiated a delay of her wedding until after she finished high school but had to scrap her plans for the Teacher Training College. Her fiancé's family did not want to wait. And Simin now has three sons, a healthy voice, untiring vigilance, and gumption enough to dominate everybody left in the house except her own children.

Abbas the rapist (maybe) eventually was caught and went to jail, but no one seems to know for which of his alleged crimes. Turan was married off to a gendarme from a town in the south. She moved there willingly, says Banu, but Nargez knows from somebody her husband works with that Turan is unhappy there, married to a man without education and living in a large family of coarse people. Nargez, more often right than wrong in her predictions (no matter how far-fetched her forecasts may seem), says that Turan will come back. She says Turan's husband will divorce her because she has no children. Nargez herself and her husband have moved back to the village for good, scratching together a living the hard way and looking back to their city days with little fondness. She is still waiting for her husband to build her a lean-to for a goat.

Banu and Mahin are doing well. Banu is sitting on her verandah surrounded by neighbors, sisters, and friends, amidst a growing family of loud and dirty children, content with the little she has and at peace with almost everybody. Mahin has married an outsider, a man of means (by local standards) and education (by her standards)—a man she herself decided to marry. (By then, all her relatives had given up trying to marry her off.) Hers is a story that most probably never will be told. It is a story of filial devotion and virtual gender-role reversal: a daughter who renounces her duty to get married, and thus provide a man with a wife, in order to assume the unusual function of caretaker to her parents. Despite criticism and disapproval she persevered in this choice, albeit with misgivings in her heart, until the conflicts around her family resolved themselves and set her free. When her father was buried and her brother got married, she turned her back to the past and moved on.

Leila fell on hard times for a while. Her husband got jealous of one of her cousins because, in his view, he misused the social freedom of close male relatives and visited the house too often. In the course of an argument the cousin was banned from the house and Leila suffered a black eye. Then she fell ill with an ulcer which was slow in healing, and with her fading strength her bubbly spirits flattened. She is much quieter now than before, and a little sad, it seems, and worried about her four sons growing up into gun-toting soldiers to be swallowed by a war no one in the village ever wanted.

Gouhar and Aftab are speaking to each other again, carefully and with expansive dignity. Maryam made a thin peace between them. The jewelry no longer is talked about. Aftab will move into a new house Bandar has built on a slope at the edge of the village, and from then on she will not see much of the women in her old neighborhood. Huri will be a new neighbor, and Simin will visit there because one of her sisters is married to a man who is building a courtyard behind Bandar's tiny speck of land. Everything will be fine there, Aftab says. They will even have an outhouse to themselves, and a shower stall, if Bandar will get around to building one.

Maryam's brother Kerim, the school principal, died of a stomach ailment. With his death his family, including Maryam, suddenly lost their spokesman, and for quite a while no man in the younger generation seemed to fill this role. His death gave Maryam a lot to do—organizing the mourning festivities for one, but more lastingly, acting as the go-between, prompter, coaxer, and kingmaker in her family. More mobile spatially and intellectually than any other of the women, she was rarely at home in these weeks. At last count, it seems that her favorite nephew, a teacher himself, is taking over some of Kerim's influence, and Maryam is backing him with admirable energy and loyalty.

In the domestic drama of Golgol and Ali, events have changed dramatically but predictably. Mehri found a husband and moved rather far away, to one of the surrounding hamlets. Akbar is a very tired old man who does not want to be bothered by anything and is quite grateful for small comforts. Begom's belligerent spirit was broken when, ill with a bad heart, she found herself too weak in body to carry enough of the labor burden to put her into a strong bargaining position, and soon also too weak in spirit to fight. She resigned herself to the role of an old woman who accepts with grace the care and service extended to her. Golgol has quit her job, is pregnant with her fourth child, and takes care of her husband's people in the spirit of an exemplary Muslim.

Tala and Yusuf have built one of the biggest houses in the village. Although feelings of sadness and rage often overcome Tala, there is friendly coming and going among most of Yusuf's people and herself, at least until the next crisis. Both have come to take their childlessness, it seems, as the will of God.

Perijan, finally past menopause now, laughs about her embarrassment when she was pregnant—"how dumb one is as a young woman," she says, mocking herself. She is happy and healthy, with two strapping sons providing a living for her better than she ever had and two little daughters who are the joy of her days and the light of the whole house. They are, she says, spoiled rotten, and may God protect them and all the other children and the whole village in these dark and sad days.

FOR THE BEST IN PAPERBACKS, LOOK FOR THE

In every corner of the world, on every subject under the sun, Penguin represents quality and variety—the very best in publishing today.

For complete information about books available from Penguin—including Pelicans, Puffins, Peregrines, and Penguin Classics—and how to order them, write to us at the appropriate address below. Please note that for copyright reasons the selection of books varies from country to country.

In the United Kingdom: For a complete list of books available from Penguin in the U.K., please write to *Dept E.P., Penguin Books Ltd, Harmondsworth, Middlesex, UB7 0DA.*

In the United States: For a complete list of books available from Penguin in the U.S., please write to *Dept BA, Penguin*, Box 120, Bergenfield, New Jersey 07621-0120.

In Canada: For a complete list of books available from Penguin in Canada, please write to *Penguin Books Canada Ltd, 10 Alcorn Avenue, Suite 300, Toronto, Ontario, Canada M4V 3B2.*

In Australia: For a complete list of books available from Penguin in Australia, please write to the *Marketing Department, Penguin Books Ltd, P.O. Box 257, Ringwood, Victoria 3134.*

In New Zealand: For a complete list of books available from Penguin in New Zealand, please write to the *Marketing Department, Penguin Books (NZ) Ltd, Private Bag, Takapuna, Auckland 9.*

In India: For a complete list of books available from Penguin, please write to *Penguin Overseas Ltd, 706 Eros Apartments, 56 Nehru Place, New Delhi, 110019.*

In Holland: For a complete list of books available from Penguin in Holland, please write to *Penguin Books Nederland B.V., Postbus 195, NL-1380AD Weesp, Netherlands.*

In Germany: For a complete list of books available from Penguin, please write to *Penguin Books Ltd, Friedrichstrasse 10-12, D-6000 Frankfurt Main I, Federal Republic of Germany.*

In Spain: For a complete list of books available from Penguin in Spain, please write to *Longman, Penguin España, Calle San Nicolas 15, E-28013 Madrid, Spain.*

In Japan: For a complete list of books available from Penguin in Japan, please write to *Longman Penguin Japan Co Ltd, Yamaguchi Building, 2-12-9 Kanda Jimbocho, Chiyoda-Ku, Tokyo 101, Japan.*

FOR THE BEST IN WOMEN'S STUDIES, LOOK FOR THE

☐ **WOMEN AND SELF-ESTEEM**
Understanding and Improving the Way We Think and Feel About Ourselves
Linda Tschirhart Sanford and Mary Ellen Donovan

Drawing on research, interviews, and the experiences of those who participated
in their Self-Esteem Enhancement Groups, Sanford and Donovan offer reasons
why many women suffer from low self-esteem, and how they can help themselves.

"A sensible book that combines intelligent analysis with a no-nonsense guide for
individual growth"—*Working Woman*
480 pages   ISBN: 0-14-008225-5

☐ **WOMEN AND CHILDREN LAST**
The Plight of Poor Women in Affluent America
Ruth Sidel

In this hard-hitting book, Ruth Sidel demonstrates how—and why—so many of
the women and children of one of the richest societies on earth must struggle to
secure the barest necessities.

"A startling expose . . . The concentration of women and children in poverty is
the scandal of the 1980s."—*U.S. Representative Patricia Schroeder*
236 pages   ISBN: 0-14-010013-X

☐ **WOMEN'S BURNOUT**
How to Spot It, How to Reverse It, and How to Prevent It
Dr. Herbert J. Feudenberger and Gail North

This sane and reassuring guide details the causes and symptoms of overexten-
sion—burnout—and provides essential advice on overcoming the accompanying
exhaustion and depression.

"A remarkably rich, thickly textured, topical analysis"—*Houston Chronicle*
244 pages   ISBN: 0-14-009414-8

FOR THE BEST IN HISTORY, LOOK FOR THE

☐ **ON WAR**
Carl Von Clausewitz
Edited by Anatol Rapoport

In his famous treatise of 1832, Clausewitz examines the nature and theory of war, military strategy, and the combat itself.

462 pages   ISBN: 0-14-044427-0

☐ **TOTAL WAR**
Causes and Courses of the Second World War
Peter Calvocoressi and Guy Wint

This bold and comprehensive account places as much emphasis on the political, social, and moral forces behind the War as on the ensuing clashes of arms. *Total War* is the definitive history of "the war to end all wars."

966 pages   ISBN: 0-14-021422-4

☐ **SIX ARMIES IN NORMANDY**
From D-Day to the Liberation of Paris
John Keegan

Keegan's account of the summer of 1944's momentous events on the battlefields of Normandy is superb; he "writes about war better than almost anyone in our century."—*Washington Post Book World*

366 pages   ISBN: 0-14-005293-3

☐ **WOMEN IN WAR**
Shelley Saywell

Shelley Saywell tells the previously untold stories of the forgotten veterans of our time—the millions of women who faced combat in some of the most important military struggles of this century.

324 pages   ISBN: 0-14-007623-9

You can find all these books at your local bookstore, or use this handy coupon for ordering:

Penguin Books By Mail
Dept. BA Box 999
Bergenfield, NJ 07621-0999

Please send me the above title(s). I am enclosing _____
(please add sales tax if appropriate and $1.50 to cover postage and handling). Send check or money order—no CODs. Please allow four weeks for shipping. We cannot ship to post office boxes or addresses outside the USA. *Prices subject to change without notice.*

Ms./Mrs./Mr. _____

Address _____

City/State _____ Zip _____

FOR THE BEST IN HISTORY, LOOK FOR THE

☐ **THE FACE OF BATTLE**
   John Keegan

In this study of three battles from three different centuries, John Keegan examines
war from the fronts—conveying its reality for the participants at the "point of
maximum danger."

366 pages   *ISBN: 0-14-004897-9*

☐ **VIETNAM: A HISTORY**
   Stanley Karnow

Stanley Karnow's monumental narrative—the first complete account of the Vietnam War—puts events and decisions of the day into sharp, clear focus. "This is
history writing at its best."—*Chicago Sun-Times*

752 pages   *ISBN: 0-14-007324-8*

☐ **MIRACLE AT MIDWAY**
   Gordon W. Prange
   with Donald M. Goldstein and Katherine V. Dillon

The best-selling sequel to *At Dawn We Slept* recounts the battles at Midway
Island—events which marked the beginning of the end of the war in the Pacific.

470 pages   *ISBN: 0-14-006814-7*

☐ **THE MASK OF COMMAND**
   John Keegan

This provocative view of leadership examines the meaning of military heroism
through four prototypes from history—Alexander the Great, Wellington, Grant,
and Hitler—and proposes a fifth type of "post-heroic" leader for the nuclear
age.   *368 pages*   *ISBN: 0-14-011406-8*

☐ **THE SECOND OLDEST PROFESSION**
   Spies and Spying in the Twentieth Century
   Phillip Knightley

In this fascinating history and critique of espionage, Phillip Knightley explores
the actions and missions of such noted spies as Mata Hari and Kim Philby, and
organizations such as the CIA and the KGB.

436 pages   *ISBN: 0-14-010655-3*

☐ **THE STORY OF ENGLISH**
   Robert McCrum, William Cran, and Robert MacNeil

"Rarely has the English language been scanned so brightly and broadly in a single
volume," writes the *San Francisco Chronicle* about this journey across time and
space that explores the evolution of English from Anglo-Saxon Britain to
Reagan's America.   *384 pages*   *ISBN: 0-14-009435-0*